DATE DUE			

Romances of Chivalry
in the Spanish Golden Age

Juan de la Cuesta
Hispanic Monographs

Series: *Documentación cervantina* Nº 3

Romances of Chivalry in the Spanish Golden Age

BY

Daniel Eisenberg

Florida State University

With a *Proemio* by

Martín de Riquer

Real Academia Española

Juan de la Cuesta

Illustrations in this book are taken from *Cirongilio de Tracia*
(Seville: Jacome Cromberger, 1545). That on the cover of the
paperback edition (also seen on p. xviii of both editions) bears
the stamp of the Alessandrina Library (see p. 15).

The decorated capital letters which begin each chapter are
from the original stock of type used in Juan de la Cuesta's
sixteenth-century Madrid print shop. These were graciously
provided by Professor R. M. Flores of the University of British
Columbia.

The Preparation of this volume was made possible in part
by a grant from the Publications Program of the National
Endowment for the Humanities, an independent Federal
Agency.

ISBN: (hardcover) 0-936388-07-2, (paperback) 0-936388-12-9
Library of Congress Catalog Card Number: 81:83663

TABLE OF CONTENTS

Proemio

L LECTOR encontrará aquí cómodamente reunidos algunos de los trabajos sobre libros de caballerías castellanos que el profesor Daniel Eisenberg ha publicado en revistas especializadas y otro que hoy se imprime por vez primera, estudios que, a pesar de haber sido redactados en fechas distintas y con intención monográfica, se enlazan perfectamente entre sí y dan al presente libro una sólida unidad y en su conjunto obedecen a una bien definida dirección.

Es seguro que, si no existiera el *Quijote*, la bibliografía de los libros de caballerías sería mucho más reducida y distinta de lo que es en la actualidad, y que el presente libro de Eisenberg, si hubiera llegado a existir, tendría un carácter muy diferente y no se plantearía ciertos problemas críticos. Es imposible soslayar esta servidumbre y grandeza de los libros de caballerías castellanos, que si gozaron de cierta popularidad en el siglo XVI, a partir del XVIII pasaron a ser un elemento decisivo para toda interpretación, correcta o equivocada, de la gran novela de Cervantes. Es bien cierto que el crítico e incluso el lector con sentido histórico y literario necesita conocer los libros de caballerías para penetrar en ciertos aspectos del *Quijote*; pero también lo es que el *Quijote*, parodia literaria, llega con su gran carga de valores a aquellos lectores que desconocen totalmente lo parodiado. La inmensa mayoría de los entusiastas de Cervantes, que son muchos, no han leído ni un solo libro de caballerías, y a pesar de ello no han dejado de disfrutar frente a las páginas del *Quijote*.

Un sector de la crítica actual estudia los libros de caballerías y, si hoy existen lectores del *Amadís de Gaula*, ello se debe fundamentalmente al *Quijote*. Y hay que destacar un significativo dato editorial: las recientes ediciones del *Amadís de Gaula*, tanto la buena como la mala, en España se agotan y hay que reimprimirlas. Y si ello no ocurre en Francia, donde no hay ediciones de gran público del *Lancelot* y del *Tristan* en prosa, es porque estas extensas y maravillosas novelas no tuvieron el revulsivo de un *Quijote* y a ellas sólo acuden los eruditos.

Cuando se habla de libros de caballerías castellanos forzosamente uno acaba cifrándolos en el *Amadís de Gaula*, aunque ello no sea estrictamente justo, porque es un libro de lectura apasionante y divertida, digan lo que digan los que temen acercarse a él, en el que el lector va de sorpresa en sorpresa, pendiente de una trama hábilmente entrelazada, y de maravilla en maravilla ante episodios de clara belleza y de magistral expresividad.

El *Amadís de Gaula* ha planteado siempre serios problemas de redacción, composición, fecha e interpretación, y en estos sentidos es de básica importancia el reciente libro de J. M. Cacho Blecua[1]; y el lector encontrará en varios de los trabajos de Eisenberg aquí reunidos puntos de vista personales y certeros sobre problemas tan decisivos. Nos vamos acercando a una eficaz comprensión del *Amadís de Gaula*, y con ella a la del género llamado libros de caballerías. Pero aun queda pendiente un aspecto capital, que es el de sus fuentes francesas. La triste incomunicación entre los medievalistas, o mejor el poco interés que demuestran muchos hispanistas por la literatura francesa, hace que muy a menudo se olvide un hecho capital: que el *Amadís de Gaula* es hijo del *Lancelot* en prosa, escrito hacia 1230, muy conocido en España, donde se tradujo a los tres romances peninsulares. Eisenberg tiene en el libro que el lector está empezando unas páginas importantísimas (de la 55 a la 74) donde configura el libro de caballerías típico, con sus temas y lugares comunes y el currículum del caballero héroe de la ficción. Es un análisis que habrá que tener en cuenta en futuras indagaciones sobre este género literario. Leyendo estas páginas advertía que todos los elementos, o llámense tópicos, si gusta más, que cataloga Eisenberg se encuentran en el *Lancelot* del siglo XIII; y basta acudir al detallado análisis que de este *roman* hizo Ferdinand Lot, en 1918, en su *Étude sur le Lancelot en prose*. Esto, en verdad, no es nada nuevo, y bien de manifiesto puso esta influencia de Grace S. Williams en el importante trabajo "The *Amadis* Question." Pero esta monografía apareció en 1909, el mismo año en que O. Sommer comenzó a publicar en Washington su monumental edición de *The Vulgate Version of the Arthurian Romances*, en la que el *Lancelot* ocupa los tomos III, IV y V, que se editaron en 1910 y 1912. A pesar de las deficiencias que se han achacado a la utilísima edición de Sommer, con ella Grace S. Williams hubiera podido ampliar y precisar mejor la vinculación del *Amadís de Gaula* al *Lancelot*. La edición

---

[1] J. M. Cacho Blecua, *Amadís: heroísmo mítico y cortesano* (Madrid: Cupsa, 1979).

de Sommer es de difícil lectura en gran parte por su ausencia de puntuación y de regularización de mayúsculas, y sólo la pueden manejar con provecho los conocedores del francés medieval, y ello sin duda ha demorado esta dirección en los estudios. Ahora, que desde 1978 disponemos de una nueva edición del *Lancelot* en prosa por A. Micha, los hispanistas podrán comparar este *roman* con el *Amadís de Gaula*, lo que a veces conduce a conclusiones curiosas, como lo es que el escudo de don Bruneo de Bonamar (*Amadís*, edición Place, III, 882, y IV, 1090) sea igual que el que Lancelot se hace confeccionar en l'Ille de Joie (Sommer, V, 403).

El *Lancelot* en prosa es el principal modelo del *Amadís de Gaula*, y como éste es el padre de los libros de caballerías castellanos, este género literario se nos presenta como la interpretación española del *roman* caballeresco de aventuras que creó Chrétien de Troyes. Es una literatura que se inspira en modelos literarios.

Pero la novela española ofrece, en el siglo XV, otro tipo de narración caballeresca: el relato ficticio que sigue la biografía de un caballero que tiene como modelo a caballeros de carne y hueso que viven en la realidad circundante. El gallego, o castellano, Pedro Vázquez de Saavedra se dio a conocer en Westminster, en noviembre de 1440, combatiendo contra Sir Richard Woodville; pasó luego, como caballero andante, a Colonia y a la corte de Borgoña, donde intervino gallardamente en el Pas de l'Arbre Charlemagne que se celebró en Dijon en julio de 1443. Mientras se celebraban estas tan lucidas fiestas caballerescas llegaron mensajeros a Felipe el Bueno, duque de Borgoña, en demanda de auxilio militar a favor de Constantinopla, gravemente amenazada por los turcos. Tal prestigio se había ganado Pedro Vázquez que fue uno de los más destacados capitanes de la escuadra borgoñona que emprendió una expedición que la llevó al Mar Negro, remontó el Danubio hasta Budapest y luego acudió al socorro de Constantinopla. Regresado a Occidente Pedro Vázquez fue el primero que pronunció los famosos Votos del Faisán en las fiestas de Lille de 1454. En 1449 había intervenido en el Pas de la Fontaine en Pleurs, organizado por el caballero andante Jacques de Lalaing. Encontramos luego a Pedro Vázquez en una nueva expedición naval por el Mediterráneo, en el norte de África y más tarde en el sitio de Perpiñán de 1473. Éste es el currículum de un caballero de veras de mediados del siglo XV, según cronistas tan solventes como Olivier de la Marche y Jean de Wavrin y documentos de archivo; pero a todos los que han leído el *Tirant lo Blanch* esto parece un resumen apresurado de la novela caballeresca catalana, ya que el currículum militar de su protagonista es muy similar y paralelo al del histórico caballero gallego o castellano. Cervantes se dio perfecta cuenta de esta realidad del *Tirant*, en oposición al mundo irreal y literario de los libros de caballerías del tipo *Amadís*; y como era hombre entendido en los secretos del arte de hacer novelas, admiró en la de Martorell—cuyo nombre ignoró siempre—que en ella "comen los caballeros y duermen y mueren en sus camas y hacen testamento antes de su muerte, con otras cosas de que todos los demás libros deste género carecen." Martorell, hacia 1460, retrató en su libro al caballero andante que entonces existía; y eran muchos: recuérdense la relación que hace Fernando del Pulgar en *Claros varones* y los pasajes de la crónica de Juan II que tan bien conocía Cervantes. Cervantes, en el paso del siglo XVI al XVII, retrató en su novela al caballero andante que en su tiempo ya no podía existir. Si el *Amadís de Gaula* se parece al *Lancelot* en prosa, el *Tirant lo Blanch* no se parece a otra obra de ficción, sino al *Victorial* de don Pero Niño.

Los historiadores de la literatura sabemos bien que nuestra disciplina no es una ciencia exacta, lo que permite defender criterios muy discrepantes y sistemas de trabajo que caducan cada cinco años, y que el panorama de trabajo es prácticamente inagotable. En el primer aspecto hay que encomiar sin reservas los presentes trabajos de Eisenberg, fundamentados en un sólido y benéfico positivismo que, apartando lucubraciones y divagaciones pseudo-culturales, a las que tan acostumbrados estamos, avanza en sus interpretaciones con el seguro apoyo del dato concreto. Queda, por otra parte, mucho que hacer en el estudio de los libros de caballerías y de la novela caballeresca. Nos faltan monografías sobre su lenguaje y estilo, indagaciones sobre el arnés del caballero, tan cambiante en la Edad Media y en el siglo XVI que nos puede suministrar datos cronológicos, y sobre la heráldica,[2] dirección ésta tan acertadamente abierta en el magnífico libro de G. J. Brault[3]; sobre el vestuario de corte, las fórmulas y ceremonias del trato, la organización de los castillos y de las villas, la situación de los villanos, y tantos otros temas que están

---

[2] Trato este aspecto en "Las armas en el *Amadís de Gaula*," *BRAE*, 60 (1980), 331-427.

[3] Gerard J. Brault, *Early Blazon: Heraldic Terminology in the Twelfth and Thirteenth Centuries with Special Reference to Arthurian Literature* (Oxford: Clarendon Press, 1972).

pidiendo la atención de jóvenes hispanistas. Eisenberg tiene en este libro un brevísimo capítulo, *Research Opportunities*, que abre grandes perspectivas. Pero, como es natural, nada de esto se puede emprender si no contamos con rigurosas y solventes ediciones de libros de caballerías, tarea que al parecer se está inciando con buena fortuna, pero que exigirá muchos años antes de que podamos darla por cumplida. Es un trabajo que pide ciencia y paciencia y una seria aplicación, de lo que Daniel Eisenberg ha dado un buen ejemplo con su edición, en seis tomos, del *Espejo de príncipes y cavalleros* o *El caballero del Febo* de Diego Ortúñez de Calahorra, aparecida en Madrid en 1975, dentro de la colección Clásicos Castellanos.

Este bello libro revela que Daniel Eisenberg tiene un profundo conocimiento de los secretos de los libros de caballerías, cuya complicada bibliografía ha ordenado en su imprescindible *Castilian Romances of Chivalry in the Sixteenth Century*, publicada en Londres en 1979 e impresa en el reino de Valencia, de donde era natural el autor del *Tirant*. Ello hace que tanto el especialista como el lector curioso de estas materias, que nunca debe ser olvidado, se acerquen al presente libro con la seguridad de que en sus páginas aprenderán mucho y encontrarán estímulos de reflexión.

MARTÍN DE RIQUER

Real Academia Española

PREFACE

THIS BOOK CONTAINS the most important of my articles on the Spanish romances of chivalry. They are preceded by an essay written at the kind suggestion of Francisco Rico, and conceived of as an introduction but grew to become the most important part of the book.

The articles themselves have deliberately been left as originally published, save for updating of the documentation and the correction of some obvious errors. One article has been reproduced from its Spanish translation in the Puerto Rican journal *Sin Nombre*, since that version contains revisions not found in its original English version published in *Hispanic Review*.

A bibliography, originally a part of this book, was published separately by Grant and Cutler (London, 1979) with the title *Castilian Romances of Chivalry in the Sixteenth Century*.

Golden Age texts taken from modern editions are quoted unchanged. Those which I have taken from old imprints have been slightly modernized, including, in most cases, the modernization of *u/v* and *i/j*, word spacing, and capitalization and punctuation. Accents have been added only to distinguish homonyms: on *sí, más, él, mí,* and similar words, on the future tense and on the preterite of first conjugation verbs, as well as on potentially confusing forms such as *sería* and *hacía*. Anyone with questions about my treatment of these texts is encouraged to consult the originals. I would be happy to make copies of my microfilms available for this or any other scholarly purpose.

References to the romances of chivalry and to the *Quijote* are most frequently given as a book or part number, followed by a chapter number. If a reference to an exact spot is needed, a volume, page, and sometimes line or note number will be cited, specifying the edition used.

Journal abbreviations are those of the MLA.

That the romances of chivalry as a genre are not treated exhaustively in this book is a fact of which I am only too well aware, and I would be glad to have its deficiencies remedied by those present or future scholars more knowledgeable than I. However, it would be, I feel, a disservice to the study of the romances to allow this sometimes overwhelming fact to delay publication of this book still further.

In addition to Francisco Rico, I would like to thank Philip Martin for reading my manuscript and for guidance in preparation of the index. I must also acknowledge Tom Lathrop's constant encouragement and good spirits. I would also like to thank *Hispanic Review, MLN, Sin Nombre, Quaderni Iberoamericani* and *Kentucky Romance Quarterly* for allowing my articles to be included in this volume; the original place of publication is specified in the first note of each.

FLORIDA STATE UNIVERSITY

August, 1981

By Way of a Prologue. *Don Quijote.*

T CAN BE SAID without fear of exaggeration that interest in and study of the romances of chivalry[1] has been an incidental by-product of the study of the *Quijote*. Diego Clemencín has been until recently the person who knew best the romances of chivalry (see *infra*, p. 132); his knowledge is found in the notes of his edition of the *Quijote*, and his *Biblioteca de libros de caballerías* was conceived of as a supplement to his edition. Collectors of romances of chivalry, such as the Marqués de Salamanca,[2] bought them because they were books which Don Quijote had owned, and Juan Sedó chose as the topic for his inaugural speech in the Real Academia de Buenas Letras de Barcelona a *Contribución a la historia del coleccionismo cervantino y caballeresco* (Barcelona, 1948), as the two topics were so closely related

---

[1] I would like to insist, as I have already several times (see "Un barbarismo: 'libros de caballería,'" *Thesaurus*, 30 [1975], 340-41, and "More on *libros de caballería* and *libros de caballerías*," *La Corónica*, 5, No. 2 [Spring, 1977], 116-18), the the only correct Spanish term to designate these books is "libros de caballerías," in the plural, and not "libros de caballería" nor much less "novelas de caballería." It is true that these works were novels, in the sense in which that word is used today, but to use this term overemphasizes their fictional nature, ignoring the acceptance of them by some contemporary readers as seemingly historical works; certainly the juggling of terms indulged in by Armando Durán (*Estructura y técnica de la novela sentimental y caballeresca* [Madrid: Gredos, 1973], pp. 176-78) in order to make the genres adapt to his conclusions, is superfluous. (See my review of Durán's book in *HR*, 43 [1975], 425-29, and those of Keith Whinnom, *BHS*, 53 [1976], 61-62 and Charlotte Stern, *RPh*, 33 [1980], 600-03.) We have in the term "libros de caballerías" something which is not so commonly found: a precise and clear expression, authorized by the authors of the very works in question. Let us use it.

[2] On the book-collecting activities of the Marqués de Salamanca, see Isidro Bonsoms y Sicart, *Discursos leídos en la Real Academia de Buenas Letras de Barcelona en la recepción pública de D. Isidro Bonsoms y Sicart* (Barcelona, 1907), and Homero Serís, "La reaparición del *Tirant lo Blanch* de Barcelona de 1497," *Homenaje a Menéndez Pidal* (Madrid: Hernando, 1925), III, 57-76.

that it was logical to discuss them at the same time. When libraries place the romances of chivalry on display, they do so in expositions devoted principally to Cervantes.[3] The romances which have received far and away the greatest amount of study, *Amadís de Gaula*, *Tirant lo Blanch*, and *Palmerín de Inglaterra*, are the ones which are praised in the *escrutinio de la librería*.[4] The authors who are seldom studied, and the most glaring abuse in this area is the treatment (or lack of it) of Feliciano de Silva, are neglected because of the censure of their works which we find in the *Quijote*.

This phenomenon has, of course, an obvious explanation. The *Quijote* is a work which all scholars of Spanish literature have read, and which much of the general public is familiar with in its broad outlines. The *Quijote*, besides its position as the most acceptable source of comment on the romances of chivalry, is the contemporary work in which the romances are discussed at greatest length. A considerable number of them are either named in the *Quijote*, or explicitly referred to; in many cases they are summarized with pithy comments, such as the priest's observation that Belianís "[tiene] necesidad de un poco de ruibarbo para purgar la demasiada cólera suya." The books are also commented on as a body. They are "aborrecidos de tantos y alabados de muchos más;" they constitute a "máquina mal fundada" (I, Prologue). They are "disparatados," and "atienden solamente a deleitar, y no a enseñar" (I, 47); none of them has "un cuerpo de fábula entero" (I, 47); nevertheless, the innkeeper "querría estar oyéndolos noches y días" (I, 32). In effect, since the romances of chivalry are a primary theme of the *Quijote*, they are commented on repeatedly, by many different characters and from many contrasting points of view.

Having said this, it must be pointed out that despite its popularity,[5] the *Quijote* is a paradoxical work, one of the most controversial

---

[3] As, for example, the two bibliographical expositions held to celebrate the fourth centenary of the birth of Cervantes (Madrid, 1947 and 1948), the *Cervantes, lector* exposition (Madrid, 1976), and innumerable others.

[4] I believe, however, that what appears to be praise for one of these books is not such. See "Pero Pérez the Priest and His Comment on *Tirant lo Blanch*," included in this volume.

[5] I have commented briefly on the popularity of the *Quijote* in "Dígalo Portugal, Barcelona y Valencia: Una nota sobre la popularidad del *Quijote*,"

ones in Spanish literature. How few things all *cervantistas* agree on! And many of the unanswered questions of the *Quijote* relate directly to the romances of chivalry. Did Cervantes admire the romances of chivalry because they "ofrecían [sujeto] para que un buen entendimiento pudiera mostrarse en ellos"? When the Toledo canon said that he had written a hundred pages of a romance of chivalry, never to be finished, was he speaking for Cervantes?[6] Was Cervantes' intent to end the popularity of the romances of chivalry, as is said many times in the work, a declaration which Avellaneda took as literal? Or was this only a pose or pretext, since the books were already dead? If he disliked the romances, how did he know them so well? In short, did he admire the romances, or find them ridiculous? Or was his true attitude some unknown compromise between these two positions?

What I mean to suggest, then, is that to take the comments in the *Quijote* as the basis for our knowledge of the romances of chivalry is to build our critical house on a foundation of sand. Too little is known with certainty about the relationship of the *Quijote* to the romances of chivalry for the often confusing or ambiguous information Cervantes offers there to be taken as reliable critical material. The romances of chivalry are, in fact, much less enigmatic works than the *Quijote*; we can read them, analyze them, and criticize them without danger of falling into the traps that await the scholar who ventures unprepared into the Manchegan countryside. What can, in fact, be done is to utilize the romances of chivalry as a tool to aid us in understanding the *Quijote*, once we have studied them and formed our conclusions about them for ourselves.

The present monograph, then, will study the romances of chivalry without taking Cervantes as a starting point. In Chapter IV, some suggestions about the relationship of the romances of chivalry to the *Quijote* will be offered.

Hispanófila, Nº 52 (1974), 71-72. See also Keith Whinnom, "The Problem of the 'Best-Seller' in Spanish Golden-Age Literature," *BHS*, 57 (1980), 189-98.

6 Most recently the subject of speculation by Alban Forcione, *Cervantes, Aristotle, and the* Persiles (Princeton: Princeton University Press, 1970), p. 169.

Romances of Chivalry in the Spanish Golden Age

❧ I ❧

A Definition

ECAUSE OF THE EXTRAORDINARY IMPRECISION of
the general conception of the romances of
chivalry, it is necessary to define clearly the
subject matter of this book. If we were discussing Golden Age epic poetry, no one would
expect to find in it a treatment of the *Cid*, or the
romancero, or of Ariosto, except perhaps as
works indirectly asssociated with the genre, as
antecedents, or as illustrations of the same forms or principles in
the literatures of other countries. Similarly, if we were discussing
the Spanish pastoral novel, one would not include Virgil, Theo-
critus, or Sannazaro, except in a discussion of predecessors.

Yet such confusion is precisely what we find among those who
write on the Spanish romances of chivalry. From the beginnings of
critical study of the genre to the present, following, perhaps, the
well-known process by which works were attributed to famous
authors (Ovid, King Solomon), the true romances of chivalry have
seen themselves classified helter-skelter with foreign works of the
most diverse languages and time periods and with original Spanish
works which can scarcely be considered romances of chivalry. In
part this is due to a confusion between chivalric material and
romances of chivalry: ballads, for example, may deal with deeds of
knights, such as Bernardo del Carpio, or even with the heroes of
the romances of chivalry, such as Amadís de Gaula and the Caballero del Febo,[1] but this does not mean that they themselves are

---

[1] Protagonist of the *Espejo de prínicpes y cavalleros*, which I have edited in
Volumes 193-98 of the Clásicos Castellanos series (Madrid: Espasa-Calpe,
1975). Ballads about the Caballero del Febo and about Amadís were

romances of chivalry. In part it is also due to the unfortunate confusion caused by the different meanings of the word "romance" in English and Spanish.[2]

Examples of this confusion are easily offered. In the first survey of Spanish romances, Vicente Salvá treated Apuleius' *Golden Ass* as if it were a romance of chivalry.[3] The French bibliographer Brunet included Tirso de Molina's *Deleitar aprovechando* with the romances,[4] and as late as the *Catálogo de la biblioteca de* [Pedro] *Salvá* (Barcelona, 1872) we find Heliodorus' *Historia etiópica de los amores de Teágenes y Cariclea*, to contemporary readers certainly the very antithesis of a romance of chivalry,[5] included in this classification.[6] A number of chivalric tales translated from French, such as *Oliveros de Castilla*, are commonly included with the Spanish romances, as are other translations, such as *Roberto el Diablo* and *Clamades y Clarmonda*, whose similarity with the Spanish romances is that they are fictional

---

published by Lucas Rodríguez in his *Romancero historiado*, ed. Antonio Rodríguez-Moñino (Madrid: Castalia, 1967), pp. 168-88.

[2] On this term see Alan Deyermond, "The Lost Genre of Medieval Spanish Literature," *HR*, 43 (1975), 231-59, and Miguel Garci-Gómez, "*Romance* según los textos españoles del Medioevo y Prerrenacimiento," *JMRS*, 4 (1974), 35-62. The confusion concerning the word "romance" has led to errors on the part of scholars who should very well have known better: see the items included under the heading "Spanish Novels and Romances" in Fernand Baldensperger and W. P. Friedrich's *Bibliography of Comparative Literature*, University of North Carolina Studies in Comparative Literature, [1] (Chapel Hill, 1950), p. 454; Edward Glaser confused "romances caballerescos" with "libros de caballerías" in his "Nuevos datos sobre la crítica de los libros de caballerías en los siglos XVI y XVII," *AEM*, 3 (1966), 393-410.

[3] *Repertorio Americano*, 4 (1827), 63-64.

[4] Jacques-Charles Brunet, *Manuel du libraire et de l'amateur des livres*, reprint of 5th edition (Paris: Fermin-Didot, 1860-65), by Dorbon-Ainé (Paris, n.d.), VI, Col. 948.

[5] See the book of Forcione, cited in note 6 to "By Way of a Prologue."

[6] Pedro Salvá y Mallén, *Catálogo de la biblioteca de Salvá* (Valencia, 1872; reprint, Barcelona: Instituto Porter de Bibliografía Hispánica, 1963), II, 74. Together with Heliodorus, we also find in the romances of chivalry section such unusual books as the *Fiammetta* of Boccaccio, *Las Habidas* of Jerónimo de Arbolanche, and Lope's *Hermosura de Angélica*.

narratives in prose.[7] Even within the strictly Spanish material, the Amadís and the Palmerín series of romances attracted to themselves, by the same process, material that did not belong: *Polindo* was confused with the Palmerín series,[8] and *Lepolemo*, the *Espejo de príncipes y cavalleros*, and *Belianís de Grecia* were all considered at different times to be part of the Amadís cycle or works of Feliciano de Silva.[9]

Nineteenth-century critics and bibliographers may perhaps be excused for this confusion concerning the nature of the Spanish romances of chivalry. Yet the same errors are perpetuated by contemporary scholars who have had more opportunity to examine the works they deal with. While Henry Thomas correctly includes the *Cifar, Tirant lo Blanch, Paris e Viana, Enrique fi de Oliva* and other early works and translations in a chapter on antecedents, "The Romances of Chivalry in the Spanish Peninsula before the Year 1500," and draws a clear distinction between them and the vogue that began about the time of the publication of the *Amadís*, in his

---

[7] This confusion has been caused, or certainly extended, by their inclusion in Volume II of the *NBAE Libros de caballerías* set; José Amezcua, in discussing the *NBAE* set, correctly points out that "este volumen peca de reunir libros que no siempre podemos situar dentro del género caballeresco" (*Libros de caballerías hispánicos* [Madrid: Alcalá, 1973], p. 70.). Amezcua's useful anthology offers a well-chosen selection, and is free from many of the misconceptions which have obstructed the studies of the romances of chivalry; see my review, in *NRFH*, 25 (1976), 138-39.

[8] Simón Díaz (see note 10 below) still includes *Polindo* as Book III of the Palmerín series. That it does not belong there was pointed out by William Edward Purser in a scholarly work which, because of its place of publication, did not receive the circulation it deserved: Palmerin of England. *Some Remarks on this Romance and on the Controversy Concerning its Authorship* (Dublin, 1904), p. 437. Purser's conclusions, however, are included in the most important work on the Spanish romances of chivalry, Henry Thomas' standard *Spanish and Portuguese Romances of Chivalry* (Cambridge, England: Cambridge University Press, 1920; rpt. New York: Kraus Reprint, 1969), p. 100, no. 1, and p. 144. There is a Spanish translation of Thomas' book by Esteban Pujals, *Las novelas de caballerías españolas y portuguesas*, Anejo 10 of the *Revista de Literatura* (Madrid: CSIC, 1952).

[9] Frederic Adolphus Ebert, in his *General Bibliographical Dictionary* (Oxford: Oxford University Press, 1837), I, 43, includes as part of the Amadís cycle the *Caballero del Febo, Belianís*, and the *Roman des Romans* (a seventeenth-century French amalgamation of various Spanish romances of chivalry). Ebert adds, "Also Primaleon, Palmerin of Oliva and of England, Olivier of

standard reference work José Simón Díaz mixes them all together and for some unknown reason includes them all under the fifteenth century.[10] Following him, Maxime Chevalier does the same in *Sur le publique du roman de chevalerie* (Talence, 1968), and neither of the two collections of romances of chivalry published in Spain in this century—Volumes 6 and 9 of the *NBAE*,[11] and the unfortunate Aguilar volume of Felicidad Buendía[12]—distinguishes between works of different countries and periods of composition.

What, then, are the romances of chivalry, the topic of the present study? We can begin with a very simple criterion: only those romances of chivalry written in Spanish can be called, or should be treated together with, Spanish romances of chivalry. We can take a great step forward in clarifying the subject matter if we exclude works that are translations into Spanish from other languages.[13] But we are still left with too large and imprecise a body of

---

Castile, and the palladian history [*Florando de Inglaterra*], are reckoned with this series of stories, but do not properly belong to it" (I, 43).

[10] *Bibliografía de la literatura hispánica*, III, 2nd ed., Volume II (Madrid: CSIC, 1965); on Simón Díaz's bibliography, see the comments of Homero Serís, *Manual de bibliografía de la literatura española*, 2nd fascicle of the 1st [and only published] part, 2nd printing (New York: Las Américas, 1968), entry No. 7012. On two occasions, first in "Mas datos bibliográficos sobre libros de caballerías españoles," *Revista de Literatura*, 34 (1968, publ. 1970), 5-14, and in the appendix to my dissertation (Brown University, 1971 [1970]), I have pointed out some of Simón Díaz's errors. The proposed corrections have been incorporated into my bibliography, *Castilian Romances of Chivalry in the Sixteenth Century* (London: Grant and Cutler, 1979).

[11] Edited by Adolfo Bonilla y San Martín (Madrid, 1907-08). This collection includes not a single work originally written in Spanish.

[12] *Libros de caballerías españoles* (Madrid: Aguilar, 1954; 2nd edition 1960). This volume, about which I have inveighed on other occasions, as has Martín de Riquer, whom Buendía plagiarized (see *Tirant lo Blanc*, ed. Riquer [Barcelona: Seix Barral, 1970], I, 98), has done a great disservice, as it perpetuates Menéndez y Pelayo's preconceived ideas about the superiority of *Cifar*, *Tirant*, and *Amadís*, and the inferiority of the later romances. It has had unfortunate effects on later students of the romances of chivalry, such as Armando Durán (see my review, cited *supra* in note 1 to "By Way of a Prologue. Cervantes.").

[13] Almost all of these are translations from the French, and this group includes many of the Hispano-Arthurian texts. I do not mean that these works are unimportant, nor that they are not deserving of study in their

texts. Consulting the nineteenth edition of the Academia dictionary, we find that a "libro de caballerías" is an "especie de novela antigua en que se cuentan las hazañas y hechos fabulosos de caballeros aventureros o andantes." The *Diccionario de Autoridades* says that "libros de caballerías se llaman aquellos que contienen hechos e historias fingidas de héroes fabulosos. Tomaron este nombre de que fingían que los héroes que hablaban en ellas eran caballeros armados."[14] And going yet further back, to Covarrubias, we find that *libros de caballerías* are "los que tratan de hazañas de cavalleros andantes, ficciones gustosas y artificiosas de mucho entretenimiento y poco provecho, como los libros de Amadís, de don Galaor, del cavallero del Febo y los demás."[15]

So the romances are books which "tratan de hazañas de caballeros andantes," and the oldest definition, the closest to the time of the romances' greatest popularity, gives us some specific references: the books of Amadís and don Galaor, his brother, the Caballero del Febo, and "all the rest," thus reflecting the common conception that the romances of chivalry are unmanageable because of their number, though certainly there were no more of them than there were epic poems.

There are also internal references in the romances of chivalry which aid us in determining what books the authors were familiar with, and which knights they considered to be in the same category

---

own right. That they are related, as predecessors, to the romances which are the subject of this book is obvious. I merely wish to point out that they are very different works and needed to be studied separately. The person who is at present carrying on Bohigas' tradition of studying Hispano-Arthurian texts is Harvey Sharrer, who has prepared a Hispano-Arthurian bibliography (Pt. I published in 1978 by Grant and Cutler, London); he has pointed out quite correctly how the relationship between these peninsular representatives of what is essentially foreign material, and the later romances, those confusedly called "indígenos" by Menéndez y Pelayo, has yet to be determined (see his position paper for the Spanish Romances of Chivalry Seminar, in *La Corónica*, 3, No. 1 [Fall, 1974], p. 5).

[14] It is not generally known that the editors of the *Diccionario de Autoridades* (Madrid, 1726-39; reprint, Madrid: Gredos, 1963) originally chose *Belianís de Grecia* and Feliciano de Silva's *Florisel de Niquea* as two of their source works (see I, lxxxvii and xci); however, they do not appear to have been much used.

[15] Ed. Martín de Riquer (Barcelona: Horta, 1943), p. 324.

or class as the heroes of the books they were writing. Marcos Martínez, the author of the *Espejo de príncipes* or *Caballero del Febo*, Part III (see *infra*, "The Pseudo-Historicity of the Romances of Chivalry," p. 126), includes Amadís and his relatives, Primaleón, Cristalián de España, Olivante de Laura, Belianís de Grecia, and Felixmarte de Hircania. In the prologue to *Olivante de Laura* we find the Amadís and Palmerín families, and Clarián de Landanís. The author of *Cirongilio de Tracia* mentions an earlier romance, *Felix Magno*.[16]

Another source which we can use to discover what the contemporaries considered to be romances of chivalry are the criticisms of the romances, in which specific works are often named. (The criticisms are discussed more fully below.) Juan de Valdés, in his *Diálogo de la lengua*, speaks of *Amadís de Gaula, Palmerín, Primaleón, Esplandián, Florisando, Lisuarte,* and the *Caballero de la Cruz,* and separates in a different group, as inferior works, other books which are actually translations: *Guarino Mezquino, La linda Melosina, Reinaldos de Montalván con La Trapisonda, Oliveros de Castilla*.[17]   Pedro Mexía refers to the *Amadís, Lisuartes,* and *Clarianes;*[18] Malón de Chaide to the *Amadises, Floriseles, Belianís,* and *Lisuarte*.[19] Mateo Alemán criticizes those women who read *Belianís, Amadís, Esplandián,* and the *Caballero del Febo*.[20]

Rather than continue with lists of names, we can summarize the results obtained from this examination of titles, distinguishing those works thought to be romances of chivalry. There are constant references to the *Amadís,* and almost as frequent ones to *Palmerín de Olivia* and *Primaleón*. Closely following in numbers of citations are the later books of the Amadís family, such as *Lisuarte de Grecia, Amadís de Grecia,* and *Florisel de Niquea,* and in the early works there are more than a few references to *Clarián de Landanís,* a lengthy cycle, which evidently, from its popularity, deserves more study than it has

---

[16] See section N of my bibliography of the romances of chivalry.

[17] P. 96 of the edition of Cristina Barbolani de García (Firenze: D'Anna, 1967).

[18] In his *Historia imperial y cesárea,* cited by Thomas, p. 158, n. 1.

[19] *La conversión de la Magdalena,* cited by Thomas, pp. 174-75, n. 1.

[20] *Guzmán de Alfarache,* in *La novela picaresca española,* I, ed. Francisco Rico (Barcelona: Planeta, 1967), p. 787.

received. In the later authors there are various references to *Belianís de Grecia*, the *Caballero del Febo*, and other later books.[21] There are less frequent references to translations, such as *Tristán*, and even fewer to works such as *Oliveros de Castilla* and *Partinuplés*. Finally, I have not found a single reference anywhere (excluding the *Quijote*) to the *Caballero Cifar*, showing that its one edition of 1512 did not remove it from oblivion, and few to *Tirant lo Blanch*.[22]

What seems clear from all this is that Golden Age readers had a clear and consistent concept of which works were, and which were not, romances of chivalry. Their preference for works written in Castilian shows that the use of language of composition as a criterion for identifying the Spanish romances of chivalry is a sensible one, and confirms that the foreign romances of chivalry available in translation were tangential works, having lost whatever influence they may have had in Castile in the fifteenth or earlier centuries. Certainly the works the contemporaries saw as being romances of chivalry had an important characteristic in common, besides their language of composition, and that was their length. These works range from moderately long to extremely long; the short, translated works such as *Partinuplés* and *Enrique fi de Oliva* are seldom referred to.

So we can arrive at a definition, partly positivist and partly empirical. A romance of chivalry is a long prose narration which deals with the deeds of a "caballero aventurero o andante"—that is, a fictitious biography. More precisely, the sixteenth- and seventeenth-century Spaniards (and I am unaware that the term "libros de caballerías" was widely used prior to the sixteenth century[23]) understood as "libros de caballerías" Montalvo's *Amadís* and the

---

[21] See the list of references to the *Caballero del Febo* or *Espejo de príncipes* in my edition, I, p. L, notes 49 and 50.

[22] One is found in a pun in the prologue to the *Caballería celestial* (cited by Thomas, p. 176, n. 4), another is by Alejo Venegas (Thomas, p. 166, n. 1), and the third known to me is of Vives (cited by Riquer in the introduction to his edition of *Tirante el Blanco* for the Asociación de Bibliófilos de Barcelona [Barcelona, 1947], p. xxxii).

[23] Alfonso Martínez de Toledo, in his curious comment in the *Corbacho* (ed. J. González Muela [Madrid: Castalia, 1970], p. 119), calls them "ystoria[s] de cavallería."

books written in Castilian subsequent to it, which are the ones we are dealing with in this book. As will be seen later, these romances have many internal elements in common, which also make them a cohesive group.

It can be noted in conclusion that the romances of chivalry which we will be dealing with are, then, those written in Castilian subsequent to the publication of the *Amadís*, including the *Amadís* itself and a few works, such as *Palmerín de Olivia*, published around that time though written slightly earlier. These books, it should be noted, were also the ones known to Cervantes, as they are the ones dealt with in the *Quijote*. Both in the "escrutinio de la librería" and in the conversations of the characters in the *Quijote*, the works named are the lengthy Castilian fictionalized biographies: *Amadís, Palmerín, Felixmarte de Hircania, Cirongilio de Tracia*, and so on. Translations into Castilian, short works, and works which are other than fictional biographies receive either the briefest and most infrequent of treatment (such as *Tablante de Ricamonte*, referred to in I, 16), or are not there at all. It is, then, the long, imaginary biographies of knights-errant, the "mainstream" works, which must be studied as potential sources of the *Quijote*.

❧ II ❧

The History and Present State
of Scholarship on
Spanish Romances of Chivalry

N CONTRAST WITH A GENRE such as the Golden Age epic poem, the subject of over 200 dense pages in which Frank Pierce outlines the history of its study in Spain,[1] there is relatively little to be said about the criticism of the romances of chivalry, especially in the Golden Age itself. The difference in prestige between the two genres is the obvious explanation for this fact; the epic was, of course, a genre in continuous existence since classical antiquity, and one of the few ways in which Spanish Golden Age authors could directly imitate classical models. Like the other forms of prose fiction, except for the so-called "Byzantine" novel,[2] with its model, the "prose epic" of Heliodorus,[3] the romances of chivalry had no classical model, no pedigree nor tradition, and thus very little prestige. Like the illegitimate son who unobtrusively exists and may even do great things, but does not share in the glory of the family, the romances of chivalry were only discussed incidentally by the literary theorists of the day.

---

[1] *La poesía épica del Siglo de Oro*, 2nd edition (Madrid: Gredos, 1968).

[2] See the comment of Forcione, *Cervantes, Aristotle and the Persiles*, p. 49, n. 1, and also the book of Armando Durán, referred to in note 1 to "By Way of a Prologue."

[3] Forcione, pp. 49-87.

9

The most familiar comments made by contemporaries about the romances of chivalry are criticisms; the romances were more often criticized, as poorly written, lascivious, "mentirosos," than they were praised.[4] These criticisms have been amply discussed and analyzed by other scholars[5] and are referred to elsewhere in this book; in my opinion they cannot be said to form part of the scholarship of the romances of chivalry, both because they are incidental comments, in many cases taken out of context (see note

---

[4] The criticisms of the romances of chivalry are summarized by Riquer on pp. xli-xliii of the introduction to his edition of *Tirante el Blanco* for the Asociación de Bibliófilos de Barcelona, already cited in note 22 to the preceding chapter, and in his *Aproximación al* Quijote, 2nd edition with this title (Barcelona: Teide, 1970), pp. 67-70. (This book was first published in 1960 with the title *Cervantes y el* Quijote.)

[5] Thomas, pp. 147-79, summarizes the data of Menéndez Pelayo and adds new material, and I offer some little-known criticisms in note 6 to "Who Read the Romances of Chivalry," *infra*, and in an Appendix to this volume. In addition, one may consult: Werner Krauss, "Die Kritik des Siglo de Oro am Ritter- und Schäferroman," in *Homenatge a Antoni Rubió i Lluch* (Barcelona, 1936), I, pp. 225-46, reprinted in his *Gesammelte Aufsätze zur Literatur- und Sprachwissenschaft* (Frankfurt, 1949), 152-76, Antonio E. Serrano Redonnet, "Prohibición de libros en el primer sínodo santiagüeño," *RFH*, 5 (1943), 162-66, Francisco Rodríguez Marín, "La lectura de los libros de caballerías," Appendix IV to his "nueva edición crítica" of the *Quijote*, IX (Madrid: Atlas, 1949), 57-68, Eugenio Asensio, "El erasmismo y las corrientes afines," *RFE*, 36 (1952), 94, Marcel Bataillon, *Erasmo y España*, trans. Antonio Alatorre, 2nd edition (Mexico: Fondo de Cultura Económica, 1966), pp. 615-24, Edmund Glaser, "Nuevos datos sobre la crítica de los libros de caballerías en los siglos XVI y XVII," *AEM*, 3 (1966), 393-410, Fernando Lázaro Carreter, "La ficción autobiográfica en el *Lazarillo de Tormes*," *Litterae Hispanae et Lusitanae* (Munich: Hueber, 1968), p. 200 (the text of Núñez de Reinoso cited there is taken from page 431, not 413, of Volume 3 of the *BAE*), Américo Castro, *El pensamiento de Cervantes*, 2nd edition (Barcelona: Noguer, 1972), p. 61, n. 20, Pierre Heugas, *La Célestine et sa descendance directe* ([Talence]: Institut d'Études Ibériques et Ibéroaméricaines de l'Université de Bordeaux, 1973), p. 14, Gonzalo Fernández de Oviedo, *Memorias [Quinquagenas]*, ed. J. B. Avalle-Arce, North Carolina Studies in Romance Languages and Literatures, Texts, Textual Studies and Translations, 1 (Chapel Hill: University of North Carolina, Department of Romance Languages, 1974), pp. 92-93, 109-10, 189-94, 221-23, 234-35, and 637, and Juan Pérez de Moya, *Philosophía secreta*, ed. Eduardo Gómez de Baquero (Madrid: CIAP, 1928), I, 8 (*apud* Alberto Blecua, in the article cited below in note 31 to Chapter IV).

30 to Chapter IV), and because most of the persons making these criticisms had not personally examined the romances, merely repeated and amplified comments of their predecessors. (The fact that these comments have been given so much attention in this century is due to their harmony with the opinions of certain modern scholars and their supposed similarity to what has been understood to be Cervantes' opinion.[6]) However, we can find among them occasional voices that show a direct contact with the romances of chivalry, and, thus, more discriminating and intelligent commentary than usual.

The first of these more intelligent comments is that of Juan de Valdés. That Valdés had some direct knowledge of the romances can be concluded from the detailed comments made about them in the *Diálogo de la lengua*, and from the fact that the character Valdés had spent "diez años, los mejores de mi vida," on no more useful occupation than reading "estas mentiras." Although he criticizes as "mentirosos" (lacking verisimilitude) *Esplandián, Florisando, Lisuarte [de Grecia]*, and the *Cavallero de la Cruz [Lepolemo]*, and as "mentirosos" and "mal compuestos" the translations of foreign works referred to previously, for reasons he does not completely explain he praises "los quatro libros de *Amadís*, como... los de *Palmerín* y *Primaleón*, que por cierto respeto an ganado crédito conmigo."[7]

A true scholar such as Alonso López Pinciano, one of the most influential literary theorists of the sixteenth century, also shows some discrimination in his comments on the romances of chivalry, prima facie evidence of more direct knowledge of them than could be gained from reading the comments of others. Although he repeatedly compares the romances of chivalry with the Milesian fables, which "tienen acaescimientos fuera de toda buena imitación y semejança a verdad,"[8] he exempts some from a general condemna-

---

6 See "Pero Pérez the Priest and His Comment on *Tirant lo Blanch*," *infra*.

7 I quote from p. 96 of the critical edition of Barbolani, cited in note 17 to "A Definition."

8 *Philosophía antigua poética*, ed. Alfredo Carballo Picazo, reprint of 1953 edition (Madrid: CSIC, 1973), II, 8. The canónigo of the *Quijote* also compares the romances of chivalry with the Milesian fables (Part I, Chapter 47).

tion: "no hablo de vn Amadís de Gaula, ni aun del de Grecia y otros pocos, los quales tienen mucho de bueno, sino de los demás, que ni tienen versimilitud, ni doctrina, ni aun estilo graue, y, por esto, las dezía un amigo mío 'almas sin cuerpo'... y a los lectores y autores dellas, cuerpo sin alma."[9]

But the well-informed, as well as the favorable, comment on the romances of chivalry is a rarity in the Golden Age. We need mention only, to conclude, the valuable information given by the authors themselves in their prologues, which have been almost completely ignored,[10] perhaps because the most accessible books, *Amadís* and *Esplandián*, lack both prologues and dedications. The criticisms to be found in the prologues—such as the famous attack of Feliciano de Silva on his predecessor Juan Díaz,[11] or the comments of Ortúñez[12]—are directed at specific works rather than at the romances as a whole. And the sometimes eloquent explanations of the romances' purposes certainly reached a larger group of readers than did the attacks of the moralists and literary critics, and presumably influenced as well as represented the attitudes toward the romances of a certain segment of the reading public. The author of *Palmerín de Olivia* said that his work "está llena de yngenio e doctrina en todas sus partes... va en sentencias poderosa, en él estilo copiosa, en ninguna parte confusa, las palabras dizen con la materia, las sentencias ygualan con las cosas, guarda la maiestad en las personas, cuenta breve, proprio, natural, sin confusión de orden, mueve passiones quando quiere, propone, incita, persuade. Ystoria es adonde conoceréys las claras hazañas de vuestros mayores: en unos alteza de ánimo que fortuna no vence, en otros esfuerço divino que peligros no teme."[13] In the prologue to *Cirongilio de Tracia* the author praises the protagonist, particularly "la piedad que en el tiempo de su mayor saña se halló en él. No se movió con yra a las

---

[9] III, 178.

[10] There is not a single example in Alberto Porqueras Mayo's *El prólogo en el renacimiento español*, Anejo 24 of the *Revista de Literatura* (Madrid: CSIC, 1965).

[11] Quoted below, in note 28 to Chapter VI.

[12] *Espejo de príncipes y cavalleros*, p. 14 of Volume I of my edition.

[13] P. 4 of the edition of Giuseppe di Stefano (Pisa: Istituto di Letteratura Spagnola e Ispano-Americana dell'Università di Pisa, 1966).

batallas, mas con misericordia y clemencia que tuvo de los afligidos. y voluntad de deshazer los tuertos y agravios, donde todos los príncipes deste tiempo pueden tomar enxemplo para más buenamente governarse, para que con justa razón sean comparados al esclarecido sol, bien como lo fue este bienaventurado cavallero en su tiempo, en tal manera que sobró a todos los del mundo en bondad, en las armas, en esfuerço de coraçon, en nobleza de ánimo, en virtud de ínclitas costumbres."[14]

These comments, although of great importance for the proper interpretation of the romances of chivalry—which always declared, sincerely or no, a moral intent—and for an understanding of their position in sixteenth-century culture, again do not constitute scholarship of the romances in the sense in which that term is usually used. Such scholarship can not be said to antedate the seventeenth century, and the first two centuries of study of the romances of chivalry were devoted almost exclusively to their bibliographical problems. It was only when there existed, first, access to texts and an accurate list of those romances which had been written, and second, information by which to distinguish the first editions and the relative order of composition of the romances, that deeper study could begin.

One cannot avoid mentioning, for its contribution to the bibliography of the romances of chivalry, the *Registrum* of Fernando Colón, illegitimate son of the discoverer,[15] and the somewhat lesser-known list of books given to a monastery in Valencia by the Duke

---

[14] Pp. 6-7 of the edition of James Ray Green, Jr., Dissertation, Johns Hopkins, 1974. An abstract of this dissertation may be found in *DAI*, 36 (1976), 6735A.

[15] Published in facsimile by Archer Huntington, *Catalogue of the Library of Ferdinand Columbus* (New York, 1905), and now reprinted by Kraus Reprint Co. (New York, 1967); items relevant to Spanish literature were published by Gallardo in his *Ensayo de una biblioteca española de libros raros y curiosos* (Madrid, 1863-69; reprint, Madrid: Gredos, 1968), II, No. 1870. Colón's other catalogue, the *Abecedarium*, has never been published. See Henry Harrisse, *Excerpta Colombiana* (Paris, 1887), Tomás Marín Martínez, *Memoria de las obras y libros del Bachiller Juan Pérez* (Madrid, 1970), reviewed in *RFE*, 55 (1972), 75-85, and Antonio Rodríguez-Moñino, *Los pliegos poéticos de la Biblioteca Colombina (Siglo XVI)*, University of California Publications in Modern Philology, 110 (Berkeley, Los Angeles, London: University of California Press, 1976).

and Duchess of Calabria,[16] both of whom were, like Colón, readers of the romances of chivalry (see *infra*, p. 115). It is from these two lists of books that we have any information at all about a number of works (*Leoneo de Hungría*) and of editions (the earliest known edition of *Esplandián*, Sevilla, 1510), which have since disappeared.

Readers of this book may be already familiar with the name of Nicolás Antonio, who published in his *Bibliotheca Hispana* (1672), later *Bibliotheca Hispana Nova*, much bibliographical information about Spanish books of all periods.[17] Antonio apparently felt a certain admiration for the romances of chivalry, and in the prologue to his bibliography offered a defense of them, comparing them to epics in prose.[18] Included in his vast repertory are all the major Spanish romances of chivalry, and many of the minor ones. He ordinarily included only one or two editions of each. We find in his work *Don Clarisel de las Flores*, which he knew only in manuscript, as well as a number of works which have apparently disappeared and cannot be positively identified; Menéndez Pelayo made the irreverent suggestion that Antonio deliberately invented one such book (*Penalva*).[19] Be this as it may, his desire to include every book, no matter how slender the evidence for its existence, led him to unintentionally invent some Spanish books which only existed in other languages, such as *Florimón*, or the thirteenth book of *Amadís* (*Bibliotheca Hispana Nova*, II, 395-96), which are still found in standard bibliographies. He

---

[16] "Inventario de los libros del Duque de Calabria," *RABM*, 1st series, 4 (1874), 7-10, 21-25, 38-41, 54-56, 67-69, 83-86, 99-101, 114-17, and 132-34.

[17] The *Bibliotheca Hispana Nova*, edited by Tomás Antonio Sánchez and others, was published in Madrid in two volumes, 1783-88, and has been reprinted in facsimile (Torino: Bottega d'Erasmo, 1963). On Antonio, see E. Juliá Martínez, "Nicolás Antonio. Notas preliminares para su estudio," *Revista de Bibliografía Nacional*, 3 (1942), 7-37, and V. Romero Muñoz, "Estudio del bibliófilo sevillano Nicolás Antonio," *Archivo Hispalense*, 12 (1950), 57-92, and 13 (1951), 29-56 and 215-44.

[18] *Bibliotheca Hispana Nova*, I, ix. The passage is reproduced at the beginning of my editon of the *Espejo de príncipes*, I, viii.

[19] See *Orígenes de la novela*, 2nd edición nacional (Madrid: CSIC, 1962), I, 413. No one has identified what books Gonsales Coutinho (*Bibliotheca Hispana Nova*, I, 554) and Simon de Silveira (II, 288) are supposed to have written.

thus attained, with some justification, a reputation for inaccuracy in the entries concerning romances of chivalry.

It is worth noting that Nicolás Antonio used one of the most important collections of romances of chivalry, that known as the "Sapienza" collection, from the Roman university which owned it, consisting of books which originally belonged to the house of Urbino. Under colorful circumstances this collection left the Sapienza's Alessandrina library, where it was housed; it is now shared by the British Library, the Biblioteca Nacional of Madrid, and the Hispanic Society of America.[20]

Nicolás Antonio's comments, which were arranged alphabetically, were extracted, collected, and supplemented by the eighteenth-century scholar Nicolas Lenglet du Fresnoy, who dedicated a section of his *Bibliothèque des romans* (1734)[21] to the Spanish romances of chivalry. He pointed out, sometimes with pleasure, the lacunae of Nicolás Antonio, indicated many more editions of the more popular romances, and mentioned for the first time some of the minor ones, such as *Arderique*, *Claribalte*, and *Felixmarte de Hircania*.

The first writer to discuss in print, however briefly, the content of the Spanish romances of chivalry was Francesco Severio Quadrio. In his *Della storia, e della ragione d'ogni poesia*, Volume IV (Milan, 1749), he gave the family trees of both the Palmerín and the Amadís families, and discussed how the latter were based, in his opinion, on the history of the early Gauls.[22]

The honor of being the first Spaniard to study the romances of chivalry must clearly fall to the Benedictine monk Martín Sarmiento (1695-1771). In his posthumous *Memorias para la historia de la poesía y poetas españoles* (Madrid, 1775; written about 1745), he discusses them briefly, commending them for their language and relating them to the medieval narrative (i.e., epic) tradition. A more interesting

---

[20] See the *Discurso* of Bonsoms and the article of Serís, cited above, in note 2 to the prologue; Bonsoms includes a list of the collection. See also Enrico Narducci, *Notizie della Biblioteca Alessandrina* (Rome, 1872).

[21] Volume II of *De l'usage des romans* (1734; reprint, Geneva: Slatkine, 1970).

[22] The complete work occupies seven volumes, and was published by various publishers in Bologna and Milan from 1739 to 1752. There is an index in Volume VII.

curiosity, however, is his still-unpublished "Disertación sobre el *Amadís de Gaula*," a copy of which is in the Ticknor collection in the Boston Public Library. According to Barton Sholod, who has studied it, Sarmiento "attempts to place the *Amadís* within the broad scope of Spanish chivalric literature which he separates into four stages or epochs. The first of these is characterized by the... *Psuedo-Turpin*, throughout the eleventh and twelfth centuries; the second is the cycle of Crusades romances most typified in Spain by the thirteenth-century prose tale, *La gran conquista de ultramar*; the third encompasses the totally fanciful tales of the fourteenth and fifteenth centuries centering about "Héroes fingidos" or "Caballeros andantes" of which Amadís is the prime example; finally, we have the most lofty but genuinely human chivalric tale which ironically breaks with the past tradition of "pure" epic-romance and creates the new realistic mode, *Don Quijote de la Mancha*."[23] A Galician himself, Sarmiento began the modern debate about the original language of the *Amadís* by suggesting it was first written in Galician (Sholod, p. 195).

Sarmiento's "Disertación" was actually "part of a more extensive unpublished essay entitled *La vida y escritos de Miguel de Cervantes Saavedra*" (Sholod, p. 189). Sarmiento was thus also the first to associate the study of the romances of chivalry with that of the *Quijote*.

At that time (the late eighteenth century), interest in *Don Quijote* as a typically Spanish work, or as *the* Spanish literary masterpiece, was beginning, and it is not surprising, then, to find that examination of the romances of chivalry became secondary to the study of the *Quijote*. We would do well to at least mention John Bowle, the first modern editor of the *Quijote*, who (the notes to his edition show) had studied well several romances of chivalry: *Amadís de Gaula* and *Amadís de Grecia*, *Olivante de Laura*, *Palmerín de Olivia*, and the *Espejo de caballerías*. He had some contact with a number of others, mentioned less frequently: *Felixmarte de Hircania*, *Tirante el Blanco*, *Belianís de*

---

[23] Barton Sholod, "Fray Martín Sarmiento, *Amadís de Gaula* and the Spanish Chivalric 'Genre,'" in *Studies in Honor of Mario A. Pei*, University of North Carolina Studies in Romance Languages and Literatures, 114 (Chapel Hill: University of North Carolina Press, 1972), p. 190.

Grecia, the *Espejo de príncipes,* and *Polindo.*[24] Bowle's comments have often been tacitly used by later Spanish editors.

Following the example of Sarmiento and Bowle in associating the study of the romances of chivalry with that of the *Quijote,* Diego Clemencín published in the first half of the nineteenth century the most important *Quijote* edition of that century (Madrid, 1833-39). Clemencín's substantial contributions to the knowledge of the romances of chivalry are discussed in *"Don Quijote* y los libros de caballerías: necesidad de un reexamen," included in this volume. Clemencín's notes to the *Quijote* are a treasure-trove of information about the romances; scarcely less valuable is his *Biblioteca de libros de caballerías,* consisting of bibliographical notes intended to be a supplement to his edition.[25]

In the early nineteenth century, bibliographical information available about the romances of chivalry was approaching a satisfactory state, and there began to appear a series of articles or catalogues devoted specifically to the bibliography of the romances of chivalry. The earliest of these, that of Vicente Salvá, dates from 1827,[26] and already we find included almost all of the titles of romances and most of the editions. Finding the romances too numerous to handle unless classified, he began dividing them into categories, a practice often followed by later writers yet a source of confusion: "Amadís

---

[24] On Bowle, see Ralph Merritt Cox, *The Rev. John Bowle. The Genesis of Cervantean Criticism,* University of North Carolina Studies in Romance Languages and Literatures, 99 (Chapel Hill: University of North Carolina Press, 1971). Cox's dissertation on Bowle (Wisconsin, 1967; see *DA,* 28 [1968], 3175A) contains transcriptions of all of Bowle's notes on the *Quijote.*

[25] Clemencín's edition of the *Quijote* has twice been reprinted by Ediciones Castilla, most recently in 1966. There is an index of Clemencín's notes prepared by C. F. Bradford (Madrid, 1885), although the Castilla edition contains much supplementary material which facilitates the use of the notes. The *Biblioteca de libros de caballerías* was published as number 3 of the series *Publicaciones cervantinas* by D. Juan Sedó Peris-Mencheta, himself the author of the already-cited *Contribución a la historia del coleccionismo cervantino y caballeresco* (Barcelona, 1948), and owner of a large library, which contained some romances of chivalry (a catalogue was published in Barcelona, 1953-55).

[26] *Repertorio Americano,* 4 (1827), 29-74.

de Gaula y su línea" (in which was included *Lepolemo*), "Palmerín de Oliva y su descendencia," "Romances [sic] españoles de caballeros independientes de las antedichas ramas," "Libros trasladados [traducidos] de otras lenguas," including those of the Round Table and of Charlemagne, "imitaciones ascéticas y morales," "historias con algún fondo de verdad, aunque desfigurados con sucesos caballerescos" (included are the chronicles of the Cid, and *La doncella de Francia*), and "libros de absoluta verdad histórica" (the *Passo honroso*).

Salvá, like a modern scholar, drew on a series of very diverse sources: bookseller's catalogues, the *Quijote* edition of Bowle as well as that of Juan Antonio Pellicer (Madrid, 1797-98), the works of Nicolás Antonio and Quadrio. Considering the handicaps he worked under, his work is a good one, marred only by his inclusion of works which no modern scholar would call romances of chivalry.

The most important contributor of the nineteenth century to our knowledge of the romances of chivalry, after Diego Clemencín, is unquestionably Pascual de Gayangos. Gayangos wrote a long introduction and the "Catálogo razonado de los libros de caballerías que hay en lengua castellana o portuguesa, hasta el año de 1800," found in Volume 40 of the *BAE*, and he published in that volume an edition of *Amadís de Gaula* that was to stand until the publication of that of Edwin Place in 1959-69, and an edition of the *Sergas de Esplandián* for which there is yet no published replacement.[27]

In his "Catálogo razonado," again divided into categories, although different ones ("libros del ciclo bretón, libros del ciclo carolingio, libros del ciclo 'greco-asiático'—los Amadises Palmerines e independientes—, historias y novelas caballerescas, libros a lo divino, libros fundados en asuntos históricos, y traducciones de poemas caballerescos, principalmente italianos"), Gayangos brought togeth-

---

[27] The *BAE* edition was first published in 1857 and has been several times reprinted; it is not known what Gayangos intended to publish in the following volumes, which are implied by the "I" found on the title page. It should be mentioned that it was Buenaventura Carlos Aribau who was originally charged with preparing a volume on romances of chivalry for the *BAE*; an introduction he wrote for it was published posthumously, in the *Revista Crítica de Historia y Literatura*, 4 (1899), 129-45.

A new edition of the *Sergas* has been prepared by Dennis Nazak, dissertation, Northwestern University, 1976 (see *DAI*, 36 [1977], 4402A-03A).

er all the previously published bibliographical information, including the rather unreliable data of the French bibliographer Brunet,[28] and added a great deal of new information. Because he lived for some time in London, he was able to include information about the copies in the great Grenville collection of the British Museum (now British Library), and those in the private library of Sir Thomas Phillipps, the greatest manuscript collector of all time;[29] he also included, for the first time, information on the many unique Spanish items in the former Imperial Library of Vienna. The only major source he did not have access to was the catalogue of Ferdinand Colón's library.

His detailed and intelligent annotations were to give Gayangos' catalogue a usefulness and reliability the previous ones had lacked. In fact, it has been the basis for all subsequent bibliographies of romances of chivalry, including, indirectly, my own. He revised his own catalogue for inclusion in Gallardo's *Ensayo de una biblioteca española de libros raros y curiosos;*[30] his information was incorporated in

---

[28] In his *Manuel du livraire et de l'amateur des livres,* cited in note 4 to Chapter I.

[29] On Thomas Phillipps, see A[lan] N. L. Munby, *Portrait of an Obsession. The Life of Sir Thomas Phillipps* (New York: Putnam, 1967), who includes references to earlier studies. Phillipps refers to his copies of works of the Amadís series in "Early Editions of *Amadis de Gaul,*" *Willis's Current Notes,* 5 (1855), 95-96, "Editions of *Amadis de Gaula,*" *Willis's Current Notes,* 6 (1856), 14, and "*Amadis de Gaula,*" *Willis's Current Notes,* 6 (1856), 48; also Phillipps, who liked to publish catalogues of his library, is reported to have published a two-page *Catalogue of Spanish Romances in Middle Hill Library* (c. 1852) which I have not seen. Some of Phillipps' romances were purchased by the Argentine poet and bibliophile Oliverio Girondo; see my edition of the *Espejo de príncipes,* I, lxxiv, n. 88, and "Búsqueda y hallazgo de *Philesbián de Candaria,*" *Miscellanea Barcinonensia,* 11 (1972), 147-57. Amalia Sarriá, of the Biblioteca Nacional of Madrid, informs me that that library has bought at least one of Phillipps' romances, his copy of *Philesbián de Candaria;* Phillipps' manuscript of *Lidamarte de Armenia* was not sold until 1973, when it was purchased by the University of California (Berkeley) Library; it has since been edited by Mary Lee Cozad, "An Annotated Edition of a Sixteenth-Century Novel of Chivalry: Damasio de Frías y Balboa's *Lidamarte de Armenia,*" Dissertation, Berkeley, 1975; abstract in *DAI,* 37 (1976), 359A-60A. On *Lidamarte,* also see David Hook, "Nota sobre la portada de *Lidamarte de Armenia* (1590)," *RABM,* 78 (1975), 873-74, and Mary Lee Cozad, "Una curiosidad bibliográfica: la portada de *Lidamarte de Armenia* (1590), libro de caballerías," *RABM,* 79 (1976), 255-61.

[30] See I, viii, where the debt to Gayangos is acknowledged.

the *Catálogo de la biblioteca de Salvá*,[31] was the subject of an article by G. Brunet,[32] and is the foundation of the most widely used modern bibliography, that of Simón Díaz.[33]

In his lengthy "Discurso preliminar" Gayangos discusses the origin of the romances of chivalry in Spain and the controversies regarding the original language of composition of *Amadís de Gaula* and *Palmerín de Inglaterra*, both of which were claimed by the Portuguese. Of more lasting interest, however, are the analyses of a number of romances of chivalry which he provides. He summarizes for us most of the chivalric production of Feliciano de Silva, *Palmerín de Olivia*, and *Primaleón*, as well as others as diverse as *Lepolemo* and *Florambel de Lucea*. He was an alert reader, and pointed out, for example, the passages which show that Feliciano de Silva was the author of *Lisuarte de Grecia* (Book 7 of the Amadís family), Pedro de Luján of *Silves de la Selva* (Book 12 of the Amadís family), and Francisco Delicado of *La lozana andaluza*.[34] He found a certain value and, in contrast with Clemencín (see *infra*, p. 140), a certain diversion in the romances of chivalry, which make his commentaries easy to read and deserving of the circulation they have received in the widely circulated collection of Rivadeneira.

Since 1857, when Gayangos published his volume, there have appeared only two studies of the romances of chivalry which even attempt any comprehensive coverage of them.[35] The first of these is that of Menéndez y Pelayo, in his *Orígenes de la novela*.[36] In this book Menéndez y Pelayo dedicates two chapters to the romances of chivalry, the first discussing foreign works translated into Spanish,

---

[31] Cited in note 6 to Chapter I; see II, 1-109.

[32] "Étude bibliographique sur les romans de chevalerie espagnols," *Bulletin du Bibliophile* (1861), 199-208, 269-80, 327-32.

[33] Items Nos. 6533-7578 in Volume III, Part 2.

[34] P. xxxi, n. 1, p. lii, and p. xxxix, n. 4, respectively.

[35] It is not generally known that Adolfo Bonilla y San Martín planned an extensive study, which apparently was never written, to accompany his editions of various chivalric texts in the *NBAE* (see p. 735 of *NBAE*, 9 [Madrid, 1908]).

[36] First published in *NBAE*, Volumes 1, 7, 14, and 21 (Madrid, 1905-15). I have used the edition cited in note 19.

and the second those which he called "indígenos," or written in the languages of the Iberian peninsula. Besides a detailed examination of *Amadís de Gaula*, he spends more time than Gayangos discussing earlier works, in particular *Tirant lo Blanch*, the *Caballero Cifar*, and the recently discovered *Curial y Güelfa*. Because of his wide reading in Golden Age non-fiction, he was able to illustrate in some detail the increasing criticism to which the romances of chivalry were subjected in the sixteenth century. These are, however, his only real contributions. Never one to disguise his prejudices, he devotes the remainder of his second chapter to a discussion of why the romances of chivalry later than the *Amadís*, most of which he had not examined, were not only bad, but monstrous. Although "el mayor defecto del *Esplandián* es venir después del *Amadís*" (p. 404), *Palmerín de Olivia* "no es más que un calco servil de las principales aventuras de Amadís y de su hijo" (p. 416), and Feliciano de Silva was "el gran industrial literario, que por primera vez puso en España y quizá en Europa, taller de novelas" (p. 407). Following well-authorized practice, Menéndez y Pelayo simply embellished the comments of previous critics when he had no direct knowledge of the works he was studying.[37] With his overemphasis on the early works and uninformed attacks on works later than the *Amadís* he has done the study of the romances of chivalry great harm.

In 1920 Sir Henry Thomas published his classic study, *Spanish and Portuguese Romances of Chivalry*, in which he joined two earlier papers with others given as lectures at Cambridge University in 1917.[38] Essentially a bibliographer, later to serve for many years as head of the British Museum's Department of Printed Books, Thomas worked extensively with that library's large collection of romances of chivalry. In discussing the romances themselves, in chapters on the Amadís and Palmerín romances, and another on "Smaller Groups and Isolated Romances," he covers, though carefully, familiar ground, bringing together the contributions of his predecessors. He summarizes Grace Williams' discussion of the origins of the

[37] See my edition of the *Espejo de príncipes*, I, xii.

[38] See note 7 to "A Definition." The earlier papers were "The Romance of Amadís of Gaul," *Transactions of the Bibliographical Society*, 11 (1909-11), 251-97, and "The Palmerín Romances," in the same journal, 13 (1913-15), 97-144.

Amadís, and its indebtedness to the French romances of the Breton and Charlemagne cycles,[39] and William Purser's definitive resolution of the question of the Portuguese or Spanish authorship of *Palmerín de Inglaterra* in favor of the former by an examination of both the Spanish and Portuguese texts.[40] Thomas also summarizes his own publication, in which he settled that Feliciano de Silva was the author of Books 7 and 9 of the Amadís series,[41] and also shows (pp. 302-09) that the second book of *Lepolemo, Leandro el Bel*, was in fact a translation from the Italian.

More than half of his study, however, is devoted to assessing the popularity of the romances of chivalry both in Spain and abroad. He arranged the romances into a list by date of publication, thus showing clearly when they found the greatest favor and when their decline in popularity began; he added to Menéndez y Pelayo's collection of comments by non-fictional writers on the romances of chivalry. The discussion of the translations of the Spanish romances into other languages could have been written by none other than a competent bibliographer, and it is only very recently[42] that any attempt has been made to improve on his treatment of the subject.

Since the publication in 1920 of the book of Henry Thomas there has been no attempt at a comprehensive treatment of the Spanish romances of chivalry. It is, however, not out of order for us to review the most important, though more limited contributions which have been made over the last fifty years. Most of this work has, for obvious reasons, centered on the romances which are most accessible. Much has been written about *Amadís de Gaula*. Edwin Place, in particular, dedicated much of his career to working with this book, preparing a critical edition based on the earliest complete

---

[39] "The *Amadís* Question," *RHi*, 21 (1909), 1-167.

[40] Palmerin of England. *Some Remarks on this Romance and on the Controversy Regarding its Authorship* (Dublin, 1904).

[41] *Dos romances anónimos del siglo XVI* (Madrid: Centro de Estudios Históricos, 1917).

[42] The article of Daniel Devoto, "Amadís de Galia," *BHi*, 74 (1972), 406-35, deals with the French translations, and the book of Hilkert Weddige, *Die* Historien vom Amadis auss Franckreich (Wiesbaden: Steiner, 1975), with the German ones. I have reviewed the latter in *JHP*, 1 (1977), 157-58.

text, that of 1508,[43] and wrote articles on its original language of composition,[44] its relationship with earlier chivalric material,[45] the date of Montalvo's redaction,[46] and to other problems related with the book.[47] Others have also discussed the interpretation of the *Amadís* of Montalvo and the characteristics of the primitive *Amadís* which preceded it,[48] and while this volume was in preparation, Frank Pierce published in the Twayne World Authors Series a volume on *Amadís de Gaula* (Boston: G. K. Hall, 1976).

---

[43] Madrid: CSIC, 1959-69, in four volumes (Volume I, "reimpresión aumentada," 1971); the reliability of Volumes III and IV of this edition has been questioned by Roger M. Walker, *RPh,* 33 (1980), 448-59. (There are earlier fragmentary texts, of course: the fragments identified by Antonio Rodríguez-Moñino, "El primer manuscrito del *Amadís de Gaula,*" *BRAE,* 36 [1956], 199-216, included in his *Relieves de erudición [del* Amadís *a Goya]* [Madrid: Castalia, 1959], pp. 17-38, and now a claim by Manuel Rodrigues Lapa that there exists in Madrid a thirteenth- or fourteenth-century fragment of the romance in *gallego-portugués,* which he has not seen ["A questão do *Amadís de Gaula* no contexto peninsular," *Grial,* No. 27 (1970), 14-28].)

[44] "The *Amadís* Question," *Speculum,* 25 (1950), 357-66. See also Place's comments in his edition, II, 585-99.

[45] "Fictional Evolution: The Old French Romances and the Primitive *Amadís* Reworked by Montalvo," *PMLA,* 71 (1956), 521-29.

[46] "Montalvo's Outrageous Recantation," *HR,* 37 (1969), 192-98, answered now by Eloy R. González and Jennifer T. Roberts, "Montalvo's Recantation, Revisted," *BHS,* 55 (1978), 203-10.

[47] "Amadis of Gaul, Wales, or What?" *HR,* 23 (1955), 99-107, "El *Amadís* de Montalvo como manual de cortesanía en Francia," *RFE,* 38 (1954), 151-69, "The Edition of the *Amadís* of Saragossa, 1521," *HR,* 21 (1953), 140-42, "¿Montalvo autor o refundidor del *Amadís* IV y V?" in *Homenaje a Rodríguez-Moñino* (Madrid: Castalia, 1966), II, 77-80.

[48] Pierre Le Gentil, "Pour l'Interprétation de l'*Amadis,*" in *Mélanges à la mémoire de Jean Sarrailh* (Paris: Centre de Recherches de l'Institut d'Études Hispaniques, 1966), II, 47-54, María Rosa Lida de Malkiel, "El desenlace del *Amadís* primitivo," *RPh,* 6 (1953), 283-89, reprinted in her *Estudios de literatura española y comparada* (Buenos Aires: Eudeba, 1966), pp. 149-56, Erilde Reali, "'Leonoreta fin roseta' nel problema dell'*Amadís de Gaula,*" *AION-SR,* 7 (1965), 235-54, and others (see section B of my bibliography). Juan Bautista Avalle-Arce's paper "El *Amadís* primitivo," was published in the *Actas del Sexto Congreso Internacional de Hispanistas* (Toronto: Department of Spanish and Portuguese, University of Toronto, 1980), 79-83.

The *Sergas de Esplandián*, available in Gayangos' edition, has been the subject of important studies by José Amezcua and Samuel Gili Gaya.[49] Two volumes of studies accompanied the recent publication of an edition of *Palmerín de Olivia*.[50] Maxime Chevalier has investigated a number of later romances in a search for the influence of Ariosto,[51] and just as Place discussed the influence of the *Amadís* on Cervantes,[52] Martín de Riquer, author of an important series of studies of *Tirant lo Blanch* and of historical chivalry,[53] has also discussed the influence of the romances of chivalry on Cervantes.[54]

---

[49] Samuel Gili Gaya, "*Las Sergas de Esplandián* como crítica de la caballería bretona," *BBMP*, 23 (1947), 103-11, and José Amezcua, "La oposición de Montalvo al mundo del *Amadís de Gaula*," *NRFH*, 21 (1972), 320-37. Gili Gaya is also the author of a lecture, "*Amadís de Gaula*" (Barcelona, 1956).

[50] The first volume (Volume II of the set *Studi sul* Palmerín de Olivia) contains the *Introduzione al* Palmerín de Olivia of Guido Mancini (published in Spanish translation in the volume *Dos estudios de literatura española* [Barcelona: Planeta, 1970], pp. 7-202) and the second volume consists of *Saggi e richerche*. The three-volume set (text, and two volumes of studies) was published in Pisa, 1966, and is numbers 11-13 of the series Pubblicazioni dell'Istituto di Letteratura Spagnola e Ispano-americana dell'Università di Pisa.

[51] *L'Arioste en Espagne* (Bordeaux: Institut d'Études Ibériques et Ibéro-américaines de l'Université de Bordeaux, 1966), pp. 254-74.

[52] "Cervantes and the *Amadís*," in *Hispanic Studies in Honor of Nicholson B. Adams*, University of North Carolina Studies in Romance Languages and Literatures, 59 (Chapel Hill: University of North Carolina Press, 1966), pp. 131-40.

[53] Editions of *Tirant lo Blanc* (Barcelona: Selecta, 1947, and Barcelona: Barral, 1970), of the Castilian translation (Barcelona: Asociación de Bibliófilos de Barcelona, 1947-49, and Clásicos Castellanos, 188-92, Madrid: Espasa-Calpe, 1974), "Andanzas del caballero borgoñón Jacques de Lalaing por los reinos de España y los capítulos del siciliano Juan de Bonifacio," in *Strenae. Estudios de filología e historia dedicados al Prof. Manuel García Blanco* (Salamanca, 1962), pp. 393-406, "Caballeros andantes españoles," *Revista de Occidente*, 2nd series, 9 (1965), 20-32, a volume in which this and other studies are collected, *Caballeros andantes españoles* (Madrid: Espasa-Calpe, 1967), and including some of the preceding, though "molto ritoccati," *Cavalleria fra realtà e letteratura nel Quattrocento* (Bari: Adriatica, 1970). Riquer also edited the collection *Lletres de batalla* (Barcelona: Barcino, 1963-69).

[54] Well-known is his *Aproximación al* Quijote, which has been referred to in note 4; less so is his "La Technique parodique du roman médiéval

Beyond this, it can safely be said that studies of the romances of chivalry have tended to deal more with tangential works, or with tangential aspects of the major works, than with the truly central works and questions. Thus, of the later books of the Amadís cycle, *Florisando*, Book 6, and the second *Lisuarte de Grecia*, Book 8, which are without any doubt the least important and least influential books of the entire cycle, have each been the subject of an interpretative essay,[55] while the vastly more important later books of the series have never been the subject of a major article. Both the Amadís and the Palmerín series have been the subject of monographs, but both of these monographs discuss the influence of the series in England.[56] Feliciano de Silva has been studied biographically,[57] as author of the *Segunda Celestina*,[58] and as friend to Núñez de Reinoso,[59] but the only study of his romances of chivalry to date is focused on the study of the pastoral elements in them.[60] Attention

---

dans le *Quichotte*," in *La Littérature narrative d'imagination* (Paris: Presses Universitaires de France, 1961), pp. 55-69.

[55] Maxime Chevalier, "Le Roman de chevalerie morigéné. Le *Florisando*," *BHi*, 69 (1958), 441-49; Juan Givanel Mas, "Una papereta crítico-bibliogràfica referent al *Octavo libro de Amadís de Gaula*," in *Homenaje a Menéndez Pidal* (Madrid: Hernando, 1925), I, 389-401.

[56] Mary Patchell, *The* Palmerin *Romances in Elizabethan Prose Fiction* (New York: Columbia University Press, 1947; reprint, New York: AMS, 1966); John J. O'Connor, Amadis de Gaule *and its Influence on Elizabethan Literature* (New Brunswick, New Jersey: Rutgers University Press, 1970). (On the latter, see my review in *Hispanófila*, Nº 45 [1972], 83-85.)

[57] Emilio Cotarelo y Mori, "Nuevas noticias biográficas de Feliciano de Silva," *BRAE*, 13 (1926), 126-39; Narciso Alonso Cortés, "Feliciano de Silva," *BRAE*, 20 (1933), 382-404; Erasmo Buceta, "Algunas noticias referentes a la familia de Feliciano de Silva," *RFE*, 18 (1931), 390-92.

[58] Isabel Monk, "The *Segunda Celestina* of Feliciano de Silva: A Study and an Edition," Ph.D. dissertation, University of Exeter, 1973.

[59] Constance Rose, *Alonso Núñez de Reinoso: The Lament of a Sixteenth-Century Exile* (Rutherford, New Jersey: Fairleigh Dickinson University Press, 1971).

[60] Sydney Cravens, *Feliciano de Silva y los antecedentes de la novela pastoril en sus libros de caballerías* (Chapel Hill: Estudios de Hispanófila, 1976), previously a Ph.D. dissertation at the University of Kansas; see *DAI*, 33 (1972), 2926A-27A.

has been drawn to an earlier romance, *Claribalte*, because of its author, Fernández de Oviedo, rather than because of its literary value, which most agree to be slight.[61] More attention has been focused on the reading of romances of chivalry in the New World[62] than has been on the reading of them in Spain.

Some recent theses suggest that this orientation of research on the romances of chivalry may be changing.[63] Nevertheless, in Chapter VII I have suggested some topics for future research and some avenues which are worth exploring.

---

[61] Juan Bautista Avalle-Arce, "El novelista Gonzalo Fernández de Oviedo, alias de Sobrepeña," *Anales de Literatura Hispanoamericana*, No. 1 (1972), 143-54; Antonello Gerbi, "El *Claribalte* de Oviedo," *Fénix*, 6 (1949), 378-90; Guido Mancini, "Sul *Don Claribalte* de Fernández de Oviedo," *Università di Padova. Annali della Facoltà di Lingue in Verona*, Serie 2, 1 (1966), 3-21; Daymond Turner, "Oviedo's *Claribalte*: The First American Novel," *Romance Notes*, 6 (1964), 65-68.

[62] See my edition of the *Espejo de príncipes*, I, lxxxiii, n. 106.

[63] James Ray Green, Jr. has prepared an edition of *Cirongilio*, cited above in note 14; Lilia F. de Orduna is preparing one of *Belianís* as her dissertation at the University of Buenos Aires; Marie Cort Daniels has included a discussion of the works of Silva in her Ph.D. dissertation, "The Function of Humor in the Spanish Romance of Chivalry (1300-1551)" (Harvard, 1976). Two minor romances have also been edited: Mary Lee Cozad edited *Lidamarte de Armenia*, cited above in n. 29., and and Magdalena Mora-Mallo did the same with *Polismán de Nápoles* of Jerónimo de Contreras (University of North Carolina, 1979).

❧ III ❧

The Birth of the
Spanish Romances of Chivalry

Amadís de Gaula

IKE MOST FORMS of literature, the Spanish ro-
mances of chivalry were not created sponta-
neously nor *ex nihilo*. Although their sudden
popularity at the beginning of the sixteenth
century might, on superficial examination,
suggest a new phenomenon, they have ante-
cessors and are derived from an earlier
chivalric tradition. Like various other types of
Spanish literature, they are directly derived from the literature of a
foreign country: in this case, French Arthurian literature. In a
word, *Amadís de Gaula*, on which, directly or indirectly, are modeled
all the sixteenth-century romances of chivalry, is neo-Arthurian
(Pierce, p. 47).

In France the romance of chivalry was more of a medieval
phenomenon than it was in Spain, more directly linked to the epic
poetry in whose prosifications it began. It was primarily French
versions of Arthurian material which, through Spanish translations
and adaptations, gave birth to the *Amadís* and the romances of
chivalry based on this work. Although the surviving Spanish texts
are neither complete nor numerous, it is clear that the Hispano-
Arthurian literature was widely circulated among the nobility, as it
was one of the few forms of fiction available in the Middle Ages,
even to that class able to indulge itself with pleasure reading in an
age of manuscripts.

Before proceeding to discuss the existing Hispano-Arthurian

literature, it is worth pointing out that I am deliberately omitting, as irrelevant, discussion of a work which some readers might expect to find here: the *Caballero Cifar*, which, I am convinced, has little in common with the Spanish romances of chivalry as they were understood by Cervantes and other readers of the sixteenth century. Even a superficial examination shows how different the work is. It is presumably based on earlier sources, perhaps some Arabic ones, but in any event, it is clearly not French in inspiration, it is not primarily a tale of love and combat, of deeds done by a knight in love with a sometimes disdainful lady, and it is much more moral and didactic in its intent than the other romances.[1] Although there is some influence of Arthurian material, particularly in Book III,[2] the work is far from being primarily chivalric in orientation, nor did it have any discernible influence on the romances which were to follow it. The supposed discovery of a source for Sancho Panza in the squire Ribaldo has been refuted so many times that it will not be further belabored here.[3]

Arthurian literature in Spain has been surveyed by Entwistle, more briefly by María Rosa Lida de Malkiel, and recently in a scholarly bibliography by Harvey Sharrer.[4] The present author can

---

[1] See the two recent books on the *Cifar*: James Burke's *History and Vision: The Figural Structure of the* Libro del Cavallero Zifar (London: Tamesis, 1972), reviewed by Ray Green and the present author in *MLN*, 89 (1974), 320-21, and Roger M. Walker, *Tradition and Technique in* El Libro del Cavallero Zifar (London: Tamesis, 1974), reviewed by the present author in *Hispania*, 59 (1976), 543-44. I have seen neither the dissertation of Marilyn Olsen, "The Manuscripts, the Wagner Edition, and the Prologue of the *Cauallero Zifar*," Wisconsin, 1975 (abstract in *DAI*, 36 [1976], 5269A), nor that of Francisco Javier Hernández-Sánchez, "A Study of *El libro del Cavallero Zifar*. The Didactic Section and Its Relevance to the Narrative," Toronto 1976.

[2] William J. Entwistle, *The Arthurian Legend in the Literatures of the Spanish Peninsula* (1925; reprint New York: Phaeton, 1975), pp. 71-75.

[3] See note 16 to "*Don Quijote* y los libros de caballerías: Necesidad de un reexamen," included in this volume.

[4] María Rosa Lida's "Arthurian Literature in Spain and Portugal" was published in *Arthurian Literature in the Middle Ages: A Collaborative History*, ed. Roger Sherman Loomis (Oxford: Clarendon Press, 1959), pp. 406-18, and was reprinted in Spanish translation in her *Estudios de literatura española y*

do little but summarize their conclusions. Prose literature is represented by texts of the Merlin, Lancelot, and Tristan families, though
the texts are either fragmentary or relatively late. Pietsch, in his
Spanish Grail Fragments,[5] published the fragmentary versions of the
Libro de Josep Abarimatia, the *Estoria de Merlin*, and *Lançarote* found in a
fifteenth-century manuscript now in the University of Salamanca. A
late 14th or early 15th-century Castilian and Aragonese manuscript
of *Tristán de Leonís* was published by George T. Northup (University
of Chicago Press, 1928). There is also a sixteenth-century copy of a
lengthy fifteenth-century manuscript of *Lançarote* in the Biblioteca
Nacional of Madrid; of this latter only a few fragments have been
published,[6] though Sharrer has promised a complete edition. The
other texts available in Castilian are late fifteenth- or early sixteenth-century imprints: *Tristán de Leonís* (Valladolid, 1501[7] and Seville, 1528[8] and 1534), the *Baladro del Sabio Merlín* (Burgos, 1498),[9]
and the *Demanda del Sancto Grial* (Toledo, 1515).[10]

The influence which these Arthurian texts, especially the *Lancelot*,
had in the creation of *Amadís de Gaula* has been discussed in greatest
detail by Grace Williams,[11] though it has also been commented on

---

comparada, pp. 134-48; Harvey Sharrer's bibliography, *A Critical Bibliography
of Hispanic Arthurian Material*, is being published in two parts, the first of
which ("Texts: The Prose Romance Cycles") has just (1978) been published by Grant and Cutler of London.

[5] *Modern Philology* Monographs (Chicago: University of Chicago Press,
1924-25).

[6] For details see Sharrer's bibliography, Aa3.

[7] Edited by Adolfo Bonilla y San Martín (Madrid: Sociedad de Bibliófilos Madrileños, 1912).

[8] Also edited by Bonilla, *NBAE*, 6 (Madrid: Bailly-Baillière, 1907), 339-
457. Hernán Colón cites an otherwise unknown edition of Seville, 1520
(No. 4008 in his *Registrum*).

[9] Edited by Justo García Morales in the series "Joyas Bibliográficas"
(Madrid, 1956-60), and by Pedro Bohigas in the series "Selecciones
Bibliófilas" (Barcelona, 1957-62).

[10] No modern edition exists of this text, of which Nicolás Antonio
(*Bibliotheca Hispana Nova*, II, 400), cites an edition of 1500. See Sharrer, Ae7.

[11] "The *Amadís* Question," *RHi*, 21 (1909), 1-167.

by Entwistle, Bohigas, Le Gentil, and Lebesque, among others.[12] Although María Rosa Lida has pointed out some influence from the Troy legends,[13] it can be safely said that *Amadís* generally follows the outlines of the central plot of the *Lancelot*. An unknown youth of royal descent falls in love with the wife or daughter of a king at whose court he serves. The knight rescues his lady from an abductor, thus earning her love or promise of love; the lady, for erroneous reasons, spurns the knight, who abandons the court and lives in solitude. Eventually he learns his true identity and is reunited with the lady. Court intrigue and discord among factions of the nobility play a major role in both works, leading to a complicated plot structure. Characters with magical powers, both friendly and hostile, appear in both works. There is an exaltation of adventure, honor, and love. *Amadís*, then, according to María Rosa Lida, from whom the foregoing is paraphrased, "offers a synthesis of the distinctive features of a typical Arthurian romance" ("Arthurian Legend," p. 413).

That the influence of the Arthurian texts is channeled almost exclusively through the *Amadís* (Entwistle, p. 225) is due to the unique circumstances surrounding the composition, revision, and diffusion of this work. The dating of the composition of the *Amadís* in the fourteenth century, when the Arthurian romances were circulating widely in manuscript, is not disputed (Pierce, p. 39). For reasons not known to us, a fifteenth-century gentleman, Garci Rodríguez de Montalvo, took this older text and revised it, abbreviating it, adapting it, perhaps, more to the tastes of the Spanish, with purer love and more emphasis on combat, and certainly improving

---

[12] For Bohigas, see "Los libros de caballerías en el Siglo XVI," in *Historia general de las literaturas hispánicas*, ed. Guillermo Díaz-Plaja, 2, reprint (Barcelona: Vergara, 1968), 213-36, especially pp. 222-24. Pierre Le Gentil's article, "Pour l'interpretation de l'*Amadís*," cited in note 48 to the previous chapter, discusses the relationship between the *Lancelot* and the *Amadís*. Philéas Lebesque's "La Matière de Bretagne et l'*Amadis de Gaule*," *Bulletin des Études Portugaises*, 3 (1937), 46-57, is of little value.

[13] "El desenlace del *Amadís* primitivo," cited in note 48 to the previous chapter. On the early *Amadís* we must also mention the important study of Edwin B. Place, "Fictional Evolution: The Old French Romances and the Primitive *Amadís* Reworked by Montalvo," *PMLA*, 71 (1956), 521-29.

its language and style. This revised version, published in the six-teenth century, was thus a link between the medieval and the Renaissance periods: a work of medieval inspiration, composition, and themes, but packaged and distributed in a way that Renaissance readers would find attractive.

It would be difficult to exaggerate the popularity of Montalvo's *Amadís* in sixteenth-century Spain. It had far and away the largest number of editions and copies printed, and has been, from its publication, the most widely read Spanish romance of chivalry, a distinction which it holds through the present day. Even among those who had not read the work, almost all literate, and many illiterate Spaniards knew the name of the work, just as most recognize the title *Don Quijote* today. *Amadís* was one of the limited number of romances made into ballads and plays; it was the ro-mance used by Bernal Díaz del Castillo in his famous comparison (quoted by Thomas, p. 82). It was "a recognized manual of chivalry and courtesy" (Thomas, p. 63). Phrases from the *Amadís*, such as "Agrajes sin obras," entered the Spanish language,[14] which hap-pened with no other romance.

Just as the writings of Aristotle defined what would later be called the field of philosophy, so the *Amadís* defined what the romance of chivalry would be in Spain. From *Amadís* the other romances took their basic framework: the traveling prince, the constant tournaments and battles, the remote setting in a moun-tainous, forested (never desert or jungle) land, the interest in honor and fame. Variations on the basic pattern, such as the *dama belicosa*, are really minor. To use a protagonist who was not of royal blood, to have a visit to a realistic Spain (or any other location the Spanish readers would know something about) would have been felt as a major break with this venerable tradition, not to be made until the *Lazarillo* broke many conventions simultaneously.

It is just as difficult to exaggerate the popularity and influence of the *Amadís* in sixteenth-century Spanish letters and culture as it is to explain the precise reasons why it was so popular. One contem-porary reader, Juan de Valdés, praised its language (the quotation is reproduced on p. 11), and certainly in an age sensitive to style this

---

[14] Discussed by Marcel Bataillon, "Agrajes sin obras," *Studi Ispanici*, 1 (1962), 29-35.

must have been a fact, though presumably not an exclusive one.
Perhaps a nationalistic factor, as well, in that *Amadís* was seen as a
clearly Castilian, rather than foreign, work,[15] may have contributed
to the book's appeal in Spain. Probably, though, the simple fact
that the book contains a good story, with lots of exciting action, was
most important.

For action the *Amadís* has, above all things. Amadís, set adrift by
his unmarried (though secretly pledged) mother, is raised at the
court of King Languines of Scotland, where he falls in love with
Oriana, daughter of King Lisuarte of Great Britain, also living with
the King of Scotland. Amadís is dubbed a knight by his father,
Perión de Gaula, though their relationship is unknown to both. He
rapidly distinguishes himself, aiding in the defeat of the evil King
Abiés of Ireland. Enchanted by the evil magician Arcaláus, then
freed, he also distinguishes himself in a great tournament held in
London, and must free Oriana and defeat the usurping king Bar-
sinán. His assistance to Queen Briolanja of Sobradisa causes the
jealousy of Oriana.

This summary, which ignores a host of minor characters and
adventures, and which could well provide material in itself for a
lengthy novel, covers only one of the four books of Montalvo's
Amadís. Book II describes the marvels of the Ínsola Firme, including
the Arco de los Leales Amadores, which Amadís successfully attempts. Upon receiving a letter from Oriana accusing him of dis-
loyalty, he makes his famous retirement to the island of the Peña
Pobre, abandoning his arms, which causes those he has left behind
to fear his death. Upon receipt of a letter assuring him of Oriana's
good graces, he sets out to meet her at the castle of Miraflores, with
further adventures on the way, but he must leave the court again
after the mind of King Lisuarte is poisoned by treasonous advice
from friends of Falangris, brother of Lisuarte.

In Book III Oriana gives birth to Esplandián, son of Amadís,
whose name is written on his body in unintelligible letters; the
infant is stolen by a lioness and raised by the hermit Nasciano.
Further adventures and travels of Amadís are highlighted by the

---

[15] Ironically so, if such is the case, considering the well-founded
arguments of A. K. Jameson, "Was There a French Original of *Amadís de
Gaula?" MLR*, 28 (1933), 176-93.

defeat of a monster, the *endriago*, on the Ínsola del Diablo. While Amadís is away, travelling in Germany, Constantinople, and other parts of Europe, King Lisuarte has made plans for Oriana to marry the emperor of Rome; Amadís must attack the fleet taking Oriana to her husband.

In Book IV, after an unsuccessful attempt to reconcile all the various dissidents, Amadís decides that war with Lisuarte is the only course open. After two great battles, peace is restored by the intervention of Nasciano, who, bringing Esplandián into the story in a more active way, reconciles Lisuarte to the marriage of Oriana and Amadís. After the various festivities which accompany the marriage of Amadís and Oriana, Lisuarte is kidnapped and enchanted. The book ends on an inconclusive note (also setting a precedent for the romances of chivalry; see *infra*, pp. 119-29), with Esplandián being armed a knight.

Once again we must emphasize the abbreviated and incomplete nature of this summary of a complicated series of characters and events, typically the despair of anyone who tries to summarize this book or any of the later romances of chivalry. Surely, however, contemporary readers, with time to spare and an interest in a captivating, complicated narrative, must have found this very quantity of characters and events to be one of the most attractive features of the book. Although the number of events and characters does not allow for any great development of personality—characters are essentially static and unchanging, always good or evil if such is their nature—this deficiency by modern standards was not seen as such by readers of the fifteenth and sixteenth centuries, whom, we may assume, were not interested in personality development, internal problems of the characters, or very much beyond the conflicts, loves, and prophecies found in the book.

These latter, which were not mentioned in the summary above, are another reflection of the Arthurian romances in the *Amadís*, since the cryptic prophecies of Merlin, usually a combination of vague comments and specific references to some contemporary events, are echoed in the frequent appearances of Urganda la Desconocida. Urganda is a mysterious character in herself, whose origin and function are not fully explained. She frequently appears in the story, assisting *Amadís*, and delivers advice—ignored at the characters' peril—about the future. In general, she is an important

contribution to the "mythic character" of the romance so well
described by Samuel Gili Gaya in his published lecture (cited above).

The Sixteenth-Century Romances

N TRACING THE CASTILIAN HISTORY of the romances of chivalry, we could begin worse than by pointing out that the romances of chivalry, as a genre, are firmly centered within the sixteenth century, give or take a few decades at each end. It is true that the *Amadís*, which would circulate so widely in printed form, existed as early as the fourteenth century, and it is also true that there are a number of Hispano-Arthurian texts of earlier centuries. But as with most texts in the age of manuscripts, these were limited in their circulation. Entwistle's affirmation that there was "an attempt to carry some knowledge of this [Hispano-Arthurian] literature by means of ballads to the unlettered masses"[1] is supported only by a very limited number of ballad texts, some of uncertain date (the ballads about Amadís were written no earlier than the sixteenth century), and a lack of evidence about the public these ballads were originally created for.

As stated in the preceding chapter, the Hispano-Arthurian texts are principally translations. As with most translations, the literary contribution they made, seen in a European perspective, is slight. The creative literary energies in Castile were not devoted to romances of chivalry: there is no figure of the significance of Chrétien de Troyes, Malory, Wace, or Layamon among those producing chivalric texts in medieval Castile, and there are no known translations from Castilian to non-peninsular languages. Also, these medieval Hispano-Arthurian texts were "not the be-

---

[1] *Arthurian Legend*, p. 230.

getters of Spanish chivalry save through their creation of *Amadís de Gaula*" (Entwistle, p. 225); in fact, they were of little interest during the last half of the fifteenth century. It was in the earlier court of Juan II when chivalry (as opposed to warfare) was most favored in the Spanish Middle Ages; Enrique IV, of course, cared little for chivalric literature,[2] and the Reyes Católicos, though not completely immune to its charms,[3] took their responsibilities too seriously, and were too interested in concluding the reconquest, to have much time for idle reading.

The romances of chivalry, then, benefited greatly in their extraordinary popularity in the sixteenth century from the possibilities that printing offered, and in this sense the so familiar Castilian *atraso*, by which this chivalric material, medieval in inspiration, arrived in Castile later, has a positive side. Because printed works, though still expensive by modern standards, were far cheaper than manuscripts, lesser nobles, and even some well-to-do bourgeois, could share in the reading of the romances, something not possible in other countries at an earlier date. Yet still, contrary to a widely-held misconception, the romances of chivalry were not among the first books published after the introduction of printing in Spain in the last third of the fifteenth century. Not only such religious works as the *Vita Christi* of Mendoza and the *Vida beata* of Juan de Lucena, not only doctrinal works such as those of Cartagena were printed during the late 1470's, 1480's, and early 1490's, but also the novels of Juan de Flores and Diego de San Pedro were published, without, however, a single romance of chivalry being published in Castile during this period.[4]

---

[2] On Enrique IV, see my article, "Enrique IV and Gregorio Marañón," *RenQ*, 29 (1976), 21-29.

[3] Isabel la Católica owned copies of *Merlín*, *Demanda del Santo Grial*, and *Lanzarote* (Diego Clemencín, "Ilustraciones sobre varios asuntos del reinado de Doña Isabel la Católica, que pueden servir de pruebas a su Elogio," *Memorias de la Real Academia de la Historia*, 6 [1821], 459). An anecdote, perhaps untrue, records Fernando el Católico as enjoying *Amadís*; see Francisco Rodríguez Marín, "*Amadís de Gaula*," in his "nueva edición crítica" of the *Quijote*, IX (Madrid: Atlas, 1949), 173.

[4] *Tirant lo Blanch*, which is somewhat closer to the form the Castilian romances of chivalry were to take than is the *Cifar*, was published in

Printers turned their attention to chivalric material rather suddenly, in the final years of the fifteenth century and beginning of the sixteenth, as if motivated by a previously non-existent demand on the part of a body of readers—the nobles—not in a position, or not needing, during the final years of the reconquest, to divert themselves with this type of literature. As with other forms of literature, the printers first began by publishing materials already available in manuscript; thus we see published a series of short, translated works with a chivalric flavor, such as *Oliveros de Castilla* (1499), *Paris e Viana* (c. 1494), *Enrique fi de Oliva* (1498), and others, and also some much longer works, such as the *Baladro del sabio Merlín* (1498), the missing *Merlín y demanda del Santo Grial* (1500), and no doubt the missing *princeps* of the *Amadís*.[5]

The brief works, the translations from the French, did not survive the competition from the publication of the *Amadís* (before 1508), the *Sergas de Esplandián* (before 1510), and the new works, such as *Palmerín de Olivia*, which began to be published about 1510, when the existing chivalric literature available to the printers had all been published.[6] We can only speculate about the reasons, and none of the potential reasons would completely explain the phenomenon. Printing, more compact than handwriting, and the use of paper rather than parchment or vellum made economically possible longer works than were possible in the age of parchment, and the increased speed with which printed material could be read also made increased length desirable.[7] The language of the earlier works may

---

Valencia in 1490, and reprinted in 1497, but it was not published in Castilian until 1511.

[5] On the changing reading public leading to a demand for chivalric material, see "Who Read the Romances of Chivalry?" *infra*, and on the translations, Thomas, pp. 31-32. Bernhard König accepts the hypothesis of a lost, perhaps fifteenth-century *princeps* of the *Amadís*, but destroys Place's evidence for a 1496 edition in "Amadís und seine Bibliographen. Untersuchungen zu frühen Ausgaben des *Amadís de Gaula*," *RJ*, 14 (1963), 294-309, but Place dismisses his comments as "las animadversiones de cierto crítico alemán," in the 2nd edition of Volume I of his edition (p. 357).

[6] Thus see, for example, the dates of the editions of *Oliveros de Castilla* (cited by Simón Díaz, III, Volume II, pp. 499-500).

[7] See on this point the learned work of J. J. Chaytor, *From Script to Print*

have seemed archaic to the readers, and the style more primitive.[8] The Castilian readers may well have preferred more sober and action-filled romances, a taste already seen in the choice of foreign works to translate.[9] In any event, as Hall points out, even the works, such as *Tristán de Leonís*, that to some extent survived this period did not retain popularity past the first third of the century.[10]

The so-called "indigenous" or native romances of chivalry, which were to set the pattern for those that would appear throughout the next half century, began to be published, as already stated, around 1510. The first "wave" of publication ended, approximately, with the publication in 1519 of Oviedo's *Claribalte* by the Valencian printer Juan de Viñao, who had, two years previously, published the little-known and curious *Arderique*.[11] With the exception of the *Amadís* and the *Sergas de Esplandián*, which apparently reached their current form in the fifteenth century,[12] it may be safely assumed that most of

---

(Cambridge, England: Heffer, 1945), and also Cedric E. Pickford, "Fiction and the Reading Public in the Fifteenth Century," *Bulletin of the John Rylands Library*, 45 (1963), 423-38; the latter includes some comments on readers of romances of chivalry in France.

[8] As I have already pointed out, those romances most censured by Juan de Valdés in the *Diálogo de la lengua*, those which are both "mentiro-síssimos" and have the "estilo desbaratado," are translations. It should not be forgotten that a romantic or nostalgic interest in old works for their own sake scarcely antedated the nineteenth century. There was, to be sure, an interest in classic authors, and a curiosity about former times, but the information or literature was desired in a contemporary form—thus, old manuscripts, even if located with difficulty, were not conserved after they had been published (L[eighton] D. Reynolds and N[igel] G. Wilson, *Scribes and Scholars. A Guide to the Transmission of Greek and Latin Literature*, 2nd ed. [Oxford: Clarendon Press, 1974], p. 124). It was only an exceptional *erudito* in the sixteenth century who saw value in preserving, for their own sake, old manuscripts and editions.

[9] María Rosa Lida, "Literatura artúrica," p. 141.

[10] J. G. Hall, "*Tablante de Ricamonte* and other Castilian Versions of Arthurian Romances," *RLC*, 48 (1974), 177-89; despite my attempts, I have not been able to see Hall's B. Phil. thesis, "Arthurian Literature in Spain. An Examination of its Popularity and Influence, 1170-1535," Oxford, 1967.

[11] Patricia Baker has begun an edition of *Arderique* as a doctoral dissertation at Florida State University.

[12] See Edwin Place, "Montalvo's Outrageous Recantation," cited in note 46 to Chapter II.

these works were written only shortly before their publication, and with publication in view. They include the sixth book of *Amadís*, *Florisando*, of Páez de Ribera (1510), and Book 7, *Lisuarte de Grecia*, of Feliciano de Silva (1514), although we should add that contemporaries apparently did not share the modern tendency to look at books such as these primarily as members of their respective "families"; it was difficult, if not impossible, for a reader of the time to assemble most of the books of any "family," for which reason these books were more often read and discussed as individual works. It includes also *Palmerín de Olivia* and its sequel *Primaleón* (1511 and 1512), and the first book of *Clarián de Landanís* (1518); perhaps we should also mention the translation of the lengthy *Guarino Mesquino* from the Italian (1512).[13]

These works, if it is legitimate to speak of them as a group, are still relatively unsophisticated works, and except for *Amadís* and *Esplandián*, only *Palmerín* and *Primaleón* were to achieve any enduring success or fame.

Before leaving this early period of the Castilian romances of chivalry, it is appropriate to mention the publication of a number of semihistorical works with some chivalric elements, either written shortly before their publication or, more often, written earlier and published for the first time in the early sixteenth century to satisfy the tastes of much the same public as that which read the romances. These include the *Crónica* and the *Estoria del noble cavallero Fernán González* (Seville, 1509, and Toledo, 1511, respectively), the two chronicles of the Cid (Burgos, 1512, and Toledo, 1526, both reprinted by the Kraus Reprint Company, New York, 1967), the *Crónica sarracina* of Pedro del Corral, published in 1499 and several times reprinted,[14] and also some lesser-known works such as the

---

[13] See on this work María Rosa Lida's "Para la génesis del *Auto de la sibila Casandra*," *Filología*, 5 (1959), 47-63, reprinted in her *Estudios de literatura española y comparada*, pp. 157-72, and I. S. Révah, "*L'Auto de la Sibylle Cassandra de* Gil Vicente," *HR*, 27 (1959), 167-93. Stephen Gilman also mentions it in *The Spain of Fernando de Rojas* (Princeton: Princeton University Press, 1972), p. 440, n. 84.

[14] Some fragments from this work, much in need of a modern edition, were included by Menéndez Pidal in his *Floresta de leyendas heroicas españolas. Rodrigo, el último godo. I. La edad media.* Clásicos Castellanos, 62 (Madrid:

Libro de dichos y hechos de Alonzo Aroa (Valencia, 1527). The current distinction made between these "historical" works and the "fictional" romances of chivalry, all of which declared themselves to be purely historical works, was certainly seen vaguely by most contemporary readers, some of whom probably did not see it at all. However, quite apart from the question of their value as historical sources, the entertainment value of these semihistorical works can easily be seen. Their elaborate descriptions of castles and armor, the numerous and fully described battles and tournaments, the almost superhuman protagonists, show that they have more in common with the romances of chivalry than is usually realized.[15] Some books, in fact, have title pages with an illustration of a chivalric scene, indistinguishable from those of the romances of chivalry.[16]

The romances of chivalry's greatest popularity in Castile coincides neatly with the reign of Carlos V (1517-1555). During this

---

Ediciones de "La Lectura," 1925), 49-140. "Más que crónica rigurosamente histórica es un libro de caballerías, tantas son las patrañas y falsedades que contiene," is how it is described by Antonio Palau y Dulcet, *Manual del librero hispanoamericano*, IV (Barcelona: Librería Palau, 1951), 197. Francisco López Estrada, *Introducción a la literatura medieval española*, 3rd edition (Madrid: Gredos, 1966), p. 243, says that the *Crónica sarracina* "trata a la manera de los libros de caballerías el tema de la destrucción de España por la derrota de don Rodrigo."

[15] See the comments of Guido Mancini, in *Dos estudios de literatura española* (cited in note 50 to Chapter II), pp. 46-50.

[16] Historical and semi-historical works with "chivalric" title pages include the *Estoria del noble cavallero el conde Fernán González* (Toledo, 1511), the *Crónica del rey don Pedro* (Toledo: Ramón de Petras [for Cosme Damián, a publisher of romances of chivalry], 1526 and Pamplona: Pedro Porralis, 1591), the *Crónica de don Álvaro de Luna* (Milán: Juan Antonio Castellano, 1546), the *Crónica del... Cid* (Medina del Campo: Francisco del Canto [publisher of several editions of romances of chivalry], 1552), the *Crónica del muy valeroso rey don Fernando [Cuarto]* (Valladolid: Sebastián Martínez, 1554), and the *Crónica del sereníssimo rey don Juan segundo* (Pamplona: Tomás Porralis, a costa de Juan Boyer [who with his brother Benito also published romances of chivalry], 1590), all of which are reproduced in Francisco Vindel's *Manual gráfico-descriptivo del bibliófilo hispano-americano (1475-1850)*, Vols. II and III (Madrid: n.p., 1930), and the *Crónica del sereníssimo rey don Juan el segundo* (Seville, 1543), reproduced by Agustín Millares Carlo, *Catálogo razonado de los libros de los siglos XV, XVI, y XVII de la Academia Nacional de la Historia* (Caracas: Academia Nacional de la Historia, 1969), lámina XIII.

time the composition and publication of new romances, and the reprinting of the classics of the genre, flourished as it never had before and never would again. New romances were published at the rate of almost one per year during this period, and there were twelve editions of the *Amadís* and eight of *Palmerín*. It was during this period that many of the romances which were to prove most popular were written: the works of Feliciano de Silva, *Belianís de Grecia*, Part I of the *Espejo de príncipes y cavalleros*.

That this great popularity of the romances was due to the model of and encouragement from the royal court is beyond question. We know that Carlos, so completely Hispanized and so given to chivalric spectacles and festivities,[17] read romances, and judged *Belianís* so pleasing that he requested the composition of a continuation.[18] Taking advantage of the interest at court, Dionís Clemente, author of *Valerián de Hungría*, pretended that he received the manuscript of

---

[17] See Carlos Clavería, Le Chevalier délibéré *de Olivier de la Marche y sus versiones españolas del siglo XVI* (Zaragoza: Institución Fernando el Católico, 1950), pp. 37-49, and for more specific examples, the "Torneo celebrado en Valladolid con ocasión de la boda del Príncipe Don Felipe con la Infanta Doña María de Portugal (1544)," and the "Relación muy verdadera de las grandes fiestas que la serenísima Reina doña María ha hecho al Príncipe nuestro señor en Flandes, en un lugar que se dice Vince," in *Relaciones de los reinados de Carlos V y Felipe II*, ed. Amalio Huarte, Sociedad de Bibliófilos Españoles, Segunda Época, 12 and 25 (Madrid, 1941-50), I, 71-94 and II, 199-221, respectively, and Juan Calvete de Estrella, *El felicísimo viaje del príncipe don Felipe*, ed. Miguel Artigas, Sociedad de Bibliófilos Españoles, Segunda Época, 7 and 8 (Madrid, 1930). Despite the references to Felipe in the titles, these works obviously reflect the tastes of the sovereign, Carlos V. For other information on the chivalric interests of Carlos V, see Prudencio de Sandoval, *Historia de la vida y hechos del Emperador Carlos V*, ed. Carlos Seco Serrano (*BAE*, 80-82; Madrid: Atlas, 1955-56), who states on p. 89 of Volume I that "como veían que el mozo rey era aficionado a cosas de guerra, [the nobles of Brussels] le procuraban entretener con justas y torneos y otras fiestas semejantes." On p. 122, we find that in Valladolid "hubo justas y torneos, con nuevas invenciones y representando pasos de los libros de caballerías. En algunas de éstas entró el príncipe rey."

[18] The quotation from the prologue to Books III and IV of the *Belianís* documenting this is reproduced by Thomas, p. 149. It is worth noting that Carlos also translated himself the allegorical *Caballero determinado* of Olivier de la Marche, on which see *Orígenes de la novela*, I, 448, and Carlos Clavería, pp. 64-65.

his work from a knight of Carlos' brother Hernando, whom he met while accompanying Carlos to the court held in Worms in 1521. Although no romances were dedicated to Carlos, several were to members of the high nobility who formed part of court society. (See "Who Read the Romances of Chivalry?" in this volume.) The French king François I first read the *Amadís*, and became enamoured of it, while being held captive in Madrid by Carlos (Thomas, p. 199), and Herberay des Essarts, who translated the *Amadís* into French, says that "maintesfois plusieurs gentilz hommes d'Espagne m'auoient loué [*Amadís*]" (prologue to the 1540 edition).

Other factors may have played some role in the romances' popularity. Their harmony with the spirit which led to the conquest and colonization of the New World, basic parts of which took place during Carlos V's reign, may possibly have been an additional factor in their popularity.[19] Yet we can hardly help but conclude that the lack of interest in chivalric fiction of Carlos' more sober son, Felipe II, was a factor in the books' decline. It is hard to picture Felipe taking a romance of chivalry to read at the Escorial.[20]

We may well pause a moment to reflect on the fact that the authors of the romances of chivalry were almost invariably obscure men, or in one case (*Cristalián de España*) an obscure woman, presumably not in close contact with the literary circles of the time. The only exceptions that could be made are Feliciano de Silva (discussed later, in Chapter VI), who achieved renown primarily from his composition of romances, Fernández de Oviedo, who rejected his own romance *Claribalte* when he reached a more mature age, Jerónimo de Urrea, whose *Clarisel de las Flores* was not published during his lifetime and still remains for the most part in manuscript,[21] and

---

[19] Though I question the degree to which the romances were a cause of the New World exploration and conquest; see note 104 to my introduction to the *Espejo de príncipes*.

[20] Although it is true that the publisher Claudio Bornat dedicated his edition of *Olivante de Laura* to Felipe II, there is no record of the King's reaction, if any; the book was not published again.

[21] See, on this book, Pierre Geneste, *Essai sur la vie et l'oeuvre de Jerónimo de Urrea*, dissertation, University of Paris III, 1973 (Lille: Service de Reproduction des Thèses, Université de Lille III, 1975). Those without access to Geneste's dissertation may wish to consult his "Les Poésies dans le *Clarisel de*

such definitely secondary authors as Jerónimo de Contreras,[22] Pedro de Luján,[23] and Antonio de Torquemada.[24] Many of the romances are anonymous, and a majority of the known authors are known only from their composition of the romance; into this category would go Diego Ortúñez de Calahorra, Pedro de la Sierra, and Marcos Martínez, authors of the *Espejo de príncipes y cavalleros*, Páez de Ribera and Juan Díaz, authors of Books 6 and 8 of the *Amadís*, Jerónimo Fernández, author of *Belianís*, Dionís Clemente, author of *Valerián de Hungría*, and so on. Similarly, none of the well-known authors of the period wrote a romance of chivalry: neither Diego Hurtado de Mendoza, nor Guevara, nor Jorge de Montemayor, nor even Ercilla attempted the composition of a romance, to say nothing of Lope, who tried virtually every other genre.

This phenomenon can only be explained when one considers that the romances of chivalry were the least "literary" type of literature being written at that time. There was a unanimous pretense that the works were true histories, only rescued from oblivion and modernized by a sixteenth-century contemporary (see *infra*, pp. 119-29); this in itself could encourage the anonymous publication of romances. Like historical writing, the chivalric romance was a form of literature in which innovation was seen as unnecessary—at least overt innovation, since there is a subtle evolution, found in the increasing sophistication of conversation and in

---

las *Flores* de Jerónimo de Urrea: mise à jour d'un ancien recueil," in *Mélanges Sarrailh* (Paris: Centre de Recherches de l'Institut d'Études Hispaniques, 1966), I, 367-78, or the older volume of Gerónimo Borao, *Noticia de D. Gerónimo Jiménez de Urrea y de su novela caballeresca inédita* Don Clarisel de las Flores (Zaragoza, 1866). A fragmentary edition of Part I was published by the Sociedad de Bibliófilos Andaluces (Seville, 1879). (I have not yet seen Geneste's *Le Capitaine-Poéte aragonais Jerónimo de Urrea* [Paris: Ediciones Hispanoamericanas, 1978], presumably a revised version of his dissertation.)

[22] Author of an unpublished romance entitled *Polismán*, as well as the *Selva de aventuras* and the *Dechado de varios subiectos*; see section JJ of my bibliography, and p. 26, n. 63, *supra*.

[23] Author of *Silves de la Selva*, Book 12 of the *Amadís* series, as well as the *Colloquios matrimoniales*; discussed in section 12B of my bibliography.

[24] Author of *Olivante de Laura*, as well as the *Colloquios satíricos* and the *Jardín de flores curiosas*; see section EE of my bibliography for several publications about his works.

the expanding love element and greater role of women. Thus, despite the comment of Cervantes' *canónigo*, there was little about the romances to attract an author who wished to win praise for his literary abilities, and the romances remained in the hands of another class of writers, not incompetent at their task, perhaps, but spiritually far from the intelligentsia of the day.

We should also remember that the world portrayed in the romances of chivalry was one which would appeal strongly to a section of Spanish society, but only to a section. It was a simple world, devoid of subtle philosophical or religious concerns. An individual could win fame and fortune primarily through his military abilities, whether exercised in serious battles or in less serious activities such as tournaments; scholarship and the world of books played, in the romances, a very secondary role. The knights-errant were often possessed of a crusading spirit and a religious element is always present. This is one of the ways these romances most reflect the values of Spanish culture, though ostensibly set in very remote kingdoms and epochs; this crusading spirit presumably influenced the young reader Teresa de Cepeda, and even more Loyola, also a reader of romances of chivalry (Rivadaneyra's life of Loyola, *BAE*, 60, 14[b]), who sometimes acted like a knight-errant *a lo divino* (Rivadeneyra, pp. 17[a] and 18[a]). Yet the knights' faith was the simple faith of the soldier, an uncritical acceptance of the correctness of Catholicism and the necessity of helping it, with arms, to vanquish infidels.

For all of these reasons, then, it is not surprising that the intelligentsia were to turn against the romances. The criticisms to which we have previously referred began, logically enough, when the romances had become sufficiently popular to attract the critics' attention; the earliest comments are from the 1520's. The early comments, such as those of Valdés, offer some intelligent observations, and I have remarked elsewhere ("An Early Censor: Alejo Venegas," in *Medieval, Renaissance and Folklore Studies in Honor of John Esten Keller* [Newark, Delaware: Juan de la Cuesta, 1981, pp. 229-41) how the scholarly humanist Venegas played an important part in the attacks on the romances. However, these attacks rapidly deteriorated from sensible observations about the inherent defects of the books themselves to a series of complaints about the pernicious effects that they allegedly had on the souls of the readers, and how the books occupied time which might have been more usefully employed in reading more spiritually uplifting material. In fact, the criticisms of the romances degenerated into a series of *topoi*, which were repeated by various moralist writers who had no direct knowledge of the works they attacked.[25]

One effect of the criticisms was to place the authors of the romances somewhat on the defensive. In the prologues and dedications of the later romances, in which the authors often discuss their works and their motives, there is a constant emphasis on the benefits readers would receive from them. One author, Diego Ortúñez de Calahorra, included explicit moral instruction in his work,[26] but all the romances, according to their authors, offered "buenos ejemplos" to their readers, showing them the model of a virtuous knight, who never acted out of self-interest.[27] In his concern for his subjects and for the persons he encountered in his travels, in his interest in seeing that justice was done and that right triumphed over wrong, in his humility, chastity, and calm temperament (*mesura*), the hero of the romances of chivalry offered to the readers the supposedly beneficial picture of the ideal medieval ruler.

Another result of the criticism of the romances as immoral and godless works was the production of the *libros de caballerías a lo divino*. As with other types of literature *a lo divino*,[28] these were works of

---

[25] One can see in Weddige, pp. 235-91, how the same clichés, taken in several cases directly or indirectly from the Spanish critics, were repeated in Germany.

[26] See the introduction to my edition of the *Espejo de príncipes*, I, liii-lv.

[27] I have quoted some statements from the prologues in n. 55 to I, liii, of my edition of the *Espejo de príncipes*.

[28] Such as Sebastián de Córdoba's *Garcilaso a lo divino*, recently edited by Glen R. Gale (Madrid: Castalia, 1971). On literature *a lo divino* in general, see Dámaso Alonso, *Poesía española. Ensayo de métodos y límites estilísticos*, 5th edition (Madrid: Gredos, 1966), pp. 220-68, and Bruce W. Wardropper, "The Religious Conversion of Profane Poetry," in *Studies in the Continental Background of Renaissance English Literature: Essays Presented to John L. Livesay* (Durham, North Carolina: Duke University Press, 1977), pp. 203-21. For a study of a specific romance of chivalry *a lo divino* (the *Historia y milicia cristiana del caballero Peregrino*, of Alonso de Soria [1601]), see Pedro Sainz Rodríguez, "Una posible fuente de *El Criticón* de Gracián," *Archivo Teológico Granadino*, 25 (1962), 7-21.

explicitly religious content, in which familiar religious and moral material—Biblical, in the case of the best known of these romances, the *Cavallería celestial* of Jerónimo de San Pedro (1554)[29]—is adapted to the external trappings of the romance of chivalry. The knights are saints or Biblical figures, and encounter adventures either taken directly from the religious material or of clear religious inspiration. None of these romances achieved any great popularity, and there is considerable doubt whether they succeeded in supplanting the original romances of chivalry as escape reading for idle readers; perhaps instead they were read by a new class of readers who were unable, because of the criticisms of them, to read the original romances. It is worth noting that despite its religious subject matter and presumably noble purpose, the *Cavallería celestial* achieved the dubious distinction of being placed on the *Index*, presumably for some doctrinal error, which none of the secular romances were (Thomas, p. 169).[29bis]

---

[29] Discussed by George Ticknor, *History of Spanish Literature*, sixth American edition (Boston: Houghton Mifflin, 1891), I, 257-60. See also on this book, and on the romances of chivalry *a lo divino* in general, *Orígenes de la novela*, I, 447-52.

[29bis] Worth mentioning at this point is a little-known book often confused with the romances of chivalry *a lo divino*, the *Cavallería cristiana* of Jaime de Alcalá. The book bears no date, and has been thought to be from the middle of the sixteenth century, but F. J. Norton (*A Descriptive Catalogue of Printing in Spain and Portugal, 1501-1520* [Cambridge University Press, 1978], p. 448) has identified it as the work of the Valencian printer Jaime Costilla and assigned it the date of c. 1515. Rather than a work of chivalric fiction, it is a treatise on religious "warfare." As Alcalá says on fol. 2^{r-v}: "Visto que algunas personas ocupavan mucho su tienpo en leer hystorias de romana cavalleria y de algunas ficiones y sueños como Amadis y otras semejantes, no por esso condenando los cavalleros y personas que con la lanca en la mano son obligados y su linaje y virtud los conbida y fuerça para morir por la justicia, que para informarse en el arte de su milicia lean a Vejecio, y para avisarse en la batalla los excelentes ardides de los romanos y troianos vean, paresciome ser cosa razonable, ya por esso no dexassen de saber la mas alta cavalleria que con pleito y omenaje en el santo baptismo.... Y asi, por informacion destos cristianos cavalleros, ocupé un poco de tiempo en hazer un libro de caballeria cristiana intitulado. Ca como diga Job a los siete capitulos que la vida del hombre es una cavalleria sobre la tierra, y segun sentencia de San Juan en su primera epistola tengamos tres enemigos spirituales, el mundo, el diablo y la carne, los catholicos cristianos que

Although the criticism of the romances was followed by a decline in the composition of new romances, it has not been possible to establish the relationship between these two trends. It is not clear that the criticisms of the romances, which are well-known today since they have been assembled and studied by scholars, were known to the readers of the romances; it is more logical to assume that the works in which these criticisms are found (*La conversión de la Magdalena*, say, or Vives' *De institutione fœminae christianae*; the *Diálogo de la lengua* was not published until 1737) were primarily read by readers of a religious or moral inclination who would not have read the romances, nor much other secular literature,[30] even if the criticisms had never been made. There are many other alternative explanations for the declining interest of potential authors in the romances. The general rise in literary standards, due in greatest measure to contacts with Italy, gave rise not only to the poetry of Garcilaso but to the pastoral novel, which made a spectacular appearance on the literary scene in the 1550's. The same period also saw the introduction of the Renaissance epic. The *Lazarillo*, with its anti-hero, as a response to the romances of chivalry has been suggested by many scholars.[31]

---

desean alcançar la corona de la gloria del cielo conviene que fielmente peleen aqui en el suelo contra nuestro principal adversario, el diablo."

[30] It should not be forgotten that the protests of the moralists, particularly the earliest, best-informed ones, were not limited to the romances of chivalry. Vives, Pineda, and Guevara all complain about the *Celestina*, Vives about a list of other works, including Poggio, Guevara about the *Cárcel de amor*, Pedro Malón de Chaide, and others following him, about the "Dianas y Boscanes y Garcilasos." Oviedo censured all fiction, not just the romances of chivalry (*Memorias*, II, 535-56 and 579-80).

[31] Ángel González Palencia, *Del* Lazarillo *a* Quevedo (Madrid: CSIC, 1946), pp. 10-11, attacked by Marcel Bataillon in *Novedad y fecundidad del* Lazarillo de Tormes, trans. Luis Cortés Vázquez (Salamanca: Anaya, 1968), p. 58; Samuel Gili Gaya, "La novela picaresca en el siglo XVI," in *Historia general de las literaturas hispánicas*, III, reimpresión (Barcelona: Vergara, 1968), 95; Alberto del Monte, *Itinerario de la novela picaresca española*, trans. Enrique Sordo (Barcelona: Lumen, 1971), p. 41, and the studies cited in his note 196, not all of which are readily accessible to me; Francisco Rico, *La novela picaresca y el punto de vista*, 2ª ed. revisada (Barcelona: Seix Barral, 1973), p. 15, and also, briefly, in his *La novela picaresca española*, I, 2nd edition (Barcelona: Planeta, 1970), p. 59, n. 80; *Lazarillo*, ed. Alberto Blecua (Madrid: Castalia, 1972), p. 16 (and we should also mention, regarding relations between the chival-

But certainly one of the principal causes, if not the single most important cause, of the decline in composition of new romances was the abdication of Carlos V in favor of his son Felipe. That Carlos' reign ended in 1555 is no coincidence. The last work of Feliciano de Silva, the *Cuarta parte de Florisel de Niquea*, was published in 1551, marking the conclusion of the Amadís "cycle" in Spanish.[32] *Palmerín de Inglaterra*, the last of the Palmerín series to be published in Spanish,[33] appeared in 1547-48. The *Espejo de príncipes y cavalleros* and *Felixmarte de Hircania*, published in 1555 and 1556 respectively, were almost surely written during the final years of Carlos' reign. *Olivante de Laura*, published in 1564, bears a dedication from the printer rather than the author, which suggests that it had been written earlier. The "true" Part II of *Clarián de Landanís* (rather than the unrelated Book 2 of Part I, mistakenly used by the Toledan printer Juan de Villaquirán in making up his set in the 1520's) was published in 1550, though written earlier. After the death of Carlos the only new romances to be published are unquestionably secondary works—*Febo el Troyano*, a plagiarism of the *Espejo de príncipes*,[34] Parts II-IV of the latter romance, *Leandro el Bel*, actually a translation from the Italian (Thomas, pp. 302-09), *Rosián de Castilla*, a short work which in several ways is not a true romance, and *Policisne de Boecia*, which was published only three years before Part I of the *Quijote*, an unfortunate coincidence which has given rise to a conclusion I believe unfounded (see p. 139, n. 16 *infra*).

It would be a mistake, however, to conclude that the romances of chivalry disappeared even though the composition of new ro-

---

resque and the picaresque, Blecua's important article, "Libros de caballerías, latín macarrónico y novela picaresca: La adaptación castellana del *Baldus* (Sevilla, 1542)," *Boletín de la Real Academia de Buenas Letras de Barcelona*, 34 [1971-72], 147-230); Hans Gerd Rötzer, *Picaro-Landtstörtzer-Simplicius. Studien zum niederen Roman in Spanien und Deutschland* (Darmstadt: Wissenschaftliche Buchgesellschaft, 1972), pp. 8-10; Ulrich Wicks, "The Nature of Picaresque Narrative," *PMLA*, 89 (1974), 245.

[32] Book 12, *Silves de la Selva*, was published earlier, and continues the third, rather than the fourth, part of *Florisel de Niquea* (Book 11).

[33] Although written and first published in Portuguese.

[34] See my edition of the *Espejo de príncipes*, I, lix-lx.

mances had been abandoned. The reprinting of the major romances, and even some of the minor ones, continued throughout the last half of the sixteenth century. *Lisuarte de Grecia, Amadís de Grecia,* and *Florisel de Niquea* (Parts I and II) were each reprinted three times during the reign of Felipe II. *Amadís de Gaula* and the *Espejo de príncipes* each went through five additional editions, the *Sergas de Esplandián* and *Palmerín de Olivia* two, *Primaleón* four, and so on. As I have explained elsewhere (*infra*, pp. 102-04), this publication of new editions of familiar texts did not occur evenly, but in several waves of publication, and the dates of these waves allow the conclusion that the romances were still read by the upper and upper-middle classes. Although the last great batch of reprints occurred during 1587-1590, stopped by the national mourning which followed the numerous deaths in the defeat of the Armada, it should be noted that Parts I and II of one romance, the *Espejo de príncipes*, were reprinted as late as 1617, after the publication of both parts of the *Quijote*, and that this edition was not a commercial failure is shown by the fact that the same bookseller (Juan de Bonilla) published an edition of Parts III and IV of the same work six years later.

Detailed information on the sixteenth-century book trade within Spain is not available, the only surviving documents being prepublication contracts, inventories of books made at death, and fragmentary information about private libraries.[35] There is no later parallel to the *Registrum* of Fernando Colón (*supra*, pp. 13-14), which notes precisely the place and date of publication of a book, plus the place, date, and cost of its purchase, information valuable for the early years of the sixteenth century which has not yet been fully exploited; the published information about Colón's library ends at 1530. But information is available, in considerable detail, about the book trade between Spain and the Spanish colonies in the New World in the later sixteenth century, because of the legal requirement for inventories of goods shipped, and the systematic conservation of such documents. These inventories are particularly valuable

---

[35] Irving Leonard, *Books of the Brave* (Cambridge, Massachusetts: Harvard University Press, 1949; reprint, New York: Gordian Press, 1964), pp. 101-02. There is a Spanish translation of this important study, *Los libros del conquistador*, trans. Mario Monteforte Toledo (Mexico: Fondo de Cultura Económica, 1963).

for the years after 1580 (Leonard, p. 132). Although the Spanish colonies' reading tastes may not have been identical with those of Spain, the mother country and her colonies were closer culturally at that time than they were ever to be again, and the publications, for example, of the Cromberger family, which benefited from its Sevillian location to publish to a considerable extent for the New World trade, do not differ as dramatically as Leonard believes from those of publishers in other parts of Spain whose New World trade was less.[36] Lacking evidence to the contrary, then, these documents provide some information about Spanish reading tastes in the later sixteenth and early seventeenth centuries.

The first, I believe, to obtain from records of book shipments to the New World information about reading tastes was Francisco Rodríguez Marín, who found that in 1605, the same year as the publication of Part I of the *Quijote*, numerous romances of chivalry of all types were sent to the New World.[37] It was Irving Leonard, however, who has most thoroughly investigated these documentary materials.[38] He found that romances of chivalry remained an important item in the book trade throughout the last years of the sixteenth century and in the opening years of the seventeenth, since the book dealers continued to sell, and the public to buy, those romances which had remained available since their last printings of ten to twenty years before.

The consequences for Cervantes of the continued circulation of the romances of chivalry in late sixteenth- and early seventeenth-century Spain are important ones, for they help lay to rest a commonly-held notion, already attacked by Rodríguez Marín,[39] that the romances of chivalry were already dead by the time of the

---

[36] Leonard, pp. 95-99. Leonard in fact argued for the similarity of taste between Spain and her colonies on pp. 256-57 of the same book.

[37] "El *Quijote* y Don Quijote en América," in his *Estudios cervantinos* (Madrid: Atlas, 1947), p. 104. This speech was delivered in 1911.

[38] *Romances of Chivalry in the Spanish Indies, with some* Registros *of Shipments of Books to the Spanish Colonies*, University of California Publications in Modern Philology, 16, No. 3 (Berkeley: University of California Press, 1933).

[39] In "La lectura de los libros de caballerías," cited in note 5 of Chapter II.

composition of the *Quijote*.[40] Were this the case, of course, Cervantes' repeated declarations that he intended to attack the romances by writing the *Quijote* could be interpreted as a disguise of his true, perhaps philosophical, intention. Yet the facts do not support this conclusion, since the romances were read right up until 1605,[41] and their disappearance was even more remote in the last decades of the sixteenth century, when Cervantes probably began the composition of Part I.[42]

It is true, of course, that no new romances, and few reprints, were published after 1602. There is evidence, however, to attack the notion, even more commonly held than the one just referred to, that the *Quijote* achieved with its publication its declared purpose of completely ending the popularity of the romances of chivalry. Quite aside from Leonard's support for the *Guzmán de Alfarache* as a more important cause of declining interest in the romances of chivalry (*Books of the Brave*, p. 264), we should avoid the conclusion that if no more romances were published after 1602 or 1605—for which reason, obviously, few copies could be shipped to the New World (Leonard, *Books of the Brave*, p. 286)—they were discarded and quickly forgotten. The reprinting of the *Espejo de príncipes* in 1617-23, the use

---

[40] Ángel Valbuena Prat, for example, in his *Historia de la literatura española*, 8th ed. (Barcelona: Gili, 1968), I, 499, says that of the romances of chivalry, "apenas quedaban débiles retoños en tiempos de Cervantes."

[41] Besides the reference in Part II of the *Guzmán de Alfarache*, cited in note 20 to Chapter I, in Tomé Pinheiro da Veiga's *Fastiginia o Fastos geniales*, written about 1605, there are many references which suggest the author's considerable acquaintance with the romances; see the translation of Narciso Alonso Cortés (Valladolid: Imprenta del Colegio de Santiago, 1916), pp. 37, 49, 70-71, 88, 106, and 132. Emma Susana Speratti Piñero points out that *La Florida* of the Inca Garcilaso, published coincidentally in 1605, was strongly influenced by them (pp. xxxix-xliii of her edition [Mexico: Fondo de Cultura Económica, 1956]).

[42] Luis Murillo, in *The Golden Dial* (Oxford: Dolphin, 1975), pp. 72-117, provides the most recent discussion of chronology of composition of the *Quijote*, pointing out that none of the books mentioned in the "escrutinio de la librería" was published later than 1591. I have also discussed the topic of the date of composition of the *Quijote* (Part II), in "El rucio de Sancho y la fecha de composición de la Segunda Parte de *Don Quijote*," *NRFH*, 25 (1976), 94-102; the revised English original was published in *Studies in the Spanish Golden Age: Cervantes and Lope* (Miami: Universal, 1977), 21-32.

made of the romances as subject for various plays written after 1605 (Thomas, pp. 78-79, 116-17, 126), the ownership of copies of the romances by individuals,[43] the appearance of the heroes of romances in masks after the *Quijote* show that "Cervantes' recent burlesquing of the fantastic adventures of these fictional supermen had not yet destroyed their vogue."[44] When Lope praises the romances in 1620 (Thomas, p. 154), and Gracián inveighs against them in the *Criticón*,[45] the composition and publication of the *Quijote* may have been more a symbol of the romances' gradual decline than a major cause of it. The simultaneous appearance of Don Quijote and the heroes of romances in masks[46] suggests that Don Quijote was seen not as an answer to the romances, but as a new type, an "Amadís a lo ridículo" as Nicolás Antonio called him,[47] a continuation rather than an antithesis.

A useful parallel can be drawn with the Western movie of the United States, also an art form of escapist intent, whose connection

---

[43] The historian Diego de Colmenares had a copy of *Amadís* (see *infra*, p. 95, n. 9). The Mexican Melchor Pérez de Soto, born in 1606, had a large collection of romances; see Donald G. Castanien, "The Mexican Inquisition Censors a Private Library, 1655," *Hispanic American Historical Review*, 34 (1954), 374-92. Irving Leonard, *Baroque Times in Old Mexico* (Ann Arbor: University of Michigan Press, 1966; first published in 1959), p. 94, summarizes as follows: "Cervantes' great masterpiece—which is also absent in this inventory—had allegedly given the coup de grâce in 1605 to the protracted vogue of the romances of chivalry. This assumption, enjoying something of the sanctity of dogma, receives a disconcerting jar as the eye roves over this book list of half a century later." Pérez owned copies of *Amadís, Lisuarte de Grecia, Amadís de Grecia, Florisel de Niquea, Palmerín de Oliva, Palmerín de Inglaterra, Belianís, Lepolemo*, and the *Caballero Peregrino* (see note 28 above). The Inquisition did not censor any of the literary works (Castanien, p. 388).

[44] Leonard, *Baroque Times*, p. 120.

[45] Ed. Miguel Romera-Navarro, II (Philadelphia: University of Pennsylvania Press, 1939), 35-36.

[46] Leonard, *Baroque Times*, p. 120; Thomas, p. 179; Rodríguez Marín, "El *Quijote* y Don Quijote en América," pp. 118, 129-37; "Relación de la fiesta que la insigne Universidad de Baeza celebró a la inmaculada Concepción (Baeza, 1618)," in Gallardo, II, cols. 182-83.

[47] *Bibliotheca Hispana Nova*, II, 133: "novum Amadisio de grege heroem ridiculum configens."

with the past on which it claims to be based can at times be very loose indeed. The Western was one of the earliest types of motion picture, which reached its greatest heights during the first half-century after the beginning of motion pictures. At the present moment it can safely be said to be moribund: few directors with artistic pretentions would wish to make a Western, and they are not paid much attention by current film critics or the discerning public (the "intelligentsia" of film-goers). The genre has been so exploited and become so hackneyed that parodic Westerns, such as *Cat Ballou*, can be made. Yet it would be a serious mistake to consider the Western film dead. Some films continue to be made, a body of fans exists who view when possible the older films, and American Westerns, like the Spanish romances, are very popular in many foreign countries, so much so that there are now "Western" film industries in several countries, particularly Italy and Japan. Perhaps most significant is the undisputed fact that even those who are bored with and contemptuous of Westerns, and would never see one, know what they are, and have a general acquaintance with the main works and the stock situations of the genre.

When, then, did the Spanish romance of chivalry die? The answer to this question must be that it did not die suddenly, on any specific day or within any specific year or even decade. Like an aged person, it lingered on, gradually failing for years, well into the seventeenth century, before it could be said to be completely dead. It is more a case of it fading away, losing gradually the interest of larger proportions of the public,[48] being restricted to ever smaller circles of active readers. Julio Caro Baroja even suggests that it never died completely, that there remained some readers, a continually smaller and less cultured group, practically up to the beginnings of modern scholarship and the first modern edition of the *Amadís*, in the nineteenth century.[49] Whether this is the case or not I have not the data to determine, but from the nineteenth century onward

---

[48] The comments of Mateo Alemán and Gracián recently referred to suggest that in the seventeenth century, the reading public of the romances included persons of lower social class than previously.

[49] *Ensayo sobre la literatura de cordel* (Madrid: Revista de Occidente, 1969), pp. 317-31. The romances discussed by Caro, however, are generally not the ones being discussed in this book.

those romances which were available have been read fairly widely, culminating in the current interest in the romances by modern novelists.[50] Certainly the present revival has not run its course, and we will see further editions and influence of the romances in this, the twentieth century.

---

[50] Besides the references given in my edition of the *Espejo de príncipes*, I, lxxiv, note 107, we can mention *Libro de caballerías*, of Juan Perucho (Barcelona: Taber, 1968). See also the addition of Julio Rodríguez-Puértolas to note 33, pp. 110-11 of *El pensamiento de Cervantes*.

❧ V ❧

A Typical Romance of Chivalry

REVIOUS BOOKS ON ROMANCES OF CHIVALRY, such as that of Henry Thomas, have tended to talk about the externals of the romances—their popularity, their publication—, rather than give the readers a complete picture of what a romance of chivalry *was*. Perhaps this is due to the fact that the complicated plots of the romances are inevitably confusing and hard to summarize, and those writers who do include such summaries often abandon them after a few pages, feeling that they are surely boring their readers and perhaps boring themselves as well.[1]

To avoid this pitfall and yet give the reader of this volume a taste of what a romance of chivalry was like, this chapter offers a composite summary of the action of a romance of chivalry, made up of the elements commonly found in them. What follows, therefore, is not a description of any one romance, but is true in spirit to all of them. I have offered in footnotes a series of selections from various romances which illustrate the points being discussed. It is hoped, therefore, that the modern reader who does not choose to read a romance in its entirety, or who gets no further than *Amadís de Gaula*, which is in some ways atypical,[2] will understand something of the

---

[1] Thomas and Menéndez Pelayo offer only brief summaries. Fuller ones are found in Gayangos' "Discurso preliminar"; for *Palmerín de Olivia*, *Primaleón*, and *Palmerín de Inglaterra* see Patchell, pp. 129-33. Some summaries may also be found in John Dunlop's *History of Prose Fiction*, ed. Henry Wilson (London: George Bell, 1896), I, 351-413. Pierce provides a detailed summary of *Amadís* in his *Amadís de Gaula*, pp. 27-36.

[2] As discussed elsewhere, *Amadís* is more sentimental than the later Spanish romances; its structure is less elaborate, and the descriptions, characterizations, and actions are less detailed.

world in which the knight-errant moved, and perhaps some of the appeal of these early works of fiction.

The romance of chivalry is always set in the past, even far in the past, though never before the birth of Christ. As is well known because of Cervantes' imitation of this feature in the *Quijote*, the romances are surrounded by trappings intended to give them an air of pseudo-historicity. (See "The Pseudo-Historicity of the Romances of Chivalry," included in this volume.) They always pretend to be true "crónicas" or "historias." The manuscript of a romance may have been found in some remote place; it will have been written in some strange language—"strange" being, in this case, non-Romance; it has been translated into Spanish with effort. There is usually an "author" or "chronicler" within the story, who may be a semi-official historian, setting down the deeds of his famous contemporary; he may be a *sabio* who takes an active part in the events he relates, helping the protagonist at crucial moments.[3]

Following classical and medieval precedent, the protagonist of a romance of chivalry is always male and invariably of royal blood—a prince. His lineage is usually specified. Through some mishap he is separated from his parents and his homeland when still a baby; he may be stolen away by evildoers, or carried off by a boat, or simply be abandoned by his mother because of the circumstances surrounding his birth, which often was illegitimate.[4] He grows up in

---

[3] Thus, for example, Artemidoro, one of the two "sabios" of the *Espejo de príncipes y cavalleros*, who, in Chapters 31 and 32 of Part I, takes the prince Rosicler to participate in a tournament in London, or, in Chapter 48 of Part III, enchants the princess Lindabrides. For other examples of "sabios," see note 34 of this chapter.

[4] After a "traidor" took the prince Cirongilio to put him to death, "oyó entre las espesuras de la montaña muy cerca de sí un estruendo tan grande que parescía hundirse toda aquella montaña.

"Y como bolviesse casi atónito e muy espantado por ver qué cosa era, vio venir para sí una serpiente la más brava y esquiva que jamás fue vista en el mundo por ninguna persona, y era tanta la furia que traýa que llamas de fuego parescía que lançava por la boca, y por las narizes humo muy espeso y negro, y los ojos parescían dos hachas encendidas. Argesilao [el traidor], que la vido venir, fue tan grande el espanto que en sí tomó que, fallesciéndole el esfuerco y espíritu de la vida, cayó amortescido en el suelo, quedando el niño entre sus braços, al qual la serpiente tomó e dixo contra Argesilao estas palabras:

the court of another king, far away, though he may have been
sheltered at first by farmers or other such humble people.[5] Usually

---

"—A lo menos desta vez no se cumplirá tu mal propósito ni tu trayción,
que muy gran mal fuera si este infante, de quien el remedio y salud de tantos
pende, al presente pereciera.

"E dichas estas palabras, dio un tan gran silvo que toda la gente de
Argesilao (que ninguna cosa avían visto hasta entonces) ovieron tanto pavor
que cada uno huyó por su parte, no teniendo ningún acuerdo de su señor.
Pues como la serpiente ovo dicho estas palabras, el niño en la boca, se metió
por lo más espeso de la montaña, donde dexaremos de contar de la serpiente
hasta que sea tiempo." (*Cirongilio de Tracia*, I, 4; p. 23, 11. 16-43 of the ed. of
Ray Green.)

Other examples: *Platir*, Chapter 5; *Lepolemo*, Chapter 5; *Belianís de Grecia*, I, 2;
Olivante de Laura, I, 5; *Amadís de Gaula*, I, 1; *Espejo de príncipes y cavalleros*, I, 15.

[5] "En la isla de Laura, que está en el mar de levante, cerca de las tierras
del Soldan de Babilonia, de la qual era señor un duque llamado por nombre
Armides, en una espessa y fragosa montaña de tan estrema sublimidad y
altura que sus cumbres sobrepujavan el lugar que las nuves comunmente
ocupar suelen, en una muy rica y hermosa morada que en ella estava,
morava una dueña hermana deste duque Armides, la qual en el arte de las
estrellas y sciencia de nigromancia de tal manera sobre quantas eran en el
mundo se aventajava, que del todo el mucho saber de las sabias Circe y
Medea en la memoria de los hombres se diminuia y estimava en tan poco,
que si en el tiempo della fueran le conocieran conocida superioridad y
ventaja. Este duque Armides, siendo natural del reino de Persia, y tiniendo
en él mucha tierra y gran señorio, como aquel que era de los principales de
todo aquel reino, y biviendo en la ley de los moros, esta dueña su hermana,
que avia por nombre la sabia Ipermea [había llevado el infante Olivante de
la corte de su padre].... Llamando la dueña que consigo traia, llamada
Polinesta, la qual avia sido casada con un muy buen cavallero cormano del
duque Armides, que pocos dias antes avia sido muerto, y esta dueña
aviendo quedado preñada dél al tiempo de su muerte, parió una hija, que
assi mismo quatro o cinco dias antes que de la isla de Laura partiessen [en
busca de Olivante] avia sido muerta, le entregó el hermoso donzel,
mandandole que con su leche lo criasse, teniendo tan entero cuidado dél
como si su proprio hijo fuesse, lo qual la dueña con toda voluntad y
diligencia puso en effecto. Mas tanto sabed, que de los que con la sabia
Ipermea vinieron de los escuderos y donzellas, sola aquella donzella que
traxo el donzel supo la tierra donde estava, y assi mismo cuyo hijo fuesse,
porque su voluntad fue que por entonces fuesse encubierto." (*Olivante de
Laura*, ff. 12ʳ-13ᵛ.)

Other examples: *Espejo de príncipes y cavalleros*, I, 18; *Cirongilio de Tracia*, I, 5.

there will remain with him some clue, either a mark on his body,[6] or some artifact which accompanies him (such as Palmerín de Olivia's cross[7]), to eventually provide the "proof" of his true identity when the anagnorisis arrives. He will eventually learn his true identity and be reunited with his parents and family, either at the midpoint or near the end of the book.[8]

---

[6] "En la misma persona del infante quiso nuestro señor Dios mostrar sus señales y grandes maravillas, poniendo y esculpiendo en el su braço derecho diez letras bermejas a manera de fuego, las quales, puesto que muchos se juntaron, no ovo persona alguna en toda aquella región que las supiesse ni acertasse a leer ni entendiesse ni penetrasse su significación, cosa dina de grande espanto y admiración. (*Cirongilio de Tracia*, I, 4; p. 21, 11. 18-26 of the edition of Ray Green.)

Other examples: see my edition of the *Espejo de príncipes y cavalleros*, I, 93, note.

[7] See Chapter 107 (p. 361 of the edition of Giuseppe di Stefano).

[8] "La reina Rosiana, que el coraçon le dezia que aun mayor alegria esperava aquella noche, pareciendole que qualquiera merced era bien empleada en Olivante de Laura, segun los servicios que el rey y ella dél avian recebido, entró en su camara a la hora que los maestros le alçaron la camisa de los pechos. Y assi como entró, le vio el coraçon que encima del suyo tenia figurado, y pareciendole lo que podia ser, porque tambien sabía la sospecha que sobre ello el rey avia tenido, dio una gran boz, diziendo:

"—¡O soberano Dios! ¡Quan gran bien sería si en mi pensamiento no recibiesse más engaño que mi coraçon dessea!

"El rey, que con el mismo sobresalto estava, viendo lo que la reina dezia, mandó salir a todos fuera de la camara. Y quedando los tres solos, el rey dixo a Olivante:

"—Mi verdadero y grande amigo, en gran confusion nos ha puesto vuestra vista. Si el secreto de lo que por nosotros os fuere preguntado quisieredes que más no sea encubierto, pues que siendo verdad lo que pensamos, aunque el amor que os tenemos, segun es mucho, no pueda crecer la obligacion en nosotros para amaros como verdadero hijo que pensamos que sois nuestro. Porque pariendo la reina uno con las mismas señales que vos teneis, nos fue llevado de nuestra presencia, sin saber de quien, más de que una donzella con grande engaño nos le pidio. Assi que, diziendonos vos quien son vuestros padres, nos podreis quitar de essa dubda . . . .

"—. . . Quien son mis padres, yo no sabria dezirlo, que nunca los vi ni conoci. Sé que me crió una dueña llamada Polinesta, a quien mucho tiempo tuve por madre, aunque despues supe no ser assi, mas que yo era natural deste reino de Macedonia, y que siendo niño de poco tiempo nacido, la sabia Ipermea me hizo llevar a la isla de Laura, donde en casa del duque Armides

The protagonist shows signs from a very early age of his royal blood and the corresponding great abilities which were thought of as the natural endowments of a great ruler. He is exceptionally handsome,[9] so much so that he captivates and gains the affection of all who see him, save those of evil nature. He may walk or talk at a younger age than normal. Being fearless, like mythological infants

---

su hermano fui criado de la manera que he dicho. La más verdadera señal que comigo llevé, fue un coraçon que sobre el mio tengo figurado, el qual, siendo todo vermejo y muy encendido, despues por cierta aventura el medio della se ha tornado blanco, por lo qual en muchas partes me han nombrado el cavallero del coraçon partido....

"—Assaz aveis dicho —respondio la reina— para que yo conozca ser vos mi verdadero hijo salido de mis entrañas.

"Y diziendo esto, con abundancia de lagrimas que por su muy hermoso rostro con la grande alegria caian, lo toma entre sus braços, besandolo en la boca, y diziendo cosas que estava fuera de sí de plazer. Pues el rey no menos estava alegre, que abriendo las puertas de la camara, a grandes bozes mandó entrar a todos, publicando el gran gozo que con el nuevo hijo aquella hora avia llegado a su anima, diziendo que no avia igualado el trabajo y tristeza del dia de su nascimiento con gran parte a la alegria que con su conocimiento entonces se sentia." (*Olivante de Laura*, 125^{r-v}.)

Other examples: *Espejo de príncipes y cavalleros*, II, 36; *Primaleón*, Chapters 8 and 169.

[9] "Mucho apuesto donzel salia Platir, e de muy valiente cuerpo, e muy buen cavallero. Bien mostrava *en su continente* [my italics] ser nieto de aquel valiente y esforçado cavallero Palmerin de Oliva." (*Platir*, 9.)

"Ansí como ivan creciendo en edad, ansí crecían sobre todos los otros en juizio y discreción, apostura y destreza, y en todo lo demás que a tales príncipes convenía, especialmente el Donzel del Febo. Que quando llegó a edad de diez años, ninguno que lo viera lo dexara de juzgar por más de quinze, y en los grandes y bien formados miembros que sacava se vía en él muy claramente de quán grandes fuerças avía de ser. Y dezían todos que según en aquella edad estava de alto y membrudo, quando llegasse a edad de veinte años parescería grande. Y ansí fue; que aunquel emperador Trebacio su padre era muy grande de cuerpo (que como la historia ha contado, tenía ocho pies en alto), el Cavallero del Febo fue algo mayor. Y con todo esto, jamás en cuerpo humano proporción igual fue vista que en el suyo, que no parescía sino que divinas manos lo uviesen fabricado. Y muchos pintores uvo, ansí griegos como asirios, que nunca avían podido alcançar la entera y acabada perfición de un cuerpo humano hasta que a este cavallero vieron, y le debuxaron, embiando su retrato por muchas partes como la más perfeta y acabada obra que uviessen hecho." (*Espejo de príncipes y cavalleros*, I, 18.)

such as Hercules, he may perform extraordinary feats as a baby or young boy. Lions, symbols of royalty, instinctively respect him. He is exceptionally strong and vigorous, possessed of excellent health, never ill unless wounded. He can easily defeat a boy of the same age, who will more than likely be physically smaller, since the protagonists of the romances of chivalry are swarthy individuals, taller and huskier than the persons they come in contact with (see the text quoted in note 9). As stated above, the prince and king-to-be, in short, conforms very closely to the image of the ideal medieval ruler.

While still at the court in which he has grown up he will receive instruction from tutors, such as a Spanish prince would; his attitude toward his studies will be respectful, not rebellious. He will learn what is taught him, which often includes a variety of languages,[10] later to serve him in good stead, but his inclination is obviously not to books nor to the world of learning. His studies do not continue past his youth.

After the prince has learned to ride and to fight with the sword and other arms, also at an early age, he will desire to leave the court where he has grown up and go in search of adventures; Rosicler, for example, simply "quería ir por el mundo a saber algunas cosas de las que avía en él" (Espejo de príncipes, I, 27). The protagonist has Wander-lust. There is always opposition to this desire of his, some attempt made to convince or force him not to leave—scarcely surprising considering that he is so young.[11] He may have to depart secretly

---

[10] "Ya que fue de edad de cinco años le mandó doctrinar e instruyr [a Cirongilio] en las letras juntamente con un hijo que él tenía llamado Antandro, que era de su edad. Y como el infante fuesse de muy grande abilidad, en pocos días deprendió tanto que hablava y entendía muchas lenguas que esto era lo que más en aquellos tiempos los príncipes y personas generosas punavan de deprender." (Cirongilio de Tracia, I, 5; p. 26, lines 41-48 of the edition of Ray Green.) We find in Chapter I, 16 of Cirongilio that the protagonist knew Greek and Arabic very well. Claribalte also knew many languages; see Antonello Gerbi, "El Claribalte de Oviedo," Fénix, 6 (1949), 378-90, at p. 381; "no avía lenguaje ninguno que Medájar [maestro de Amadís de Grecia] supiese qu'él [Amadís de Grecia] no la sabía tan bien como él" (Amadís de Grecia, I, 2). For other examples, see my edition of the Espejo de príncipes, I, 229, note to lines 23 and 24.

[11] "En esta sazon Lantedon tenia gran desseo de ser cavallero; platicavalo

(an action that Don Quijote was to imitate).¹² By this time he will have been or will seek to be dubbed a knight, by the person of highest status he can manage to find and convince to do so—a king or an emperor is ideal—,¹³ and will have received as gifts his first set

---

esto mucho vezes con su hermano Gedres. El rey Tanabel [his father], siendo desto sabidor, e teniendo recelo que Lantedon, a quien él e la reina su muger en desigual grado amavan, se partiria en breve dellos, tomóle un dia por la mañana, e levando le para la camara de la reina, le dixo:

"—Amado hijo, tu madre me ha rogado que los dos juntamente te demandemos un don, por ende te rogamos que nos lo otorgues.

"Lantedon respondio con mucha humildad:

"—Señor, no ay cosa que demandarme quisierdes que assi por me la pedir tales dos personas, como por ser este el primer don que me aveis demandado, que yo no haga.

"—Pues mi buen fijo —dixo el rey— el don que te pedimos es que no rescibas orden de cavalleria ni partas de nuestra corte por espacio de un año.

"Oido esto por Lantedon pesóle mucho, mas aun que contra su voluntad, otorgólo.

"Gedres del fuerte braço, como esto supo, viendo que el rey su padre dél no se avia acordado ni hecho mencion, y considerando que aquel reino despues de sus dias era de Lantedon, y que a él por el valor de su persona le convenia alcançar bien e honra en este mundo, e acordó de ser luego cavallero e partirse de alli. Yendose para el rey, que en su palacio, con muchos de sus ricos hombres, estava, hincandose de hinojos en tierra, le pidio que le armasse cavallero. El rey, como quiera que se escusó mucho dello, fue dél assi aquexado que se lo ovo de otorgar.

"Sabido por Lantedon que su hermano, siendo menor que él, queria ser cavallero y meterse a buscar las aventuras, y que a él convenia a estar mal de su grado, mucho pesar ovo en su coraçon." (*Clarián de Landanís*, I, introductory, unnumbered chapter.)

Another example: *Platir*, Chapter 74.

¹² "El donzel Lucencio, despues que la dueña salvaje le dixo como venia de alto lugar, nunca descansó su coraçon, contino pensando como podria armarse cavallero, si lo diria a su madre Florisma o no. En fin de muchos pensamientos acordó, sin le dezir cosa, de se ir para Constantinopla, a suplicar al emperador Esplandian que lo armase cavallero, dandole todas las armas y cavallo que para ello le convenia.... Otro dia, diziendo que ivan [Luciencio y su escudero Florindo] a monte como solian, se fueron secretamente en una nao que al puerto hallaron." (*Amadís de Grecia*, I, 14).

¹³ When Cirongilio is asked by whom he wishes to be armed a knight, his answer is "de la mano del emperador Corosindo de Grecia, que grandes cosas avía oýdo de su virtud y nobleza" (I, 7; p. 31, 11. 1-3 of the ed. of Ray Green).

of arms and armor, his shield white as befits a new or *novel* knight.[14]
Later, after some especially noteworthy or significant adventure, he
will take as a heraldic symbol an animal, natural phenomenon,
flower, or some similar item, such as are found in any inventory of
coats of arms, which in their origin were based on just such a
practice.

Once he has left the court where he has grown up, the knight-
errant (for such he now is) will travel extensively. His travels will be
both through familiar and unfamiliar parts of the world: Europe,
Asia, sometimes North Africa, sometimes to imaginary places made
up by the author. (The New World, of course, had not yet been
discovered.) He may visit London, Paris, or Constantinople, cities
already with some chivalric tradition, but never Rome, Jerusalem,
nor a Spanish city such as Toledo or Santiago. The travels of the
knight offered the author of the romance an opportunity to enter-
tain his readers, always eager for discussions of new and marvellous
places, and display whatever geographic knowledge he might have,
and his powers of imagination.

The knight will primarily travel by land, on horse or occasionally
on foot, but he may well have occasion to journey by sea or by
means of some supernatural means of transportation. His travels
may be for various purposes: to see, serve, elope with, or retire
from his lady, to attend a tournament announced in some more or
less distant city, to go to the aid of kings or queens in need of
military assistance to repel invaders or to claim what is rightfully
theirs, to obtain a healing agent for someone ill, to help free
someone held captive, to catch a glimpse of some beautiful woman,

---

[14] When Lucencio appears before the emperor Esplandián, he orders a
courtier: "llevad con vos por huesped este donzel, y mandalde dar las mejores
armas de mi guardaropa, y un cavallo de los mejores que tengo, y otro para el
escudero que consigo trae, con tanto aver qu'él sea contento, porque me da el
coraçon que deve ser bueno.... El marques hizo luego lo que le era mandado
por el emperador, y armando al donzel de muy ricas armas blancas, tales que
les convenian a cavallero novel, él quedó tan apuesto y bien hecho a ellas
como si fuera criado en ellas." (*Amadís de Grecia*, I, 14.) Artemidoro gave
Rosicler, one of the protagonists of the *Espejo de príncipes*, "unas armas...
hechas por su arte y gran saber de suerte que jamás pudieron ser cortadas, y
tan ricas y vistosas como ningún príncipe del mundo las podía tener. Eran
blancas como de novel.... Y con ellas le dio un cavallo..." (I, 31).

to get to know the identity of or to find his parents.[15] There may be no more significant reason than the fact that someone he encounters has requested his company.

The knight never seeks money; indeed, money is so seldom mentioned, as Don Quijote correctly points out to Sancho, that it seems that the protagonists of the romances live in a primitive era, outside the money economy altogether. The only times we find money mentioned at all is in terms of a prize or reward (more often a valuable object), or as a tribute or tax demanded by an evil ruler (as, for example, in *Cirongilio de Tracia*, III, 10). The knight expects and receives hospitillity from those he meets along his way; similar to the modern Indian holy man, it was considered both a duty and an honor to provide for someone as valuable to society as the knight. His physical needs, modest in any event, are thus easily met.

To the extent that the knight seeks anything, he seeks prestige, fame, and reputation, and his adventures are a means of obtaining these. However, besides his extraordinary deeds, he also attains fame and reputation because of the qualities of his personality—the gracious way the knight treats others, for example, magnanimously setting free the enemies he has vanquished. Although he will never boast of or even recite his feats—for that would be a symptom of pride—, and may often disguise his identity, using, for example, borrowed armor with a different heraldic symbol, the news traveled fast in the chivalric world, and the knight-errant rapidly became well known and sought after. He is, in effect, proving that he is of royal abilities, and a fit ruler for the kingdom or empire which he will in the course of time inherit.

---

[15] We can find examples of all these means of and motives for traveling in a single romance of chivalry, the *Espejo de príncipes*. An enchanted boat, for example, takes the Caballero del Febo to the island of Lindaraxa, from which he helps his enchanted and as yet unrecognized father Trebacio to escape (I, 44). Rosicler travels from the house of his presumed mother to England in order to participate in a tournament organized by the king of that country (I, 28-32). The Cavallero del Febo departs rather suddenly on a trip to the kingdom of Lidia, in order to help King Liseo, whose kingdom (Lidia) had been taken from him (II, 44). The Caballero del Febo travels from Constantinople to China after having fallen in love with, and earned through combat, the princess Lindabrides (see II, 53). Rosicler tries through travel to find Theoduardo, whom he believes to be his father (I, 28).

Part of the knight's reputation, as we have just indicated, is based on something besides his ability as a fighter. He will, in fact, have a great many desirable qualities: intelligence, a calm temper, magnanimity. His *mesura* and cool temper were important virtues, for one with a hot temper too easily gets into unnecessary fights. The knight has a highly developed ethical sense, and always helps the more deserving of two parties to a conflict; in fact, he feels he has a responsibility to help those deserving persons in need of his help, of which there are many. The knight does not seek occasions for serious fighting, though he does for the less serious fighting which was intended as entertainment. He avoids conflict whenever possible, and only engages in it when reconciliation with his opponent is impossible, when the adversary cannot be made to see the inevitable error of his ways.

He will be a good courtier, even though court life is not to his taste.[16] He is neither wordy nor taciturn, and may be able to play musical instruments and compose verses. He may have a good sense of humor and sometimes enjoy verbal repartée.

With all these desirable qualities and abilities, it is scarcely surprising that the knight is widely liked and respected. Nevertheless, there are evil persons in the world, "traidores" and "malvados," and thus he will have enemies. They may be simply jealous of him, jealousy being both a sin and a flaw in one's personality, or they may seek revenge for some defeat they have received at his hand.[17]

---

[16] Miguel Hierónymo Oliver, "notario de Valencia," comments thus in a prefatory poem to *Valerián de Hungría*: "Vereis la pintura de un buen cortesano/ y las calidades que en él se requieren./ Vereis dela corte las leyes que quieren/ que cumpla quien viste l'arnes de Vulcano."

[17] Before the emperor of Constantinople, Validos accuses Primaleón:

"Vengo acusar a tu hijo Primaleon de una traicion que hizo en matar tan cruelmente a un cavallero de alta guisa que vino por honrar sus fiestas, y este se llamava Perequin de Duaços, principe de Polonia, que no me negará él, si aqui está, que no le mató falsamente, e sobre acuerdo, lo qual él no deviera fazer, pues avia segurado a todos los cavalleros que al torneo viniessen. Que Perequin, por aver gana de se provar con él, no merecia muerte tan airada; pues que otros muchos cavalleros fazian lo que él. E vos, Primaleon, si aqui estais, no sé que escusa me deis a su muerte; que yo vos acuso que lo matastes falsamente.

"Primaleon, que esto oyo, levantóse en pie (que estava assentado delante del emperador, e muchos altos hombres con él), e dixo contra Validos:

Not infrequently he may gain an enemy as a consequence of an interest in, or from, a female. Such enemies may invent falsehoods about the knight, accusing him of treason which he would never dream of committing. He may be accused of love for an inappropriate person, such as a (married) queen.[18] Or the accusations may be less serious. Usually the ultimate fate of the knight's evil accusers is death, either because a battle is required to show, through combat, which party is telling the truth and to cleanse the knight's honor and reputation, or because the malcreants are put to death by the king when exposed, or because they cannot bear living in humiliation, which in the chivalric world, again reflecting contemporary Spanish values, was felt to be intolerable. The knight-errant and protagonist will not, however, seek the death of his enemies.

Among the evil characters the knight will come into contact with on his travels are giants. As I have explained elsewhere,[19] the giants were not supernatural beings but merely very large and ugly men, who believed themselves to be superior to ordinary men and therefore free from the troubling need to follow society's rules. Giants are clearly the villains of the romances of chivalry. Never Christians,[20] they usurped kingdoms because of their whim, and carried off women with the intent of raping them and men to be sold as slaves. (One may well note here a reflection of the Spaniards'

"—Cierto, cavallero, mal aconsejado fuistes en tomar tal demanda, en querer vengar muerte de cavallero que murio en torneo. Yo no negaré que lo maté, que sí fize, e aun sobre acuerdo, como vos dezis. Mas esto causó su gran sobervia e locura; que en tres torneos no me podia dél defender. Que en todos lo hallava delante con voluntad de matarme, e antes que la hiziesse, pues él no buscava otra cosa, quise yo adelantarme. Pues que lo pude hazer no me pesa. E digo que si vos traeis gran voluntad de combatiros comigo, yo lo hare, porque todo el mundo vea que vuestra acusacion es falsa." (*Primaleón*, 68.)

[18] For an example, see Chapter I, 5 of *Amadís de Grecia*, in which the traitor Mauden falsely tells king Magadén, in whose court Amadís lived, that Amadís had slept with Magadén's queen.

[19] In my edition of the *Espejo de príncipes*, I, 46-47, note. For a list of numerous giants of the romances of chivalry, see note 14 of Diego Clemencín to Chapter 49 of Part I of the *Quijote*.

[20] While the religious beliefs of giants are usually not explored in detail, there is a colorful description of the moon-worship of one giant family in Chapter 39 of Part III of the *Espejo de príncipes y cavalleros*.

attitude toward the Moors.) The giants are haughty and disrespect-
ful. They offer the knight the chance to show his extraordinary
abilities in defeating and killing them; in the case of giants, he does
not hesitate to put them to death. Occasionally one finds a good or
reformed giant,[21] and sometimes dwarfs,[22] evil or otherwise.

Several other characteristics of the knight in the romances of
chivalry need mentioning. Because he is such a likeable person and a
good companion, the knight is seldom alone. This is not because he
has a squire, since the role of squires in the Spanish romances of
chivalry, as Don Quijote knew, is a very secondary one. It is rather
because friends of similar age, or relatives, accompany him on his
travels. Often he travels with knights that he meets by chance on
the road.

The knight is also an outdoorsman. He is not upset by the
discomforts of travel in those primitive times, and frankly enjoys
the nature by which he is usually surrounded. He goes through
beautiful forests, climbs gentle hills, comes across fresh, clear riv-
ers,[23] is woken in the morning by the singing of the birds, and

---

[21] "En los confines de Albania avía una pequeña ysla de la qual era señor
un gigante llamado Epaminón. Era tan diferente e diverso de la condición y
sobervia que los tales suelen tener que de todos sus vasallos era muy amado y
querido, que no solamente no les fatigava con tirano imperio, pero antes eran
por él defendidos y amparados de la violencia de sus contrarios." (*Cirongilio de
Tracia*, I, 5; p. 26, lines 16-22 of the edition of Ray Green.)

[22] *Primaleón*, 29; *Clarián de Landanís*, I, 34; *Cirongilio de Tracia*, III, 17.

[23] "Tres días anduvo sin aventura hallar, y el tercero, porque era tarde y
la noche venía muy escura, determinó de alvergar en un hondo valle que
cerca de la carrera estava, debaxo unos robles muy altos y espessos, que con
sus estendidas ramas causavan un deleytoso frescor y semblante, y en medio
dellos manava una clara y hermosa fuente que mucho al príncipe agradó,
recreando allí sus espíritus que muy fatigados del trabajo passado venían,"
(*Cirongilio de Tracia*, I, 12; 51, lines 31-40 of the edition of Ray Green.)
"Poniendo los ojos en la ínsula, vio que era la más fresca y deleitable y la
más estraña tierra que jamás uviesse visto. Era todo lo que él podía alcançar a
ver poblado de arboleda, y los árboles muy olorosos y floridos, y algunos avía
tan altos que la vista parescía cansarse en mirar sus verdes y fronduosos
remates. Debaxo de los quales era toda la tierra un prado muy verde, lleno de
olorosas y silvestres flores, entre las quales se hazía un suave y dulce ruido de
muy claras y cristalinas aguas, que en pequeños arroyos corrían por ellas.
Veíanse por entre los árboles passar los ligeros gamos muy descuidados. Y los
hermosos unicornios, con los aspados ciervos y medrosos corços, y otras mil

makes his meals when necessary from what nature provides. His main diversion, aside from tournaments or an occasional *sarao* with the ladies, is *caza de monte*.

Correspondingly, the knight does not like urban life. Cities, as well as creature comforts, make him uneasy and restless. To visit a castle, palace, or court (the latter usually set in a city) may be attractive for a time, but once the tournament is over or his business concluded, the knight feels he must be on the road again, an attitude clearly reflected by Don Quijote in II, 57 and 58 of the *Quijote*. The knight may even be surmised to have a certain scorn for those who do not share this view. One of the saddest moments in the life of a knight-errant (or in the life of a king, perhaps the protagonist's father, a former knight-errant) is when he finally accedes to his throne. Then he can no longer be "errant," for custom and good sense require that the king remain more or less in one spot, chained by his duty, and unable to travel as a younger person is free to do.

While the knight feels comfortable in small groups and is glad to have company, he dislikes large gatherings of people. In a military action, conscious of his status, he will not mix with the common soldiers, though he will quite routinely accept a meal from shepherds if he encounters them on his travels. The tournament is the only exception to this, since tournaments are a basic element of the Spanish romances of chivalry, and they bring together a large body of knights.

It may safely be concluded that the tournaments are as frequent as they are because the Spanish readers found them entertaining, strange as this may seem to the modern reader who has lost the taste for this type of sport. A tournament would be given by a king, who himself gained status by staging one and by having distinguished knights in his court, even for a short time; the king also would enjoy recapturing some of the pleasure of the company of other knights, which he cannot enjoy as frequently as in his youth.

---

diversidades de animales silvestres grandes y pequeños con celosas corridas y enamoradas luchas retoçavan sobre la verde yerva. Juntávase con esto una dulcíssima y muy estraña armonía que tenían las aves en los verdes ramos, que a qualquiera hombre que triste y afligido fuera bastara a consolar." (I, 44 of the *Espejo de príncipes*; II, 175-76 of my edition.)

A tournament usually had some prize or prizes to be awarded, some attraction which would draw knights. They came not so much for the prize to be awarded (since the winner, our protagonist, would invariably give it away in his turn, often to a woman present at the tournament whom he wished to impress). The knight entered the competition for the *honor* of winning the prize, the status gained thereby, and the social obligations he created with his gift. The most common sport at the tournaments was the fight with lances, long, thick poles with which two knights at a time ran at each other, on horseback, each attempting with the blow of the impact to knock the other from his horse. The force of the impact was considerable, and often the thick lances would break; the two knights would continue using additional lances until one was victorious.[24] Al-

---

[24] The tournaments of the romances of chivalry are so abundant that it is only possible to cite a selection and to give some brief extracts. For examples: *Belianís de Grecia*, I, 32-33, II, 4 and ff., 22, *Platir*, 22, *Lepolemo*, 125, *Espejo de príncipes*, I, 32, II, 64, *Clarián de Landanís*, I, 6, 9-11, *Olivante de Laura*, I, 27-28, *Primaleón*, 24-25, 59, 62, 78-80, 210, *Cirongilio de Tracia*, III, 36, 38-41, etc., etc. Here is an extract from *Primaleón*, Chapter 59:

"El primero que fue a justar con él fue el marques Penarado, que era cavallero muy preciado y de alta guisa, e venia del linaje de los emperadores de Constantinopla, y desseavase casar con Melisa. Y porque oyo dezir que aquellos cavalleros le embiaron aquel mandado que aveis oido dezir, los desamava, y tomóle voluntad de provarse con ellos. Y armóse de ricas armas, y entró en el campo, cubierto de su escudo, e sin dezir ninguna cosa abaxó la lança e assi hizo Recindos, e vinieronse a encontrar con tanto ardimiento e poder que no ay hombre que vos lo pudiesse dezir. Mas el encuentro de Recindos fue con tanta fuerça que sacó al marques de la silla por las ancas del cavallo, e dio con él en tierra, y fue tan maltrecho que por una pieça no bullio pie ni mano, e un su primo, hermano del marques, que era muy buen cavallero, ovo tan gran pesar que luego se fue a armar, y entre tanto los del marques lo sacaron del campo e lo llevaron a su posada. Bimer, que assi avia nombre el primero del marques, vino con gran voluntad de justar con Recindos, y venia tan desacordado que faltó de su encuentro, y Recindos lo derribó en tierra muy ligeramente. Bimer se levantó muy ligero, e dixole:

"—No podeis, don cavallero, de vos ir. Assi que a las espadas veremos que sabeis fazer.

"Recindos se apeó, y enbraçó su escudo, y començaron su batalla, mas presto fue despartida. Que Recindos andava ligero; que de gran fuerça y coraçon era, y prestamente vencio al cormano del marques, y le tomó sus sobreseñales, y los suyos lo llevaron a la posada del marques, que iva malferido.

though physical injury was not the object in this sport, which was often a game among friends, it was not uncommon for someone to be hurt.

A sort of impromptu tournament, semi-serious, which the knight might encounter was the *paso*, in which someone would block the road, or a bridge, and the knight could not continue his travel unless he admitted something unacceptable (that his lady was less beautiful than another, for example[25]), or defeated in battle the knight maintaining the *paso*. That this type of adventure antedated the Spanish romances, and is found in the fifteenth-century *Passo honroso*—itself a reflection of literature—,[26] is so well known as almost to make it unnecessary to mention it here.

Along with tournaments and *pasos*, battles are also an essential part of the romances of chivalry, and here again the knight-errant is able to show his exceptional abilities. Always held for a serious and

---

"—Pareceme —dixo el emperador— que no es de menos bondad este otro cavallero quel primero. Mucho los querria conocer, que de gran bondad son.

"Recindos mandó al paje de Belcar que llevasse las sobreseñales del marques y de Bimer a Melisa, y que le dixesse que le pedia por merced que las recibiesse; que gelas embiava un cavallero que mucho la desseava servir."

To see the variety in these potentially monotonous descriptions, contrast the preceeding one with this combat between Primaleón and Don Duardos:

"Movio el uno contra el otro al más correr de sus cavallos, con tan gran poder que no parecia sino que la tierra tremia. E vinieronse a encontrar con tanta fuerça que ninguno faltó de su encuentro, y ambos fueron a tierra, falsados los escudos e las lorigas, e cada uno uvo una llaga pequeña de la lança. E como cada uno dellos ovo verguença de aver caido, levantaronse a priessa, e embraçaron sus escudos y sacaron sus espadas, y començaronse de ferir de esquivos golpes. Primaleon de sañudo contra aquel que lo avia derribado, que jamas lo avia sido de cavallero, e Don Duardos de ver a Flerida ante sus ojos, hazian ambos maravillas; que rajavan los escudos y desmallavan las lorigas de los fuertes golpes que se davan. E en poca de hora se pararon tales que quantos los miravan eran espantados, y más el emperador, que no tuvo por segura la vida de su hijo, segun vido la gran bondad del cavallero con quien se combatia. E como ambos traian buenas espadas, hazian las llegar a la carne, por manera que eran mal heridos." (*Primaleón*, 83)

[25] Don Quijote imitates this practice in his challenge to the *mercaderes* in his primera salida (I, 4). For examples of *pasos*, see *Espejo de príncipes*, I, 52, *Primaleón*, 56, *Platir*, 61, *Olivante de Laura*, I, 26.

[26] For information on the *Passo honroso* of Suero de Quiñones, see entry NN41 of my bibliography.

just reason—to repel an attack, for example—the battles are invariably bloody affairs in which many are killed,[27] unless, as occasionally happens, the two sides to a conflict decide to have a limited number from each side determine, through fighting, the outcome.[28] The protagonist is usually not a main participant at the beginning of a battle, since he remains calm and somewhat detached, and the duty of fighting would first be assumed by the person(s) the knight is aiding. But when the knight-errant, the hero of the story, has his anger aroused, he becomes a terrifying opponent. He wields his sword and charges through the battle, cutting off heads and arms, penetrating armor with the force of his blows. Not unusual is the blow which descends through the helmet, the neck, and part of the trunk, severing an opponent almost into two parts. There is often a religious element to these battles, in which the knight, though not necessarily a Christian, helps the Christian side, which will in any event be more deserving for other reasons. The knight not born a Christian will at some point be converted to the "true" religion.

Women and love usually play a secondary role in the Spanish romances of chivalry, serving more as background, or providing motives for action,[29] than taking part in the action themselves. Ladies did not travel for pleasure or amusement; in fact, except for women

---

[27] *Palmerín de Olivia*, 136-42, *Belianís de Grecia*, I, 53, *Platir*, 26, *Espejo de príncipes*, III, 17-25.

[28] *Belianís de Grecia*, II, 47; *Espejo de príncipes*, III, 26 and 30. This practice was really engaged in the sixteenth century, though whether a source of the practice in the romances or a result of it is not clear. See the "Relación muy cierta y verdadera de un desafío que se hizo en Orán el año de 1553 entre veinte cavalleros christianos y otros tantos cavalleros moros," in *Relaciones de los reinados de Carlos V y Felipe II*, ed. Amalio Huarte, I, Sociedad de Bibliófilos Españoles, 2ª época, 12   (Madrid, 1941), 95-136. In Sandoval, *Carlos V*, II, *BAE* 81, 285-86, we find Carlos responding to François I's request for a duel "por evitar efusión de sangre, y poner fin a esta guerra."

[29] "Para defender las dueñas y donzellas que tuerto reciben principalmente se dava la orden de cavalleria," the narrator states in *Amadís de Grecia*, I, 14, while the protagonist reiterates in chapter 18, "no dexaré de serviros, si de mí teneis necessidad por algun tuerto que se os haga. Que para esto recebi la orden de cavalleria; que en otra guisa mal empleada sería en mí y en todos los que armas traen si consintiessen contra justicia hazerse enojo a dueña ni donzella."

in search of assistance or carrying out some vow, they did not travel at all unless forced to by evil-doers. We can summarize by saying that both literally and figuratively, women are the spectators at the tournament. Love, of course, was seen as a refining element, felt to improve men, and the knight will fall in love at some point with the woman he will eventually marry, though not much significance was given to the marriage vows, to judge from the number of children conceived out of wedlock. But love was still a pretext for adventures, rather than a main focus of attention. The knight's courtship of his lady, consequently, will usually be secret, and beset with external difficulties, even if the lady is agreeable, which is not always the case, especially at the beginning.[30] The romance will usually end with the marriage of the knight (perhaps a joint marriage, together with some of his friends or relatives), the birth or conception of a son, and the protagonist's accession to the throne.[31]

Women in need of assistance, ranging from queens to humble servant girls, are the basis for many of the knight's deeds.[32] A woman whose honor had been attacked could only cleanse it through battle with her accuser or dishonorer, and had to seek a knight to take her part and defend her (a practice reflected in the episode of Doña Rodríguez, in the Quijote). The protagonist will not resist the request to help such a deserving person.[33]

Adventures with the supernatural will also present themselves to the knight, though not in the sense the Quijote has given us to understand. He will not be pursued by enchanters; more often he will have sabios with some magical powers—those consistant with Christianity, usually—who will be working to help him, and may deter-

---

[30] María Rosa Lida points out how one of the differences between Arthurian texts and the Spanish chivalric literature influenced by them is that the Spanish works "no logra[n] acentuar suficientemente el elemento sobrenatural característico de las aventuras de la 'materia de Bretaña,' ni la fuerza irresistible del amor" ("Arthurian Literature," p. 412; p. 141 of the Spanish translation).

[31] For further details, see "The Pseudo-Historicity of the Romances of Chivalry," infra.

[32] Some examples: Primaleón, 115-18, 152; Cirongilio, pp. 52-54, Platir, 20; Lidamor de Escocia, 40; Clarián de Landanís, I, 74-75.

[33] Palmerín de Olivia, 85-86; Espejo de príncipes, I, 50, 53-54, III, 43-45.

mine the course of the plot.[34] (Thus the knight, like Don Quijote in the Cueva de Montesinos, may find that adventures have been "reserved" for him.[35]) But the knight will still have to combat with unnatural beasts of all sorts,[36] penetrate obstacles created by magic in order to reach some protected place, fight and find the inevitable weak point of a combatant with magical gifts, or travel in a boat, carriage, or other conveyance sent and moved by magical means. He may be misled by apparitions, or be held enchanted in a castle or island for a period of time.[37]

So far we have been discussing the ways in which the romances of chivalry are similar, and they can seem surprisingly similar and even monotonous to the casual reader. But this is merely a reflection of the fact that the customs of another age, seen from the perspective of some five hundred years, will seem uniform and will not reveal their nuances and details until one is familiar with the broad generalities. One would scarcely expect the readers of the romances to purchase and read numerous works if these were all seen by them to be identical. The differences were what made the romances, as a genre, possible.

---

[34] Besides Artemidoro, mentioned in note 3 to this chapter, the Caballero del Febo and Rosicler have another "sabio," Lirgandeo. Belianís is helped by Fristón (to whom Don Quijote frequently refers), Amadís de Grecia has Alquife, Florisel de Niquea has Cirfea, Queen of Argines, etc.

[35] "Bien paresce, buen cavallero, que todas las aventuras grandes están guardadas para vos, como aquel que para las acabar fue por el alto Dios elegido," is how it is put to Cirongilio, I, 15 (p. 85, lines 35-38 of the ed. of Ray Green.)

[36] "Aquí viérades maravillas estrañas. Demonios con formas y vissiones muy espantables e fieras, con aspecto de tigres, leones, onças, serpientes, y otras infernales ymágines le ponían muy gran temor. Unas vezes de lexos hazían acometimiento de despedaçarle, otras de cerca le tomavan de los braços y con sus agudos dientes asían de su muy tajante espada, y hazían tales cosas y representaciones que a todo el mundo pusieran pavor. Unas vezes oyeras los silvos que davan, que de mejor grado padecieras mill muertes, y otras con bramidos espantables y temerosos atronavan y hazían temblar los ayres e firmamento." (Cirongilio de Tracia, I, 16; pp. 95, lines 32-44 of the ed. of Ray Green.) See the description of the "fauno," offspring of the devil, in Chapters 14 and 15 of Part III of the Espejo de príncipes.

[37] Platir, 14, 44, 60, 65, 70; Primaleón, 165; Lidamor de Escocia, 32; Olivante de Laura, 20; Espejo de príncipes, I, 8-9.

The countries in which the romances were set varied considerably, and in fact no two, save different members of the same "family," were set in exactly the same locale. The travels that the knight undertook were thus similarly varied—he might travel to China, at one end of the world, or to England, at the other. The romance may have numerous subplots, with many simultaneous stories and many secondary characters, sometimes taking center stage for a period of time. However, this is a difference of degree, for even those romances concentrating more specifically on one protagonist had, by modern standards, an extremely confusing number of characters. The types of adventures encountered by the knight, the problems he is beset with, the ways in which he is tested, the various and diverse fantastic beasts or magical apparitions, the military situations, all could provide for variety within the standard framework of the romance. Even the various and seemingly endless and uniform tournaments actually have subtle differences within them to maintain the readers' interest, just as each soccer game, for example, is different, though to one who has not seen many games and does not understand the strategy, they will all be alike.

Within the limitations provided by the ideal of knighthood (and by implication, manhood) to which the knights of the romances must conform, the various protagonists of the romances of chivalry are in fact diverse individuals. One may be more interested in love than another; one a more constant lover than other. One knight may have a particularly fierce temper, and though a calm, even excessively calm, individual normally, particularly fierce temper, and though a calm, even excessively calm, individual normally, become a particularly terrfying warrior when he is aroused. Though all the protagonists of the novels are exceptional fighters, their interests in music, poetry, and travel, to cite a few examples, may vary. A knight may have an overriding purpose or goal which stays with him and underlies his varied actions through much of the romance—finding the secret of his ancestry, for example—or such a general purpose may be lacking, and his motivations be more specific and of more limited duration.

We see also in the romances attempts by the authors to impress and divert the reader through creation of specific set pieces, often with reference to well-known Classical events. The author may state that his readers are about to see a new battle of Troy, fought over a woman more beautiful than Helen. A knight may even, as does the

Caballero del Febo (*Espejo de príncipes*, II, 55), pass through the scene of the original battle of Troy, and find there descendants of the participants in that conflict. A series of chapters may be centered around a particularly marvelous castle, with transparent walls, extremely elaborate and rich decoration, and superlative inhabitants.[38]

Several times in this chapter I have referred to the Spanish nature of the romances, and it is worth referring to it once again in conclusion. The world presented in the Spanish romances of chivalry is an idealized version of Spain itself, not so foreign as to be truly surprising, just enough so as to be entertaining. The values are Spanish, and all characters save clearly identifiable outsiders share them. The value system is more specifically that of the Spanish nobility at the end of the Middle Ages and beginning of the Renaissance; the only difference is that the characters endorse these values so firmly, just as they themselves are obviously idealized individuals—ones that the readers, perhaps, would like to identify with.

The romances of chivalry, then, presented to their Spanish audience a world which was familiar in its basic values even though different in details. For this reason it was a reassuring world, one free of the moral and political confusion characteristic of early modern Spain (and of most other times as well). Black is black and white is white in the romances of chivalry, heroes and villains are clearly distinguished; women are either virtuous or common, beautiful or ugly. The books, while entertaining to the spirit, were relaxing to the intellect, as one would expect from a type of literature which was essentially escape or pleasure reading. One should not be surprised that the romances were as popular as they in fact were.

---

[38] Such as the Casa de la Fortuna, discussed in *Olivante de Laura*, 4-6, the Castillo del Universo of *Amadía de Grecia*, or the pentagonal castle of Cupid which Cirongilio de Tracia visits in Chapter 19 of Part III of his history.

Amadís de Gaula and *Amadís de Grecia*

In Defense of Feliciano de Silva

UR POINT OF DEPARTURE in this chapter is the imbalance in Spanish literary history, from the eighteenth century to the present, between the treatment of Garci Rodríguez de Montalvo, editor of most of *Amadís de Gaula*, author of the remainder and of its continuation, the *Sergas de Esplandián*, and Feliciano de Silva, favorite author of Don Quijote and the author of many romances of chivalry, of whose works the most representative and perhaps the best is *Amadís de Grecia*, Book 9 of the Amadís series.[1] While Montalvo's works have been edited and studied in depth for over a century, the works of Silva, with the partial exception of his *Segunda Celestina*,[2] have not been reprinted since the

---

[1] An earlier version of this chapter was given before the Third Romances of Chivalry Seminar, Modern Language Association of America Convention, December 27, 1975, also before the Department of Hispanic and Italian Studies, SUNY Albany, April 25, 1977.

[2] There is no published, critical edition of the *Segunda Celestina*. The edition of Monk, referred to above (note 58 to Chapter II), has not been published; the only published editions since the *princeps* are those of José Antonio de Balenchana, in the Colección de libros españoles raros y curiosos, 9 (Madrid, 1874), of María Inés Chamorro Fernández (Madrid: Ciencia Nueva, 1968), and of Manuel Criado de Val, in a volume including the *Celestina* of Rojas and its three continuations (Barcelona: Planeta, 1976).

sixteenth century, and have been studied incompletely by a small handful of specialists.[3]

The modern scorn for the works of Silva is surely derived from the negative comments of Cervantes' humor-loving priest, who enthusiastically dispatches all the chivalric works of Silva, along with the *Sergas de Esplandián*, to the bonfire in the *escrutinio de la librería*,[4] and from the attack in the first chapter of the *Quijote* on Silva's "entricadas razones," including the famous quotation "la razón de la sinrazón...," the only sentence from Silva's works to be generally known today.[5] Scholars have generally felt it superfluous to look at Silva's works for themselves after these comments from such an authority as Cervantes himself. Menéndez y Pelayo's comments on the dramatic decline in quality of the romances after *Amadís de Gaula*, and the "taller de novelas" which Silva allegedly set up, have already been quoted (p. 21). Even such a well-informed critic as Henry Thomas, however, states that "this [*Esplandián*] and the succeeding continuations of *Amadís* are for the most part but poor exaggerations of their original" (p. 67). John O'Connor, author of the only monograph on the entire Amadís cycle, can only complain about the "extravagant length" of the books.[6]

We can contrast this imbalance with the attitude towards Silva in Golden Age Spain, in which a scholar like López Pinciano excepted *Amadís de Grecia* from the general condemnation of romances of chivalry (p. 12, above). Silva was thought of by some as a writer of the same stature as Antonio de Guevara,[7] and he was a friend of

---

[3] Most studied has been the pastoral element in his works; besides the monograph of Cravens, mentioned above, see Juan Bautista Avalle-Arce, *La novela pastoril española*, 2nd ed. (Madrid: Istmo, 1974), pp. 37-42.

[4] In "Pero Pérez the Priest and His Comment on *Tirant lo Blanch*," reproduced *infra*, I have suggested that the priest's opinions are not necessarily those of Cervantes.

[5] Sydney Cravens has identified the probable source of Cervantes' quotation in words of Darinel in Part IV of *Florisel de Niquea* ("Feliciano de Silva and his Romances of Chivalry in *Don Quijote*," *Inti*, No. 7 [Spring, 1978], 28-34). However, Constance Rose, without specifying a specific passage as Cravens does, says it is taken from his *Segunda Celestina* (*Alonso Núñez de Reinoso*, p. 29, n. 20).

[6] *Amadis de Gaule and its Influence on Elizabethan Literature*, p. 6.

[7] See "De la Academia de los Humildes de Villamanta," quoted by Avalle-

Jorge de Montemayor, who dedicated to him an epitaph and an elegy.[8] We can also gain information about the esteem in which the works of Silva were held by looking at the printing history of his works. Although *Amadís de Gaula* was the single most popular romance, the various chivalric works of Silva together had more editions, and therefore more circulation. *Lisuarte de Grecia* went through ten editions, and the longer *Amadís de Grecia* seven. Montalvo's own work, the *Sergas de Esplandián*, was not more popular, and went without an edition for almost forty years (1549-1587). Irving Leonard, from his study of ship inventories, comments on the distinct popularity of Silva's *Florisel de Niquea*, during some part of the century the most popular romance.[9]

All of this suggests that the modern imbalance in the popularity of Silva's and Montalvo's works did not exist in the sixteenth century, nor even later, to judge from the adaptations made of Silva's works,[10] and from the fact that, like Homer or Ovid, he was such a famous author as to have attributed to him works that were not his.[11] There are a number of factors one can point to in order to explain why this was so. Montalvo, about whom we know very little,[12] was a man of the fifteenth century, and he was working with a text, the *Amadís*, which was even older. The *Amadís* was a text of relatively unsophisticated structure[13] and a simple style, with

---

Arce, p. 37, n. 5, and the "Carta del Bachiller de Arcadia," in *Sales españolas*, ed. A. Paz y Melia, 2nd ed., *BAE*, 176 (Madrid: Atlas, 1964), p. 35.

[8] *Cancionero del poeta George de Montemayor*, ed. Ángel González Palencia, Sociedad de Bibliófilos Españoles, 2ª época, 9 (Madrid, 1932), pp. 443-47.

[9] *Books of the Brave*, p. 115.

[10] Thomas, pp. 78-79. For the operatic adaptations of Silva's works, particularly *Amadís de Grecia*, see Hilkert Weddige, pp. 286-308; the best-known of the operatic composers is Handel.

[11] Nicolás Antonio attributed to him part of the *Espejo de príncipes* (I, 365); Gayangos states that he was generally considered to be the author of *Don Silves de la Selva* ("Discurso preliminar," p. xxxvi).

[12] Even his name needed to be definitely established, by Narciso Alonso Cortés, "Montalvo, el del *Amadís*, *RHi*, 71, Part 1 (1933), 434-42. No biographical information has come to light since this article was published.

[13] Thus the comments of Armando Durán, pp. 127-39 and elsewhere.

a sentimentalism more typical of medieval works of French inspiration, or of some *cancionero* poetry, than of the Spanish renaissance, prior to the pastoral novel and the advent of neo-Platonism.

Montalvo was also an author of limited output. Though his statement in the prologue to *Amadís* that he had "corr[egido] estos tres libros de Amadís" could have been taken as merely another formula to disguise his authorship, that Montalvo was not the work's author was apparently widely known in sixteenth-century Spain.[14] Modern scholarship has questioned even his composition of Book IV of the *Amadís* and of the *Sergas de Esplandián*.[15] Furthermore, Montalvo was a writer of a distinctly moralist outlook. He wanted to "clean up" the *Amadís*, eliminating sensual passages, and he wanted to create in Esplandián a knight not stronger, but more virtuous than his father. Montalvo criticized the characters of his source, such as Oriana, and tried to de-emphasize the role of personal combat.[16]

In contrast with Montalvo, Silva was a voluminous writer, the only author of romances of chivalry to achieve renown from his fiction. The fact that he was a moderately well-known writer in his own day, so much so as to offer a target for parody,[17] has led in part to the conservation of considerable biographical material. His will, documents concerning the *limpieza de sangre* of a descendant, the verse *Sueño* dedicated to him by "un su cierto servidor," and various comments by his literary friends and enemies, supplement the

---

14 "Del autor del famoso libro poético de Amadís no se sabe hasta hoy el nombre, honra de la nación y lengua española, que en ninguna lengua hay tal poesía ni tan loable" (Luis Zapata de Chaves, *Miscelánea*, ed. Isidoro Montiel [Madrid: Castilla, 1949], II, 162 [Chapter 164]). Juan de Valdés talks of "el que compuso a *Amadís de Gaula*," not of Montalvo (*Diálogo de la lengua*, p. 68).

15 Edwin Place, "¿Montalvo autor o refundidor del *Amadís* IV y V?" cited above.

16 See the articles of Gili Gaya and Amezcua, cited above, in note 49 to Chapter II.

17 See the "Carta del D. Diego [Hurtado] de Mendoza en nombre de Marco Aurelio [note again the allusion to Guevara together with the attack on Silva], a Feliciano de Silva," in *Sales españolas*, pp. 85-86. One conclusion which can be drawn from this parody is that Hurtado was familiar with Silva's works, as also was Francisco López de Úbeda, author of the *Pícara Justina* (see *BAE*, 33, p. 92).

information taken from his works, and allow a fairly complete picture to be drawn.

Whereas the information we, and presumably the sixteenth century as well, have about Montalvo is limited to the fact presented at the beginning of the *Amadís*, that he was "regidor de Medina del Campo," we know that Silva was of a noble family of Ciudad Rodrigo, of which he succeeded his father to the office of Regidor.[18] (Ciudad Rodrigo was also the home of the author of *Palmerín de Olivia* and *Primaleón*,[19] with whom Silva may have had contact.) His father bore the chivalric name of Tristán de Silva, which surely explains the unusual name Feliciano (Tristán-Feliciano). Feliciano studied in Salamanca, and acquired at an early age literary tastes which were to remain with him: his friend Núñez de Reinoso, whose work shows great influence of Silva,[20] has him "leyendo de contino en Ciceron/y lo mas primo de lenguas floridas," in a verse epistle directed to him (Rose, p. 295; Cravens, p. 29, n. 28; it is also discussed by Eugenio Asensio in the article cited in note 20.) Silva received "criança y mercedes" from the Archbishop of Seville, Diego de Deza,[21] and he served two years under Carlos V, quite possibly fighting on the side of the King during the revolt of the Comunidades.[22] The collector of curiosities Luis Zapata records his

----

[18] Narciso Alonso Cortés, "Feliciano de Silva," *BRAE*, 20 (1933), 382-404, at pp. 383-84. "La obra es de cavallero, y tan insigne como Feliciano de Silva," says Benito Boyer in his preface to the 1564 edition of *Amadís de Grecia*.

[19] The colophon of the first (1512) edition of *Primaleón* states that it and its predecessor, *Palmerín de Olivia*, were "trasladado[s]... en la muy noble ciudad de Ciudadrodrigo por Francisco Vasquez vezino dela dicha ciudad" (quoted by Giuseppe di Stefano in his edition of *Palmerín*, p. 783). Also, the name "Augustobrica" used in the verses at the end of *Primaleón* (Di Stefano, p. 766) is most easily explained as the Latin name of Ciudad Rodrigo.

[20] Rose, pp. 29-35, 39. See also Eugenio Asensio, "Alonso Núñez de Reinoso, 'gitano peregrino,' y su égloga *Baltea*," in *Studia Hispanica in honorem R. Lapesa*, I (Madrid: Gredos, 1972), pp. 119-36.

[21] *Lisuarte de Grecia* is dedicated to Deza; see below, p. 111.

[22] This information is taken from his will; see the article of Alonso Cortés cited in note 18. Cravens, to whom the reader who wishes more extensive biographical information on Silva is referred, gives (pp. 23-24) plausible reasons to support the hypothesis that Silva served under Carlos in the Guerra de las Comunidades.

strange ability to predict the winners of battles and *oposiciones*.[23] The love element in his life was an important one, as we shall see shortly, but once married, he led a calm family life. Despite his abundant literary production, Silva was far from wealthy at his death, his printer Portonariis owing him a sizeable quantity of money.[24] Nevertheless, he is reported to have been helpful to those in need, though whether this was financially or otherwise is not specified.[25]

While Montalvo was a conservative, and in some ways a reactionary, Silva was an innovator, and gave the Amadís series new life after it almost ended with the unfavorable reaction to *Florisando*, Book 6, and the second *Lisuarte de Grecia*, Book 8.[26] He was the first to continue the *Celestina*, in which he was imitated directly by two others and indirectly by several more; it was he who introduced the pastoral into Spanish prose fiction, in *Amadís de Grecia*, setting an important precedent for the pastoral novel which would come later.[27]

Silva also attempted to improve the romances of chivalry, and shows a consciousness of his romances as "his" and a strong sense of what is appropriate in these works.[28] We see in his chivalric

---

[23] *Miscelánea*, II, 158 (Chapter 161).

[24] Alonso Cortés, "Feliciano de Silva," p. 393. The epitaph of Montemayor states that Silva possessed "más honra que dinero" (*Cancionero*, p. 446).

[25] Gaspar Gómez de Toledo, *Tercera parte de la tragicomedia de Celestina*, ed. Mac E. Barrick (Philadelphia: University of Pennsylvania Press, 1973), p. 76.

[26] See the comments of Pierre Geneste, *Essai sur ... Jerónimo de Urrea*, II, 632-33.

[27] On this topic see Cravens, *passim*, and the work of Avalle-Arce cited in note 3; however, Maxime Chevalier, *L'Arioste en Espagne*, p. 175, and Francisco López Estrada, *Los libros de pastores en la literatura española. I: La órbita previa* (Madrid: Gredos, 1974), p. 323 and ff., have contrary opinions.

[28] Thus the comment of the "Corrector," found at the beginning of *Amadís de Grecia*, a statement obviously written by Silva himself. Although this passage is known at least to those who have read the book of Thomas, who quotes it from the edition of 1542 (p. 73, n. 1), or the "Discurso preliminar" of Gayangos, who reproduces it, apparently, from the edition of 1596 (p. xxxi, n. 1), I have thought it worth reproducing here, because of what it reveals about Silva's conception of his own works. I quote from the

works, and particularly in *Amadís de Grecia*, a desire to create a literarily sophisticated composition and to cause "admiración" in the reader. The plots of his romances are more complicated than those of his predecessors, with more characters and as a result more narrative threads and subplots, to the point where it is virtually impossible to make an intelligible summary of the plot of any of them.[29] But even when the adventures are the same as those found in the works of Montalvo, the difference between the two authors is clear. For example, Montalvo set up a battle between the father Amadís and his son Esplandián, but it is not much developed, takes about a page in the *BAE* edition (p. 434), and there is a definite victor. In *Amadís de Grecia* there is also a conflict between Amadís de Grecia and his father Lisuarte de Grecia, but as both were equally irresistible and neither could win, the horrendous battle lasts a long time and is only stopped by Urganda la Desconocida. Urganda, who had been enchanted, is freed in time to stop the battle when Amadís, desperately searching for a weapon to replace his broken

---

princeps (see *infra*, p. 85), replacing the Tironian sign with "e," resolving abbreviations, and correcting one misprint:

No te engañe discreto lector el nombre deste libro diziendo ser Amadis de Grecia y nono libro de Amadis de Gaula: porque el octauo libro se llama Amadis [actually Lisuarte] de Grecia enlo qual ay error en los autores: porque el que hizo el octauo de Amadis y le puso nombre de Amadis no vio el setimo y si lo vio nolo entendio ni supo continuar: porque el setimo que es Lisuarte de Grecia y Perion de Gaula hecho por el mismo autor deste libro enel capitulo vltimo dize auer nacido el donzel dela ardiente espada hijo de Lisuarte de Grecia y dela princesa Onoloria: el qual se llamo el cauallero dela ardiente espada y despues Amadis de Grecia. de quien es este presente libro Assi que se continua del setimo este nono y se auia de llamar octauo: y porque no vuiesse [hubiese] dos octauos se llamo el nono puesto que no depende del octauo sino del setimo (como dicho es). Y fuera mejor que aquel octauo feneciera enlas manos desu autor y fuera abortiuo que no que saliera a luz a ser juzgado y a dañar lo enesta gran genealogia escrito: pues daño a ssi poniendo confusion enla decendencia y continuacion delas historias. Vale.

[29] A summary is given by Pascual de Gayangos in his "Discurso preliminar," pp. xxxi-xxxiv, who complains that "no es fácil dar idea del intricado argumento de este libro caballeresco." A shorter summary is given by John Dunlop in his *History of Prose Fiction*, I, 366-69. These summaries are easiest to follow when one has already read the novel.

one, removes the sword which Urganda had been run through with (reminiscent of Arthur's feat with Excalibur).

In *Amadís de Gaula*, as is well known, there is found the adventure of the "Arco de los leales amadores," which is a test or "prueba" of love. Those who do not succeed in passing it are tormented by blows, while those faithful lovers who pass "sienten gran deleite," and in the case of Amadís himself, the arch plays music and dispenses flowers. This, however, is but little compared with the adventure of "La gloria de Niquea," in *Amadís de Grecia*.[30] The first knight to attempt it is not just turned back, but is burned to a crisp, "él y su cavallo convertido todo en carbones" (II, 50; fol. clxxii of the edition of 1530). The "gloria" which the successful knight was to receive was the sight of the princess Niquea herself, who was so beautiful that all who saw her died, or lost their minds, for which reason she was shut up in a tower, later surrounded by flames—the "aventura" itself—to protect her from the passion of her brother Anastarax.

There are certainly enchantments in the works of Montalvo, but what such episode can compare with the Castillo del Universo, built by Urganda and Alquife in *Amadís de Grecia*? In this castle a group of the protagonists is enchanted, to remain there a hundred years. The Castillo del Universo is so named because it contains a working model of the universe, made up of a series of rooms in a tower, one above another, corresponding respectively to the various elements of the Ptolomean universe—the planets, the sun, the stars, with God above them all, who makes the parts of the model move, "haziendo sus influencias naturales en cada parte del universo, segun sus operaciones" (II, 76; fol. 204 of the edition of 1530).

A final point in the comparison of the works of Montalvo and those of Feliciano de Silva is the contrasting treatment of love. As we have said, the love which is a main theme of *Amadís de Gaula* is a sentimentalized love, similar to that of courtly poetry, in which Oriana "fue hecha dueña... más por la gracia y comedimiento de Oriana que por la desemboltura ni osadía de Amadís" (ed. Place, I, 285). In the works of Silva love is just as present, but it is of a

---

[30] "La gloria de Niquea" is the subject of the most famous play of the Conde de Villamediana; see Luis Rosales, *Pasión y muerte del Conde de Villamediana* (Madrid: Gredos, 1969), pp. 69-77.

different sort, less idealized and more sensual. Amadís de Grecia is by no means the same faithful lover as is his great-grandfather, Amadís de Gaula. His grandson, Rogel de Grecia, is even more licentious. In the romance which bears Rogel's name, he says to his companion near the beginning: "Dexad en mal punto essas sandezes y lealtades de amor, y tratad pendencia de amores con una de las infantas, y démonos a plazer, en cuanto podamos" (I, fol. 5' of the edition of 1568).

This change in focus may perhaps be explained by examining the personality of Silva. (Of the love element in Montalvo's life we know nothing.) Silva was certainly a person who married for love—not unknown in that period, but not so common either—since he married, against the strong opposition of his family, a girl, Gracia Fe, of Jewish descent.[31] (Her last name was concealed and is unknown.) In an attempt to overcome the opposition, Silva attributed her paternity to Diego Hurtado de Mendoza, to whom *Amadís de Grecia* was dedicated, whose reputation was such that he could not deny that Gracia was his daughter. (Mendoza did not know how many illegitimate children he had.[32])

In the "Sueño de Feliciano de Silva"[33] which is found at the end of Book I of *Amadís de Grecia*, Silva describes himself as "cansado y quebrantado de mi gloriosa y excelente passion de amores, aunque no harto de padecella, por la causa que más me obliga, y tanto, que muchas vezes del dios de amor me quexo, porque puso tanta gloria **adonde avia de faltar** con tantos quilates la pena" (fol. 111ᵛ of the edition of 1530). Guided by "aquel buen amador" Juan Rodríguez del Padrón, author of the fifteenth-century *Siervo libre del amor*, Silva has an interview in this dream with the god of love, who exclaims, when he sees Silva, "este es mi hijo muy amado, con el qual yo

---

[31] Henry Thomas, *Dos romances anónimos del siglo XVI. I. El sueño de Feliciano de Silva...* (Madrid: Centro de Estudios Históricos, 1917); Emilio Cotarelo, article cited in note 57 to Chapter II.

[32] See my article, "Two Problems of Identification in Parody of Juan de Mena," in *Oelschläger Festschrift* (Chapel Hill: Estudios de Hispanófila, 1976), pp. 157-70.

[33] Not to be confused with the verse "Sueño," based on it, mentioned in note 31.

mucho me he gozado" (fol. 113ᵛ). When Silva sees his lady there as
well, she says: "Yo sé que una de las cosas [causas] porque as sacado
tan bien al natural los amores de aquellos preciados cavalleros
Lisuarte y Perion³⁴ y Amadis de Grecia fue por la esperiencia de los
que tú por mi causa passas, y sé que tienes gran congoxa por saber
de la parte segunda desta grande historia. Y porque yo assi mismo
tengo el desseo que tú tienes, para satisfazer al tuyo y al mio y al
servicio de aquel que la obra quieres dirigir, ... te hago saber que la
hallarás en una cueva que se llama los Palacios de Hercules, metida
en una caxa de madera, que no se corrompe, en un lado de la pared;
porque quando España fue perdida la escondieron en aquel lugar,
porque la memoria destos cavalleros no se perdiesse" (fol. 114ᵛ).³⁵

These comments clearly suggest a man in whose life love has
played an important role, and whose experiences are reflected in his
fiction. It is not surprising, then, that Silva differs in two ways from
his predecessors in his portrait of love. His portrayal of the courtly
lover, the one who suffers from his love for an idealized woman, is
more developed than anything found in any earlier Spanish text. At
the same time, in different sections of his works, we find a physical
element to the love among men and women which had also been
missing from the romances of chivalry. (We should not forget that
Silva was the author of the *Segunda Celestina*, much less moralistic
than the work of Rojas.) If Darinel is a versifying courtly shepherd,
Florisel seeks physical rather than spiritual love (Cravens, pp. 58-
59). While Urganda la Desconocida, present since *Amadís de Gaula*,
finally marries Alquife, we have a stimulating contrast to her in the
figure of Zahara, a lady knight who fights like a man. On the other
hand, in a chapter of *Amadís de Grecia* with the tittilating title of
"Cómo Nereyda conosció carnalmente a Niquea," the situation is
the reverse: Amadís de Grecia dresses as a girl, Nereyda, and
arranges to be sold as a slave. This is the only way he can sleep in
the chamber of the beautiful Niquea; the results are predictable. At
the same time Niquea's father, seeing the beautiful "girl," falls in

---

³⁴ Additional evidence that Silva was the author of *Lisuarte de Grecia*, on
which point I believe no further doubt is in order.

³⁵ A possible allusion to the recent burying of manuscripts by those
expelled from Spain.

love with her and wishes to seduce her, causing further complications for Amadís.

It is difficult to imagine how, within the framework of the Spanish romance, an author could produce works which differed more from the chaste and simple novels of Montalvo. If Silva's works were attractive for all the above reasons to sixteenth-century readers, and the modern literary public has shown that it can appreciate some of the romances of chivalry, could it not, also, recapture some of the pleasure that contemporaries found in the works of Silva? Believing that it can, I have begun an edition of *Amadís de Grecia*, based on the rediscovery in Germany of the only known copy of the *princeps*, the missing edition of Cuenca, 1530.[36]

---

[36] See Elena Lázaro and José López de Toro, "Amadís de Grecia por tierras de Cuenca," *Bibliofilia*, 6 (1952), 25-28.

Don Ci rõgilio

⁊ Libro tercero del valeroso
⁊ inuencible cauallero don Cirongilio de
Tracia que trata delas proezas y ha
zañas que hizo:legũ elcriue el la
bio y excclentiſſimo coro-
nista ſuyo Nouarco.

❧ VII ❧

Research Opportunities

HE ROMANCES OF CHIVALRY offer great possibilities of research for the young as well as the mature scholar. In the hopes of stimulating some research in areas where I believe it would be useful, as did Homero Serís,[1] I too am offering a series of "nuevos temas."

We still need to make the bulk of the romances accessible through modern, critical, published editions.[2] *Lepolemo, o el Caballero de la Cruz,* different from the other romances in its North African setting and almost complete lack of supernatural elements, would be an ideal candidate. Part I of *Clarián de Landanís* would be another, as would be *Valerián de Hungría.* More accessible editions of both the Spanish and Portuguese texts of *Palmerín de Inglaterra* are clearly in order.

There are a number of analytical or stylistic studies that could properly be made by scholars with an inclination to this type of investigation. It would be worthwhile to analyze Book 2 of Part I of *Clarián,* for example, to see if it is possible to confirm or deny the statement in the prologue that the author was, like Fernando de Rojas, continuing a work already begun by another. A comparison of *Platir* with *Florambel de Lucea* could determine whether they are by one author, as one might suspect from the dedications.[3]

A study of a theme in various romances would be useful—the

---

[1] I allude to Serís' *Guía de nuevos temas de literatura española,* ed. D. W. McPheeters (New York: Hispanic Society of America, 1973).

[2] Some unpublished editions are referred to in note 63 to Chapter 2, *supra.* Federico Curto Herrero informs me that he is preparing an edition of *Primaleón;* as previously stated, I am preparing one of *Amadís de Grecia.*

[3] See the appendix to "Who Read the Romances of Chivalry?" *infra.*

giant in the Spanish romances of chivalry, the architecture, the flora and fauna of the romances of chivalry. An index of the motifs or themes of the romances of chivalry, a task too large to be carried out comprehensively at present, would be a very useful research tool.

One versed in fifteenth- and sixteenth-century history might well study allusions to contemporary events in the romances. (For example, Gayangos ["Catálogo razonado," p. lxxvii] states that the deeds of Rodrigo de Mendoza, "marqués del Zenete," are to be found in *Valerián de Hungría*.) Is the Greece found so often in the romances of chivalry exclusively the ancient Greece of Homer and Alexander the Great, or does it reflect something of the medieval Greece with which the Catalans, at least, had contact?

Although the translations of the Spanish romances, especially the *Amadís*, into other languages have been studied for themselves, there has not been sufficient study of the characteristics of the translations compared with the characteristics of the Spanish originals; it would be surprising if these translations were faithful, by twentieth-century standards. Such an investigation could perhaps help scholars such as O'Connor, who prefer to work with the translations, and would help us see how France, England, and Germany saw Spain at that time.

Particularly valuable for comparatists would be a study of the interest in the romances of chivalry during the romantic period, when Southey and Rose translated romances into English, when Hispanophiles such as Sir Walter Scott were inspired by them in their portrayal of remote times, when even a poet such as John Keats was influenced by them.[4]

A study of the influence of the romances on the learned Spanish epic has yet to be undertaken. Even more important, however, is the fact that by no means have all the chivalric allusions in the *Quijote* been discovered. It is true that because of the similarity of many of the romances, it is difficult to be sure that a parallel indicates a borrowing, but by the same token, some of the parallels already discovered may be coincidental and it may be for some new scholar to find the true sources. It would be valuable even to go through any one romance, identifying all the potential parallels with the work of Cervantes; with a series of such analyses one would then be in a position to begin a serious study of the chivalric sources of the *Quijote*.

---

[4] See items Bd88 and 4FFd9 of my bibliography; also Patchell, pp. 23-24.

Who Read the
Romances of Chivalry?

HE ROMANCES OF CHIVALRY which are the subject of the present discussion are those which were written in Castilian in the sixteenth century.[1] The conclusions should also be valid for *Tirante el Blanco, Amadís de Gaula,* and the *Sergas de Esplandián,* all of which were probably consider-ed to be sixteenth-century Castilian works by the readers of the period. Specifically excluded are those short French works, of the fifteenth century or earlier, translated into Spanish, such as *Oliveros de Castilla, Partinuplés de Bles,* or *Enrique fi de Oliva;* they are quite different works, and to a degree were translated and published for a different public. (They are scarcely mentioned in the *Quijote.*) In any event, they do not form part of Spanish literature.[2]

---

[1] Published in *Kentucky Romance Quarterly,* 22 (1973), 209-33. My re-search was greatly facilitated by the Smith Fund and the University Research Council of the University of North Carolina, and by the Brown University Library.

I would like to express my appreciation to Keith Whinnom, Merritt Cox, and James Burke for reading this paper and making helpful sugges-tions; to Juan Bautista Avalle-Arce for his assistance with sections of the Appendix; and to Ricardo Arias, who is publishing with the CSIC an edition of *Rosián de Castilla* [published in 1979], for permitting the Hispanic Society of America to make a copy of this work for my examination.

[2] Maxime Chevalier includes them together with the romances which we are considering here in his treatment of the topic, in which he arrives at the same conclusions for somewhat different reasons: *Sur le publique du*

The accepted opinion concerning the Spanish romances of chivalry during their heyday, the sixteenth century, is that they were
works which were read by all classes of society, from the highest to
the lowest, but with a considerable predominance of the more
numerous lower classes. Thus, we find Rodríguez Marín making a
distinction between the readers of the fifteenth and those of the

---

roman de chevalerie (Talence: Institut d'Etudes Ibériques et Ibéro-Américaines de l'Université de Bordeaux, 1968). These works, printed in large
quantities at modest prices, are lumped together as "menudencias" in the
book order reproduced by Irving Leonard, "Best Sellers of the Lima Book
Trade, 1583," *HAHR*, 22 (1942), 30-31, and in another, of 1599 (Rodríguez Marín, "La lectura de los libros de caballerías," p. 68), where they are
called "para niños." They are also called "para niños" in book dispatches of
1605 (Rodríguez Marín, "El *Quijote* y Don Quijote en América," p. 104); it
is, of course, to them that Julio Caro Baroja, *Ensayo sobre la literatura de cordel*
(Madrid: Revista de Occidente, 1969), pp. 317-27, and Antonio Rodríguez-
Moñino, *Construcción crítica y realidad histórica en la poesía de los siglos XVI y XVII*,
2nd ed. (Madrid: Castalia, 1968), pp. 45-49, refer.

   This discussion is also limited to Castilian readers; excluded are the
Portuguese, about whom it is often hazardous to extrapolate from data
gathered in Spain. Although the romances were virtually dead in Castile
by 1590, for after that we have only the publication of *Policisne de Boecia* in
1602 (written before 1600; see Luis Astrana Marín, *Vida ejemplar y heroica de
Miguel de Cervantes Saavedra*, V [Madrid: Reus, 1953], 493-94) and the
reprint in 1617-23 of the *Espejo de príncipes* (the 1636 edition of *Florisel de
Niquea* found in Simón Díaz is a ghost), we see not only that the Spanish
romances continued to find favor in Portugal (a Lisbon, 1596 reprint of
Amadís de Grecia, and a 1598 one, though "alimpiado," of *Primaleón*), but that
Portuguese romances continued to be written and reprinted in both the
seventeenth and eighteenth centuries, I would be surprised if the conclusions reached in this article did not hold true for Portugal, but I prefer to
leave this demonstration, as well as the whole topic of chivalric literature
in Portugal, for another scholar. [Much work remains to be done on the
Portuguese romances of chivalry. The most recent studies are those of
Massaud Moisés, *A novela de cavalaria no quinhentismo português:* O Memorial
das proezas da Segunda Távola Redonda *de Jorge Ferreira de Vasconcellos*,
Boletim nº 218 da Faculdade de Filosofia, Ciências e Letras da Universi-
dade de São Paulo (São Paulo, 1957), and the three theses on *Palmeirim de
Inglaterra*, Antona Morales Rodríguez, "Estudio sobre el *Palmerín de Inglaterra*," Diss. Barcelona, 1961; Richard Otto Wolf Goertz, "Strukturelle und
thematische Untersuchungen zum *Palmeirim de Inglaterra*," Diss. Michigan,
1967 (summary in *DA*, 28, 5053A), published in Lisbon, R. B. Rosenthal,
1969, and Jerusa Pires Ferreira, *O tapete preceptivo do* Palmeirim de Inglaterra
(Salvador, Brazil: The author, 1973).]

sixteenth centuries: in the fifteenth century, the works were read by the nobility, but in the sixteenth century "cuantos y cuantas supieron leer perecíanse por el dañoso pasto de los libros de caballerías," inasmuch as "siempre lo que habla a la fantasía se llevó de calle a las gentes."³ For Salvador de Madariaga, the romances of chivalry were the melodrama of the time, "género, como es sabido, favorito del pueblo. Porque el pueblo, a quien no se le da un bledo la construcción estética ni la consecuencia, cuyas ideas sobre la verosimilitud se apartan sabiamente de las exigencias de nuestra científica edad, y cuyo instinto se pone siempre de parte de la juventud y del amor, el pueblo busca ante todo en la literatura una distracción a la monotonía de su vida."⁴ "Los campesinos leían los libros de caballerías," baldly affirms Aubrey Bell.⁵

The immediate sources of these observations need not concern us here. Their ultimate source is undoubtedly the *Quijote*, since in it

---

³ *Don Quijote*, "nueva edición crítica," IX (Madrid: Atlas, 1949), 58. Quotations from the *Quijote* are taken from this edition.

⁴ *Guía del lector del* Quijote, 6th ed. (Buenos Aires: Sudamericana, 1967), p. 42.

⁵ As translated by Eduardo Juliá Martínez, *El renacimiento español* (Zaragoza: Ebro, 1944), p. 81. Actually, what Bell originally wrote, in *RHi*, 80 (1930), 296, was that "the peasants listened to the romances of chivalry," a statement obviously inspired by the *Quijote*. The slight mistranslation is itself revealing.

The examples can easily be multiplied: Irving Leonard, *Books of the Brave* (Cambridge: Harvard, 1949), pp. 13, 20; Ángel Valbuena Prat, *Historia de la literatura española*, 8th ed. (Barcelona: Gili, 1968) I, 489; Martín de Riquer, *Aproximación al* Quijote, 3rd ed. (Barcelona: Teide, 1970), p. 19, Alban Forcione, *Cervantes, Aristotle, and the* Persiles (Princeton: Princeton Univ. Press, 1970), p. 13; with salutary doubts, Jole Scudiere Ruggieri, "Per uno studio della tradizione cavalleresca nella vita e nella cultura spagnola medioevale (I)," in *Studi di letteratura spagnola* (1964), p. 59. Indeed with the lone exception of Menéndez Pelayo, *Orígenes de la novela*, 2nd edición nacional (Madrid: CSIC, 1962), I, 461, to find someone who rejects this view we must go back to Diego Clemencín (see p. 992 of the reprinting of his edition of the *Quijote*, 2nd edition [Madrid: Castilla, 1966], whose direct acquaintance with a large number of romances of chivalry enabled him to speak with an authority which on the whole remains unsurpassed. (See my article "*Don Quijote* y los libros de caballerías: necesidad de un reexamen," included in this volume).

the romances of chivalry are discussed in more detail than in any other contemporary work. Don Quijote himself says that the romances "con gusto general son leídos y celebrados de los grandes y de los chicos, de los pobres y de los ricos, de los letrados e ignorantes, de los plebeyos y caballeros, finalmente, de todo género de personas de cualquier estado y condición que sean" (I, 50). Cervantes' unnamed friend of the Prologue to Part I is more specific: "Esta vuestra escritura no mira a más que a deshacer la autoridad y cabida que en el mundo y en el vulgo tienen los libros de caballerías." The canon from Toledo concurs in naming the *vulgo* as the most important group of readers: "Yo he tenido cierta tentación de hacer un libro de caballerías... [pero] no quiero sujetarme al confuso juicio del desvanecido vulgo, a quien por la mayor parte toca leer semejantes libros" (I, 48).

These passages are important, and we will return to them, but they should not be accepted uncritically as the final word on the subject. There is, in fact, a considerable quantity of other data which bears on the problem. We may begin by noting that although many moralist writers of the period criticized the romances of chivalry, with varying degrees of justification, we will look in vain among their comments for any indication that the books affected members of the lower classes.[6] There is evidence to the contrary, in

---

[6] Elsewhere (notes 4 and 5 to Chapter II) I have given references to those scholars (Thomas, Krauss, Bataillon, Riquer, and Glaser) who have collected these attacks. I have only one note to add here, a scrap of information found in a forgotten work of eighteenth-century criticism, Francesco Henrion's *Istoria critica e ragionata. Sull'origine, incontro generale, successiva persecuzione costante, esterminio, e rarità singolare di tutte l'Istorie o Romanzi de Cavalleria e Magia dei Secoli XV e XVI, come quelle della Tavola Redonda, di Amadis di Gaula, ec. Con la Biblioteca Italiana di tutte le Istorie predette, di cui son mancanti al presente i bibliografi, e le biblioteche e collezioni più scelte. E perciò offerta alla repubblica letteraria da...* (Florence, 1794). On p. 76, he says that the romances of chivalry, and specifically the *Amadís*, were denounced at the Diet of Worms by Cardinal Girolamo Aleandro il Vecchio, a papal representative, as a force contributing to the Reformation. Citing a "Commentarius de Lutheranismo, Tom. I, Lib. I, p. 149, Ediz. II" (Johannes Cochlaeus' *Commentaria... de actis et scriptis Martini Lutheri?*), he adds "che in Vittemberga, prima residenza de Lutero, si facessero andare in giro con tanto credito i romanzi di cavalleria, e segnatamente quello di Amadis di Gaula per eccitare colla lettura de essi i cristiani ad avere in ludibrio le cose sacre e gli ordini religiosi."

that several critics (and the unsuccessful petition of 1555, requesting the prohibition of the romances) speak of the uselessness of guarding a daughter when she has the *Amadís* to read, or of the time which boys waste in reading the romances which they could better spend studying more useful books.[7]

This note on the youthfulness of readers corresponds with the familiar names of several nobles who "wasted time" with them when young (Juan de Valdés, the future saints Íñigo de Loyola and Teresa de Cepeda), and many of the books were dedicated to young patrons.[8] Other nobles, however, remained interested in them as

---

Three considerations cast suspicion on this statement: the romances did not in fact have anything to do with the Reformation, the later critics of them do not associate them with Protestantism, and it seems incredible that Hispanists who have studied the documents connected with this event, so important for Carlos V, would not have noticed such a comment. Nevertheless, were it true, it explains admirably the moralist writers' constant protests against them, which began only three years later, with the publication of Vives' *De institutione fœminae christianae* (1524). Also see, on this point, the fascinating note of Julius Schwering, "Luther und Amadis," *Euphorion*, 29 (1928), 618-19, Thomas, pp. 217-18, Rodríguez Marín's "nueva edición crítica" of the *Quijote*, IX, 174, and p. 61, n. 20 of the second edition of Américo Castro's *El pensamiento de Cervantes* (Barcelona: Noguer, 1972).

[7] Similarly, Jerónimo de San Pedro says, in the "Epístola proemial" to Volume I of his *Caballería celestial* (Amberes, 1554): "para que después deste pasto, como suelen algunos padres recitar a sus hijos las patrañas delos cavalleros de burlas [= fiction], les cuenten y hagan leer las maravillas de los guerreros de veras." This is no doubt the point of Cervantes' criticism implicit in the words of Dorotea, who "había leído muchos libros de caballerías" (I, 29), but who still does not know such an elementary fact as the location of Osuna (I, 30).

We may safely assume that adult members of the lower classes would even less have had the idle time in which to read these lengthy books, in an age when reading speed was far lower than today, nor could they afford the cost of illuminatin to read them by. (See Rodríguez Marín, *Quijote*, IX, 58 and 63, for two texts which mention the time necessarily spent on them.)

[8] The predominance of youthful readers has been seen as more striking than it is through comparison with other genres, in which dedication to a very young patron is more exceptional. I have not in every case been able to determine the age of the recipient of the dedication at the time of publication of the first edition of the work, but the following

adults⁹—notably Carlos V and many of his court, which set a model

figures, if not exact, will give a reliable picture: Luis de Córdoba and Cristóbal de Guardiola were both addressed as sons of their fathers and referred to as being of "tiernos años," Felipe (II) was 18; Rodrigo Sarmiento, Martín Cortés, and María de Austria, 23; John III of Portugal, about 24; Juan de la Cerda, 25; Fernando Álvarez de Toledo, 26; Luis Cristóbal Ponce de León and Íñigo López de Aragón, 29; Mencía de Mendoza, 32; Pero Álvarez Osorio was almost certainly in his 30's; Charles de Lannoy, 36; Pedro Fajardo, 39; Diego López Pacheco, 42; Jorge, Duke of Coimbra, 45; Juan Vázquez de Ávila could hardly have been less than 50; Diego de Deza, 67; Diego Hurtado de Mendoza "el Grande," 69.

If the anecdotes referred to in the following note concerning Diego Hurtado de Mendoza, the poet, are true, he would have been in his early 20's.

The question of the age of the authors of the romances is neither as relevant nor as easy to settle as that of the patrons, since the authors are generally more obscure than their patrons, and authors of many periods have written, for financial gain or other reasons, books which were tangential to their own literary tastes. I summarize briefly those cases in which there is any indication of the author's age: Diego Ortúñez de Calahorra excluded himself from the "ancianos," but was at least in his 20's; Marcos Martínez, author of Part II of the Espejo de príncipes, confessed himself to be, although a licenciado, of "tiernos años." Jerónimo López, in the prologue to Clarián de Landanís, Part II, says that "dos causas me movieron [to write this book]. La primera, fallarme de aquellos negocios familiares que la cargada edad suele consigo traer tan desocupado que tuve por mejor en esta ocupacion honesta ocuparme, que no seguir aquellos apetitos que la floreciente juventud a los de mi hedad suelen traer." Oviedo was 41 when Claribalte was published in 1519. Antonio de Torquemada, author of Olivante de Laura (1564), was perhaps born about 1510, conjectures J. H. Elsdon, On the Life and Work of the Spanish Humanist Antonio de Torquemada, University of California Publications in Modern Philology, No. 20 (Berkeley: University of California Press, 1937) p. 128; according to Latassa, Fernando Basurto, author of Florindo (1530), fought with distinction in the conquest of Granada. Pedro de Luján, usually accepted as author of Silves de la Selva (1546), probably was rather young. Feliciano de Silva might have been born in 1492, which would mean that he was still writing romances in his 50's (E. Cotarelo y Mori, "Nuevas noticias biográficas de Feliciano de Silva," BRAE, 13 [1926], 137). Silva comments on his age in the prologue to Part IV of Florisel de Niquea (cf. the prologue to the Novelas ejemplares, or the words of Don Quijote in the final chapter).

Francisco Delicado was probably in his 50's when he published his editions of the Amadís and the Primaleón.

⁹ We know of various noble figures who owned copies of romances, such as Isabel la Católica (though not the indigenous Castilian ones), the

for the country by its interest in romances of chivalry and in chivalric spectacle.[10] When we examine the dedications of the romances, we find they are dedicated not just to nobles, but to the very highest nobility of sixteenth-century Spain—Diego Hurtado and Íñigo López de Mendoza, Dukes of the Infantado, Pero Álvarez Osorio, Marquis of Astorga and count of Trastamara, Juan de la Cerda, Duke of Medinaceli, and many others, including various members of Carlos V's court (see Appendix). Some of these dedications are perfunctory and formal, in that they are an appeal on the

---

contents of whose library are itemized by Diego Clemencín in his *Elogia de la reina Católica Doña Isabel*, Memorias de la Real Academia de la Historia, 6 (Madrid, 1821), pp. 431-81, Diego de Colmenares, the historian of Segovia, who owned a copy of *Primaleón*, noteworthy at so late a date (*apud* E. García Dini, "Per una bibliografía dei romanzi di cavalleria: Edizioni del ciclo dei 'Palmerines,'" in *Studi sul* Palmerín de Olivia. *III. Saggi e richerche.* [Pisa: Istituto di Letteratura Spagnola e Ispano-americana dell'Università di Pisa, 1966], p. 31), and Pedro Guerrero, Archbishop of Granada, who owned a copy of *Amadís* (see Juan Martínez Ruiz, "La biblioteca de don Pedro Guerrero," in *Actas del Tercer Congreso Internacional de Hispanistas* [Mexico: El Colegio de México, 1970], p. 598), Diego Hurtado de Mendoza (Sir Henry Thomas, *Spanish and Portuguese Romances of Chivalry* [Cambridge, England: Cambridge University Press, 1920], p. 80), to whom are attributed two attacks on Feliciano de Silva, that in the "Carta del Bachiller de Arcadia," and the "Carta de D. Diego de Mendoza en nombre de Marco Aurelio, a Feliciano de Silva," both of which may be found in Paz y Melia's *Sales españolas*, 2nd ed. by Ramón Paz, *BAE*, 176 (Madrid: Atlás, 1964), pp. 35 and 85-86 (the authorship of these is questioned by R. Foulché-Delbosc, "Les oeuvres attribuées a Mendoza," *RHi*, 32 [1914], 13-15 and 20, whose opinions are copied without comment by A. González-Palencia and E. Mele, *Vida y obras de Don...*, III [Madrid, 1943], 205-06 and 223, among the surviving lists of whose books I find only a vague reference to a "Profecías de Merlín," *ibid.*, III, 542), and the Duke and Duchess of Calabria, whose considerable library, including many romances of chivalry, was given to the monastery of San Miguel de los Reyes (Valencia); an inventory of this library was published in the *RABM*, 4 (1874), 7-10, 21-25, 38-41, 54-56, 67-69, 83-86, 99-101, 114-17, and 132-34. (For further information on the Duke of Calabria, see *Claribalte* in the Appendix.)

[10] One discussion of this topic can be found in the speech of Juan Menéndez Pidal upon his reception into the Real Academia (Madrid, 1915). A sizable bibliography of contemporary accounts of chivalric practices and festivities may be found in Jenaro Alenda y Mira, *Relaciones de solemnidades y fiestas públicas* (Madrid, 1903); some of these are accessible in recent reprintings.

part of the author to someone he knew slightly or not at all,[11] but it should be remembered that a dedication was more meaningful in the sixteenth than in the seventeenth century, on which our image of them is based,[12] and moreover, some of the dedications, such as those to *Palmerín de Olivia* and the *Espejo de príncipes*, have a familiar air about them, suggesting that the author knew the person to whom the work was dedicated and had reason to expect that he would like it. (Were this not a factor, one would expect the books to be dedicated to older patrons, who might be more pleased by the flattery and in any event in a better position to reward the author.) There are a significant number of cases (again, see Appendix) in which an author dedicated successive books to the same person, or in which one romance was dedicated to a husband, and later a different one to his wife,[13] or to a father and then to his son. Still

---

[11] Such as, for example, those of the second *Lisuarte de Grecia* (*Amadís*, Book VIII) or *Felixmarte de Hircania*.

[12] See the discussions of Rodríguez Marín, *Quijote*, IX, 9-19, and Gracián, *Criticón*, ed. M. Romera-Navarro, III (Philadelphia: University of Pennsylvania Press, 1940), 197-98 and notes. Dalmiro de la Válgoma y Díaz-Varela, in the introduction to his *Mecenas de libros. Su heráldica y nobleza*, I ([Burgos, the author?], 1966), is primarily concerned with dedications as biographical sources.

Theodore Beardsley, Jr. has pointed out, in his important bibliography of *Hispano-Classical Translations Printed between 1482 and 1699* (Pittsburgh: Duquesne, 1970), p. 121, how the whole question of Golden Age patronage has hardly been explored. Yet for those who would dismiss these dedications as purely formal and not indicating anything about the tastes of their recipients, it is revealing to compare the list in the Appendix with the dedications recorded in Beardsley's study, which can be taken with, I believe, less cause for objection as indicating patrons of learning. There is surprisingly little overlap, which suggests that both the authors of romances of chivalry and the translators of classical works exercised at least a modest amount of care in choosing a patron.

[13] A knotty problem is the question of the sex of the readers of the romances, or more specifically, whether or to what extent their readers were members of the fair sex. Besides the sources already referred to, there are in the moralist writers references to female readers; some romances are dedicated to women, and in other cases, such as Part III of the *Espejo de príncipes*, the author directs himself to them. There are also other contemporary references, usually derogatory ones, to women as

other romances, as can be seen from the dedications, were written by members of the same household, and there is no doubt that in certain cases the publication of the work was subsidized by the *mecenas* involved.

It is still true, of course, that the receiver of a dedication might not be pleased by a book, but we can nevertheless safely assume that he would not have felt the dedication to be an insult; works printed expressly for popular consumption, such as the *pliegos sueltos* and the *libros de cordel*, had no dedications at all.

The books themselves, as physical objects, offer us considerable information. They are, almost without exception, folio volumes; the exceptions are themselves significant, since they were printed outside of Spain.[14] The editions were small. The printing, except for a

---

readers of romances; Santa Teresa's comment on her mother, quoted by Menéndez Pelayo, *Orígenes*, I, 459, n. 1; Oviedo, *Memorias*, ed. cit., pp. 110, 234-35; Cervantes, *El vizcaíno fingido*, p. 530 of the edition of Francisco Yndurráin, *BAE*, 156 (Madrid: Atlas, 1962); *Guzmán de Alfarache*, II, iii, 3 (p. 787 of the edition of Francisco Rico in *La novela picaresca española*, I [Barcelona: Planeta, 1967]; for an earlier period, Hernán Mexía, in Menéndez Pelayo, *Antología de poetas líricos*, edición nacional, II (Madrid: CSIC, 1944), 335.

Without being able to resolve this question completely, two comments can be made: I have already noted elsewhere (n. 13 to the introduction of my edition of the *Espejo de príncipes*) that not all the romances of chivalry are identical, and that certain later ones, in which the love element is more pronounced, may have been directed to a female audience. Beyond this, however, it should be kept in mind that whatever influence women may have had in the field of contemporary secular literature was not restricted to the romances of chivalry alone, and that one should indeed go with leaden feet in qualifying the leadership of the romances as exceptionally feminine. In the "courts" with a literary orientation the women played a very active role, and we find such works as the *Diana enamorada*, the *Selva de aventuras* and the translation of Strapanarola dedicated to women. In this case, of course, the participation of women is even more obviously an upper-class phenomenon.

[14] The priest, in *Don Quijote*, I, 6, clearly realizes this: "Estos [pequeños] no deben ser de caballerías, sino de poesía."

There are only two editions of the "indigenous" romances which were not in folio: the Venice, 1534 edition of *Palmerín de Olivia*, and the Louvain, 1551 edition of *Amadís de Gaula*, which was inexplicably chosen as the basis of the unreliable Aguilar "Libros de caballerías" edition by Felicidad Buendía.

few reprints of the final quarter of the century, ranges from good to excellent in quality;[15] some of the editions are illustrated with woodcuts. Their purchasers had them bound in bindings of high quality.[16]

Some documents provide us with concrete evidence that these books commanded a high price. An important source for the early part of the century is the well-known catalogue of the library of Fernando Colón, reproduced in facsimile by Archer Huntington in 1905.[17] This partial listing of the contents of his library includes for each entry the price paid, as well as the place and date of purchase, information invaluable for a study of contemporary book distribution. He evidently purchased as many romances of chivalry as he could obtain; the prices he paid for them are as follows:

---

[15] Of most romances which I have examined the same could be said as of *Claribalte*: "La impresión del *Claribalte* es realmente primorosa: papel magnífico, tipos bellísimos, anchos márgenes, composición limpia, en suma, un conjunto tipográfico exquisito" (Agustín G[onzález] de Amezúa y Mayo, prologue to the facsimile of *Claribalte* [Madrid: Real Academia Española, 1956]).

[16] Books were, as today, usually sold in paper bindings (*Viaje del Parnaso*, ed. Rodríguez Marín [Madrid, 1935], p. 127), although among the small stock of leather-bound books of Benito Boyer, partially reproduced by Pérez Pastor (see n. 23, *infra*), we find 2 copies of *Cristalián* and one each of the *Caballero del Febo* and the *Amadís*, at 102, 152, and 51 maravedíes for the binding, respectively, and in the order reproduced by Leonard (v. *supra* n. 2), most of the books are ordered "en pergamino."

[17] *Catalogue of the Library of Ferdinand Columbus, reproduced ... by Archer M. Huntington* (1905; facsimile, New York: Kraus Reprint, 1967). The items relevant to Spanish literature may be more easily consulted in Gallardo's *Ensayo de una biblioteca de libros raros y curiosas*, II (Madrid: Rivadeneira, 1866), Item No. 1870.

Item Number		(1 real = 34 maravedíes)
4000	Lisuarte de Grecia (Amadís, Book 7) (1514 edition)	130 maravedíes
4076	Arderique	95 maravedíes[18]
2708	Floriseo	128 maravedíes
4118	Leoneo de Hungría "encuadernado en pergamino"	170 maravedíes
4069	Lepolemo (1521 edition)	95 maravedíes
3976	Tirante el Blanco	260 maravedíes[19]
3331 & 3332	Sergas de Esplandián (1510 edition) and Florisando (Amadís, Book 6; 1510 edition)	13 reales (together)
4120	Clarián de Landanís. Part II (1522 edition)	6½ reales
4119	Clarián de Landanís. Part III, "encuadernado en pergamino"	7 reales
4124	Palmerín de Olivia (1516 edition)	4 reales
4125	Primaleón (1524 edition)	5 reales

[18] Arderique is a romance deserving of considerably more attention than it has received, which is, in a word, none whatsoever. None of the writers on Spanish Arthurian literature (Entwistle, Bohigas, María Rosa Lida), has realized that, superficially at least, it is an Arthurian work. It was written some years before it was published, probably in the fifteenth century, and its original language may well not have been Castilian. Although the declaration on the title page—"traduzido de lengua estrangera en la comun castellana"—could merely be a topos (see my "The Pseudo-Historicity of the Romances of Chivalry," in this volume: but why did it mislead the compiler of Fernando Colón's catalogue to note that it was "en español"?), the names are foreign in origin, and a valuable document reproduced by José María Madurell Marimón, Documentos para la historia de la imprenta y librería en Barcelona (1474-1553) (Barcelona: Gremios de Editores, de Libreros y de Maestros Impresores, 1955), No. 179, provides us with solid evidence of a Catalan version, or possibly original, existing in 1500.

In the document, a book inventory, Arderique is given a low value, possibly because it was written on paper rather than parchment; it also might reflect the lack of interest in chivalric works in Cataluña, which Madurell found noteworthy: "Ni una vez tan sólo he visto citado el Amadís y el Tirant lo Blanc únicamente en el contrato de edición" (p. 103*).

[19] As noted at the beginning, Tirante el Blanco does not, rigorously speaking, have a place in the present discussion, as it is not a Castilian

In comparison, Colón purchased his copy of the *Visión deleitable* (item 2076) for 36 maravedíes, the *Corbacho* (item 4024) for 40 maravedíes, and the lengthy *Propaladia* (item 4032) for only 75 maravedíes. The romances of chivalry are clearly the most expensive Spanish literary works in his library.

We also find evidence of these high prices later in the sixteenth century. In the 1529 inventory of the possessions of Jacob Cromberger,[20] in the inventory of the books of Juan de Timoneda made at his death in 1583,[21] and in registers of book shipments reproduced by José Torre Revello,[22] we find that the romances consistently commanded a high relative price (irrespective of the inflation which affected Spanish money in the period).[23]

---

work. Yet it is revealing to note how it is by quite a margin the most expensive of the romances of chivalry in Colón's library. Its cost may have contributed to its rapid fall into oblivion.

[20] Reproduced by José Gestoso y Pérez, *Noticias inéditas de impresores sevillanos* (Seville, 1924), pp. 36-56; the *Visión deleitable* is valued at 40 maravedíes, unspecified "Amadises" are 150, *Clarián* is 108, etc.

[21] José Enrique Serrano y Morales, *Reseña histórica... de las imprentas que han existido en Valencia* (Valencia: F. Doménech, 1898-99), pp. 548-59.

[22] *El libro, la imprenta y el periodismo en América durante la dominación española*, Publicaciones del Instituto de Investigaciones Históricas de la Facultad de Filosofía y Letras, no. 74 (Buenos Aires, 1940); his document No. 30, dated 1594, is an inventory of a shipment to Indies, with prices; see also No. 24.

[23] The standards used in assigning the values, as well as the prices charged Colón, need some discussion. In a similar document reproduced in part by Cristóbal Pérez Pastor, *La imprenta en Medina del Campo* (Madrid, 1895), pp. 456-62, the inventory of the possessions and stock of the wealthy bookseller Benito Boyer, who died in 1592, we find book values assigned exclusively on the basis of number of pages. It is likely that the cost of the paper exceeded the value of the printing, and that both of them exceeded any factors such as the book's subject, or rights due the author, which affect modern prices (see Agustín G[onzález] de Amezúa, *Cómo se hacía un libro en nuestro Siglo de Oro* [Madrid: Imprenta de Editorial Magisterio Español, 1946], pp. 22-31; reproduced in his *Opúsculos histórico-literarios* [Madrid: CSIC, 1951], I, 348-59). Similarly, the concerns of modern bibliophiles about a book's printer or edition were completely irrelevant (Colón never or rarely bought more than one edition of the same text, although in many cases he could have); the age of a book was a

Upon examining the printing history of the genre, we can also draw some conclusions. The number of romances of chivalry is

---

negative, not a positive factor, which could perhaps explain why, in a seventeenth-century inventory, we find reasonable, but not high, values assigned to *Policisne de Boecia* and to the 1588 edition of the *Sergas de Esplandián* (inventory of the books of Pedro de Párraga by Martín de Córdoba, published by the Marqués de Saltillo, "Bibliotecas, libreros e impresores madrileños del siglo XVII," *RABM*, 54 [1948], 261-63).

The inventory of Boyer, which can be taken as indicating the stock-in-trade of a large peninsular bookseller of the time, whose trade with the new world was only a small portion of his business, provides evidence that the romances had not completely fallen into disfavor in the peninsula as the century drew to a close, but still retained some popularity. In his unbound stock, he had 70 copies of *Palmerín de Olivia*, a book which, like the "cuatro del Amadís," had lost much of its earlier popularity, 43 of *Primaleón*, 64 of the *Sergas de Esplandián*, 34 of the "segunda de la quarta" of *Florisel* (*Amadís*, Book XI), 53 of both parts of the *Caballero de la Cruz* [*Lepolemo*], and 31 more of the first part alone, 59 of the Tercera Parte of the *Caballero del Febo* [*Espejo de príncipes*], and 18 of *Cristalián*; on the other hand, he only had 13 copies of the *Amadís*, 2 of *Belianís*, 3 of Parts I and II of the *Caballero del Febo*, and 6 of *Celidón de Iberia*. (My attempts to identify the editions from the number of "pliegos" have not been overly successful.) The quantity of romances of chivalry contrasts with lesser qualtities of works one would have thought to be more popular; 8 *Dianas* of Montemayor, 16 of the *Lazarillo*, 2 of the *Flos Sanctorum*, 10 of the *Jardín de flores curiosas*, 2 of the Chronicle of Ocampo, 24 of Garcilaso and 27 of the *Celestina*.

It may be objected that these figures represent the books that Boyer did not sell, rather than those he did, and perhaps this is why he had 19 copies of *Olivante de Laura*, whose unique edition appeared 25 years previously (though it is also found in document No. 30 of Torre Revello). Yet the same pattern is found in the inventory of the books of Juan Cromberger (Gestoso Pérez, pp. 90 ff.), and it can be safely assumed that Boyer would not have been as successful as he was if he had not been possessed of shrewd business sense (some idea of his business methods may be found in documents reproduced by [Francisco Fernández del Castillo], *Libros y libreros en el siglo XVI*, Publicaciones del Archivo General de la Nación, 6 [Mexico City, 1914], pp. 260-88, in which is also found an inventory including some romances of chivalry), and at the same time other booksellers were underwriting editions of romances of chivalry, as Benito Boyer himself had underwritten the 1563 edition of *Primaleón*: among them his cousin Juan Boyer, who had printers bring out the 1586 edition of *Espejo de caballerías*, and the 1583/86 edition of the *Espejo de príncipes*.

itself revealing. Although the romances began as a genre, like the pastoral novel, with some works which were great commercial successes, and there were several later works which were frequently reprinted, there is an extensive list of works published which were reprinted only once or not at all, indicating a modest sale. Some of these publications, as stated above, were subsidized, but the majority were treated by their publishers like any other work. Surely it was not the case that publishers brought out, year after year, expensive books which would fail commercially. The figures seem to point instead to a small but consistent demand, which these publications filled, on the part of a limited group of *aficionados* with the means to indulge this expensive taste. [24]

It is also revealing to look at the dates of the reprints of the popular works, which are more closely tied to public favor than is the production of new works.[25] After the abdication of Carlos V, which marks a cut-off point for the writing of new romances,[26] we

---

[24] The sudden growth in popularity of the romances in the opening years of the sixteenth century—which led printers desperately to publish whatever chivalric material they could lay their hands on, such as the ancient *Caballero Cifar*, and perhaps *Tirante el Blanco*—is also explained by noble preoccupations. As Marañón has pointed out, in *Los tres Vélez*, 2nd ed. (Madrid: Espasa-Calpe, 1962), pp. 45-46, these years were not the happy ones they are commonly said to have been. The great military endeavor of the reconquest was concluded, and the army suffered a sudden decline in importance. The discovery of America was of no particular interest. The centralizing tendencies which we see as the foundation of a modern state were seen by many as the erosion of traditional aristocratic privileges. The marriage of Ferdinand and Isabella meant that after her death, Castile was ruled by an Aragonese king, who did not hide the fact that his interests were Aragonese and not Spanish. (And even he was preferable to the Flemish Carlos V.)

It is not hard to understand why, at this time especially, the nobility would turn to the romances of chivalry to read about a world which was in many ways superior to the one they lived in, in which the nobility still had a clear-cut and essential function, where life was varied, exciting, and adventurous, and in which the individual still had abundant opportunities to show his abilities and win status.

[25] Beardsley, pp. 129-30.

[26] We only have *Olivante de Laura* (with a dedication by the printer, not the author, which suggests an earlier date of composition), *Rosián de*

find that reprints were not produced uniformly throughout the conclusion of the century (as was the case with *pliegos sueltos*[27] and other popular literature), but instead appeared in groups. We find between 1556 and 1562 not a single reprint, but in 1562 we find printings of *Palmerín*, of *Lepolemo*, and of the *Espejo de príncipes*, in 1563 of *Primaleón*, of *Amadís*, and two of *Lepolemo* (with the publication of its Second Part), and in 1564 of *Belianís*, *Lisuarte de Grecia*, and *Amadís de Grecia*, with the publication of *Olivante de Laura*. The production then abruptly drops off again, with a lone reprint of the *Amadís* in 1565, and aside from minor exceptions[28] there are no further reprints until 1579. In this latter year we find both parts of *Belianís* printed, and the *Espejo de príncipes*; in the following year two editions of the *Amadís*, one each of *Belianís* and *Palmerín*, and the publishing and reprinting of Part II of the *Espejo de príncipes*, as well as a reprint of the first part. After editions of *Amadís de Grecia* in 1582 and two of *Florisel* in 1584, the last great surge of publishing of romances of chivalry gets underway, with three reprints in 1585, five in 1586, and eight in 1587, including the publication of Part III of the *Espejo de príncipes* and the first edition in 45 years of the *Sergas de Esplandián*.[29] But once again the commercial interest in the romances disappears abruptly, with only a possible

---

Castilla (a short work and not a true romance), *Lidamarte de Armenia, Febo el Troyano*, and *Policisne de Boecia* published after this date, although there were written and published continuations of earlier works, such as those of the *Espejo de príncipes* (whose first edition is of 1555—during the reign of Carlos V—not of 1562, the date usually found in bibliographies.)

[27] This can be seen from the splendid bibliography of Antonio Rodríguez-Moñino, *Diccionario bibliográfico de pliegos sueltos (siglo XVI)* (Madrid: Castalia, 1970), pp. 34-45 and 643-46.

[28] The 1568 *Florisel* edition and the 1575 *Amadís* edition; the publication in 1576 of *Febo el Troyano* was almost certainly subsidized by its patron.

[29] In 1585, two reprints of the *Espejo de príncipes*, Part II and one of the *Primaleón*; in 1586 the *Amadís*, *Cristalián*, the *Espejo de príncipes*, and two of the *Espejo de caballerías*; in 1587 the *Amadís*, two of the *Sergas* and of *Lisuarte de Grecia*, *Belianís* and its second part, and the publication of Part III of the *Espejo de príncipes*.

In 1588 was published the version of Fray Juan de Pineda of the *Passo honroso*, with its description of chivalric life under Juan II, whose court was the most recent Castilian model for that of Carlos V.

reprint of *Florisel* in 1588, reprints of the *Espejo de príncipes* in 1589, and the mysterious and probably non-existant edition of *Lidamarte de Armenia* in 1590. Except for the anomalies mentioned in n. 2 above, this completes the Castilian printing history of the romances of chivalry.

In the truly popular genres, as just mentioned, we find a much more constant production. Moreover, the dates of the fluctuations, which parallel, though imprecisely, the changes in popularity of the epic poem,[30] themselves suggest an upper-class audience. The first "low point," from 1556-1561, can be explained as caused by the upheaval surrounding Carlos V's abdication and death, and the adjustments needed by the installation of a new king. The second lacuna, from approximately 1567-1579, corresponds well to the military activities directed by Don Juan de Austria—first the *morisco* rebellion, then the naval activities in the Mediterranean, in which he was accompanied by a significant portion of the Spanish nobility.[31] That the final rise and decline were situated around the year of 1588 cannot be a coincidence, for whatever the effect of the Armada's defeat on Spain's naval power, there can be no doubt that the expedition aroused interest in chivalric matters, and that in its defeat was lost a considerable sector of the cream of the nobility.[32]

---

[30] Lest it be thought that this fluctuation was present in all types of publishing except the very lowest, it can quickly be confirmed that the two periods referred to as virtually devoid of commercial interest in the romances of chivalry (1556-61, 1567-79) witnessed an intense activity in the fields of scientific and religious publishing, fields less subject to external vicissitudes, and to a somewhat lesser but still significant degree in the fields of belles-lettres and poetry (cf. the printing history of Montemayor and Garcilaso, for example).

The publication in 1554 of the first Spanish translation of Heliodorus and of the *Lazarillo* is surely coincidental.

[31] Croce has already stated how "innumerevoli attestazioni" (of which he unfortunately gives but one—a quotation from Jerónimo de Urrea) pointed to the romances of chivalry as the soldiers' reading matter (*La Spagna nella vita italiana durante la rinascenza*, 4th ed. [Bari: Gius, Laterza, 1949], p. 210). Probably the editions of the romances published outside the peninsula were printed with the soldiers in mind.

[32] "Los historiadores de aquel tiempo no convienen en la pérdida total

Taking all the factors mentioned into consideration, is it reasonable to conclude that the romances were read by the upper or
noble class, and perhaps by a few particularly well-to-do members
of the bourgeoisie.[33] Certainly they were not read by, nor to, the
peasants.[34] We have still, however, to reconcile this with the

que tuvo la escuadra de los españoles.... Lo cierto es que la desgracia fue
tal que cubrió de luto toda la España, porque no había familia ni casa de las
distinguidas en todo el reino donde no se llorase la muerte de algún hijo,
hermano o pariente, de manera que Felipe, temiendo el efecto que podría
producir sobre el pueblo este luto general, publicó un edicto como hacían
los romanos en semejantes circunstancias, mandándolo cesar" (José Sabau
y Blanco, chronological tables to Mariana's *Historia general*, XVI [Madrid,
1820], lxxii).

[33] An example of a member of the middle class who read romances of
chivalry would be Fernando de Rojas, a *converso* who never rose above the
position of mayor of Talavera. Among the books he owned when he made
his will (1541) we find two "libros del *Amadís*" (two books of the Amadís
cycle), *Esplandián, Palmerín, Primaleón, Platir*, and the *Segunda Parte de Don
Clarián* (see Appendix). In the inventory it was noted that these books
were "traídos y viejos y algunos rotos," presumably from use, as no note
is made on the condition of a group of legal books he also owned. (Taken
from Fernando del Valle Lersundi, "Testamento de Fernando de Rojas,"
RFE, 16 [1929], 382.)

[34] I am convinced that were it not for Juan Palomeque's comments, no
one would even have suggested that the indigenous Castilian romances
were read to the peasantry.
    Honesty compels me to mention the *proceso* of Román Ramírez, sum-
marized by A. González Palencia in "Las fuentes de la comedia *Quien mal
anda en mal acaba*, de Don Juan Ruiz de Alarcón," *BRAE*, 16 (1929), 199-222
and 17 (1930), 147-74 (reprinted in his *Historias y leyendas. Estudios literarios*
[Madrid: CSIC, 1942], pp. 217-84), yet the data it presents is so contradic-
tory and difficult to evaluate that I prefer not to include it with my main
argument. In 1595 Ramírez, a *morisco* of Deza, was denounced to the
Inquisition. He was a farmer (*labrador*), the son of a farmer, and lived from
an orchard "arrendado del Duque de Medinaceli," and as a *curandero*.
According to his own declaration, he had once owned romances of
chivalry, whose titles he specified (the bad spelling no doubt due to the
amanuensis): "Floranuel [Florambel], los doce [!] de Amadís, Don Cristalián, Don Olivante del Aura [de Laura], Primaleón y Don Duardo [I do not
believe, as González Palencia suggests, that he is referring to the Portuguese *Duardos*, Book VII, in Gayangos' enumeration, of the *Palmerín*
"cycle"; rather to the same *Primaleón*, which on the title page promises to
present as well the deeds of Duardos, prince of England], Don Clarián del

statements in the *Quijote* quoted at the outset. With regard to Don Quijote's remark, we are free to dismiss anything he says, particularly in Part I, as the misconceptions of an insane person, for if he can believe windmills to be giants and sheep to be soldiers, he could just as well fantasize that the romances of chivalry were read with enthusiasm by all; he is not a reliable source. Furthermore, considering the tone of the Prologue to Part I, and the narrow interpretation Cervantes' friend takes of the purpose of

---

Amadís [de Landanís], el Caballero del Febo, Don Rogel de Grecia, Don Felís Malo [Felix Magno]... y otros que al presente no se acuerda" (257-58). When he was tested and it was found he could only read with great difficulty, he declared that he knew these books because "antes que él supiese leer ni lo hubiese deprendido, sabía ya de memoria los más libros de caballerías de los cuales dichos, porque Román Ramírez, padre deste confesante, leía muy bien y muchas veces en presencia deste y así este confesante iba tomando en la memoria lo que le oía leer" (260). He also claimed to have written a romance of chivalry, entitled Florisdoro de Grecia.

Because of his extraordinary memory, which he first claimed to have lost and then explained he never had (he memorized the main plots of the romances and then invented details to fit them), he was often called upon, as a curiosity, to recite romances of chivalry before various nobles, and as a result of a petty squabble because one evening he could not be two places at once, he was denounced to the Inquisition out of spite, as having a memory inspired by the devil. He died before his case was settled, in 1509, having confessed to being a *cripto-moro* (and the Inquisition, with its usual thoroughness, went on to condemn him to death posthumously).

All of this seems suspect in the extreme. An illiterate farmer could scarcely, from his earnings, afford even one of the books which Ramírez said he had in such abundance, but which he no longer owned and could not produce. It seems more likely that he claimed this extensive knowledge to make himself more in demand as the owner of a prodigious memory, which was, no doubt, highly profitable for him. I wish, likewise, that it could be concluded from his testimony alone that the romances of chivalry were regularly read aloud among the nobles of this period, but it seems that the interest was more in his memory than in what he actually recited. (Roger M. Walker tackles the always knotty problem of oral reading of written texts with regard to the *Cifar*, in *FMLS*, 7 [1971], 36-42, without reaching any firm conclusion.)

I hope it is unnecessary to point out, finally, that the romances of chivalry were only incidental to his denunciation and later condemnation. [On Román Ramírez, see more recently L. P. Harvey, "Oral Composition and the Performance of Novels of Chivalry in Spain," *FMLS*, 10 (1974), 270-86.]

the *Quijote*, the statement there could be merely another ironic note.

The comment of the canon from Toledo is not to be so easily dismissed. Whether or not he speaks for Cervantes,[35] he is presented as a sober and serious man, deeply concerned about the course literature is taking. He is knowledgeable, and he does not make jokes.

We can understand this comment properly if we remember that *vulgo*, in a literary context, meant in practice "the uneducated," without reference to a particular social class.[36] This is

---

[35] Bruce Wardropper maintains that he does not, in "Cervantes' Theory of the Drama," *MP*, 52 (1954-55), 217-21, although F. Sánchez Escribano and A. Porqueras Mayo, without giving any reasons, reject this article as "totalmente desenfocado," in *Preceptiva dramática española del renacimiento y el barroco* (Madrid: Gredos, 1965), p. 21, n. 21. Wardropper is supported, on different grounds, by Alban Forcione, *Cervantes, Aristotle, and the* Persiles (Princeton: Princeton University Press, 1970), pp. 108-27, on whom see E. C. Riley, *HR*, 41 (1973), 566.

[36] This is probably what the friend in the Prologue to Part I meant by the term.

There is on the word *vulgo* a considerable bibliography. In a penetrating article, which deserves to be reprinted in a more accessible form, Werner Bahner discusses the change in the term from its original sense of, more or less, the peasantry, to mean the uneducated or the half-educated ("Die Beziechnung 'vulgo' und der Ehrbegriff des spanischen Theaters im Siglo de Oro," *Omagiu liu Iorgu Iordan*, ed. B. Cazacu et al. [Bucharest: Editura Academiei Republicii Populare Romîne, 1958], pp. 59-68). It might be added as well that *vulgo* is invariably defined negatively, as being people lacking something which the writer possesses; none of the writers who use the term include themselves in it (except, satirically, Cosme de Aldana, in a work which has been overlooked by the critics writing on the topic, despite its accessibility in BAE, 36: "Invectiva contra el vulgo y su maldiciencia," opening sonnets, p. 496: "No creas que esta inventiva [sic]/contra el vulgo, de autor compuesta sea/que se exima del vulgo, y que no crea/ser del mismo en cuanto obre, hable y escriba"), even though they might be of obscure or non-existent lineage.

[While this article was in press, two other scholars pointed to this poem in Aldana: Américo Castro, in the second (only) edition of his *Pensamiento de Cervantes*, p. 214, and Alberto Porqueras Mayo, in "Sobre el concepto *vulgo* en la Edad de Oro," an article in his *Temas y formas de la literatura española* (Madrid: Gredos, 1972), pp. 114-27, originally published in *Actele celui de-al XII-lea congres interaţional de linguistică şi filologie romanică* (Bucharest: Editura Academiei Republicii Socialiste România, 1971), pp.

spelled out in the well-known comment of Don Quijote to the

713-22. Also on the topic *vulgo* may be consulted Hans-Jörg Neuschäfer, "Lope de Vega und der Vulgo. Über die soziologische Bedingtheit und die emanzipatorischen Möglichkeiten der populären Comedia (am Beispiel von Fuenteovejuna)," in *Spanische Literatur im Goldenen Zeitalter. Fritz Schalk zum 70. Geburtstag* (Frankfurt: Klostermann, 1973), pp. 338-56, A. Porqueras Mayo and F. Sánchez Escribano, "Función del vulgo en la preceptiva dramática de la Edad de Oro," *RFE*, 50 (1967), 123-43, George Boas, *Vox Populi: Essays in the History of an Idea* (Baltimore: Johns Hopkins Press, 1969), and A. A. van Beysterveldt, *Répercussions du souci de la pureté de sang* (Leiden: Brill, 1966), pp. 15-29.]

The following may also be consulted: Otis Green, "On the Attitude toward the *Vulgo* in the Spanish *Siglo de Oro*," *Studies in the Renaissance*, 4 (1957), 190-200; Américo Castro, *El pensamiento de Cervantes*, Anejo 6 of the *RFE* (Madrid, 1925), pp. 210-12; Aubrey F. G. Bell, *Renacimiento*, pp. 113-17; Amado Alonso, *Castellano, español, idioma nacional*, 4th ed. (Buenos Aires; Losada, 1968), pp. 68-74; Werner Bahner, "El vulgo y las luces en la obra de Feijóo," *Actas del Tercer Congreso Internacional de Hispanistas*, ed. Carlos H. Magis (Mexico: El Colegio de México, 1970), pp. 88-96; A. Porqueras Mayo, *El prólogo como género literario*, Anejo 14 of the *Revista de Literatura* (Madrid: CSIC, 1957), pp. 156-58, *El prólogo en el renacimiento español*, Anejo 24 of the *Revista de Literatura* (Madrid: CSIC, 1965), pp. 21-25, and *El prólogo en el manierismo y barroco españoles*, Anejo 27 of the *Revista de Literatura* (Madrid: CSIC, 1968), pp. 17-19; Lope de Vega, *El sembrar en buena tierra*, ed. William Fichter (New York: M.L.A., 1944), pp. 198-99; E. C. Riley, *Teoría de la novela en Cervantes*, trans. Carlos Sahagún (Madrid: Taurus, 1966), pp. 178-82. Two other references to the *vulgo* in which the uneducated are the class referred to are found in Fernández del Castillo, p. 563: "no sólo se consumían en cenizas libros prohibidos, sino otros muchos 'porque no fuesen en el vulgo ocasión de errar,'" and Prudencio de Sandoval, *Historia de Carlos V*, BAE, 80, 116: "Ninguno que lo fuese [dotor] hacía caso de Lutero, ni le tenía en más de lo que merece un . . . instrumento de Satanás, para ganar infinitas ánimas de predición, de gente vulgar y idiotas semejantes a él, sin letras ni entendimiento verdadero. . . ."

Aside from a passage in the prologue to the *Quijote* of Avellaneda, obviously based on the passage in Cervantes' prologue quoted at the outset, and an isolated and undated scrap of information in Gayangos (BAE, 40, p. lxxii, col. a, l. 6), I have found only one other contemporary reference to the *vulgo* as readers of romances of chivalry, in the *Florisando*, Book VI of the *Amadís* series, a work which Cervantes almost certainly did not know (see n. 16 of my *"Don Quijote y los libros de caballerías,"* *infra*). In the prologue to this work, the author says that the *Amadís* and the *Sergas de Esplandián* were read "ansí del palacio como del vulgo," and expresses his concern that "rústicos" might not have been able to tell the good in them from the bad. I think that this statement from the author of so tangential

Caballero del Verde Gabán: "Todo aquel que no sabe, aunque sea señor y principe, puede y debe entrar en número de vulgo" (II, 16). In the light of this passage, the canon's comment is indeed explicable. The intelligentsia (of which the canon would have formed a part) was never the class that read the romances of chivalry; they were responsible for the Erasmian and moralist complaints against them. If, but only if, the word *vulgo* is understood without class implication, as merely meaning "todo aquel que no sabe," is it true that the romances were read by the *vulgo*.[37]

In conclusion, we should note that the evidence deduced from the *Quijote* about the readers of the romances of chivalry was never as unequivocal as it might have been. It is not true, as Madariaga says, that there is no one in the *Quijote*, except "perhaps" Sancho, who has not read the romances or heard them read.[38] When did Don Quijote's *ama*, or Tomé Cecial read them? Had la Tolosa or the galley slaves heard them read? A moment's reflection shows how extreme this statement is. Neither should the fact that the innkeeper Juan Palomeque had two romances of chivalry be taken to mean that they were read at every harvest in all the remote corners of Spain. The books were there because

---

a work, who has such a hostile attitude toward the romances as they then existed (see Maxime Chevalier, "Le roman de chevalerie morigéné. Le *Florisando*," BHi, 60 [1958], 441-49) is of little value. (See also the prologue to Part III of *Espejo de cavallerías*.)

[Although Oviedo in his *Memorias* also refers to the *vulgo* as readers of the romances of chivalry, it is obvious from his comments that he uses the word in the sense discussed here (ed. cit., pp. 110, 189, 192).]

[37] I would thus accept, though for different reasons, Pérez Pastor's statement in *Bibliografía madrileña* (Madrid, 1891), xiii-xiv: "La falta de libros de caballerías impresos en Madrid desde 1566 hasta 1600, aunque es una prueba negativa, dice mucho en contra de la opinión generalizada por varios cervantistas, pues viene a demostrar: 1º que entre la gente ilustrada de esta época, los libros de caballerías estaban en completa decadencia; 2º que en la Corte no habia un solo autor, traductor, ni editor que se atreviera a poner manos en libros de caballerías..." (If this latter argument were extended, it would imply that because romances of chivalry were printed in Salamanca, that they were read by the university community, which was on the whole quite untrue—but see n. 34 to the introduction of my edition of the *Espejo de príncipes*).

[38] P. 34 of the edition cited. The qualification concerning Sacnho is not **Sancho**

some traveller forgot them, and the illiterate innkeeper has no plans to buy any others. His wife didn't listen to them being read, his daughter didn't understand them, and Maritornes, who did not know what a *caballero aventurero* was (I, 16), listened for the worst possible reason.

From a slightly different perspective—looking at those characters who were *well* acquainted with the romances of chivalry—we find that the *Quijote* in fact confirms the thesis of this paper, that the romances were read by the middle and upper classes. Don Quijote, the priest, and perhaps the barber,[39] the canon, Dorotea, the various people at the ducal palace, and, perhaps, Luscinda and Sansón Carrasco, knew the romances well, but there is no representative of the peasantry among them. Yet only one, the canon, can clearly be excluded from the *vulgo*, as defined above.

---

[39] On the evidence of his discussions with the priest in I, 1 and his use in I, 46 of a type of prophecy found in the romances of chivalry (see my editon of the *Espejo de príncipes*, V, 81).

❧ Appendix ❧

Dedications of the

Spanish Romances of Chivalry

The date(s) of the edition(s) consulted are given for those cases in which I have not been able to consult the *princeps*. No works which I have been able to examine have been omitted.

Amadís de Gaula, Books I-IV: No dedication.

Sergas de Esplandián (*Amadís*, Book V): No dedication.

Florisando (*Amadís*, Book VI): Juan de la Cerda (1485-1544), second Duke of Medinaceli. His son, Luis de la Cerda, married Ana de Mendoza, daughter of Diego Hurtado de Mendoza, to whom Book IX was dedicated (Diego Gutiérrez Coronel, *Historia genealógica de la casa de Mendoza*, ed. A. González Palencia [Madrid: CSIC, 1946], I, 236).

Lisuarte de Grecia (*Amadís*, Book VII; 1548 edition, and according to Gayangos, 1525 edition): Diego de Deza (1443/44-1523), archbishop of Seville, "para descanso del trabajo de su mucho estudio." A. Cotarelo y Valledor, *Fray Diego de Deza. Ensayo biográfico* (Madrid, 1905), states that Deza was in the 1480's catedrático de prima de teología in Salamanca, inquisidor general of Castile from 1501 to 1507, and from 1504 on archbishop of Castile, but Mariano Alcocer y Martínez, head of the Archivo de Simancas, reveals in his *Fray Diego de Deza y su intervención en el descubrimiento de América* (Valladolid, 1927) the close relations of Fray Diego with the family of the Reyes Católicos: preceptor del príncipe, confesor of Fernando el Católico and of Juana la Loca, "doncel" de su Magestad, etc., which may, perhaps, explain why a romance of chivalry was dedicated to him. (Deza, of course, was one of the key figures to encourage Colón in the 1480's, and to intercede with the monarchs for him.)

Silva says in the prologue to *Lisuarte* that he received "criança e mercedes" from Deza, but not enough is known of the lives of either to identify where this took place.

Fernández de Oviedo, who was *mozo de cámara* of the same prince (Juan) of whom Deza was preceptor, also mentions Deza, *Quinquagenas*, ed. cit., pp. 524-25; his *extracto de la vida del Arzobispo Deza*, which I have been unable to locate, is cited by Alcocer, p. 27.

Lisuarte de Grecia (*Amadís*, Book VIII): Jorge, Duke of Coimbra (1481-1550), bastard son of John II of Portugal.

Amadís de Grecia (*Amadís*, Book IX): Diego Hurtado de Mendoza (1461-1531), third Duke of the Infantado, Marquis of Santillana, called "el gran duque." Silva, before his marriage (which took place near 1520; Cotarelo [*supra*, n. 8], p. 138), had falsely attributed the paternity of his wife Gracia Fe to this licentious figure.
The author of the *Guerra de Granada*, about whom the anecdote referred to in note 9 is told, belonged to a different branch of the family.

Florisel de Niquea (*Amadís*, Book X; 1566 edition): No dedication.

Rogel de Grecia (*Florisel de Niquea*, Part III; *Amadís*, Book XI): Francisco de Zúñiga de Sotomayor, third Duke of Béjar, the great-grandfather of the sixth Duke of Béjar, to whom Part I of the *Quijote* was dedicated.
Perhaps it was in the Duke of Béjar's library, if there was a collection of romances of chivlary, that Cervantes read these books which he knew so well (see my article, "*Don Quijote* y los libros de caballerías," in this volume). I hasten to point out that this is pure speculation, based on what may well be a coincidence.

Florisel de Niquea, Part IV (*Amadís*, Book XI): María de Austria (1528-1603), daughter of Carlos V and wife of Maximilian II of Hungary. Juan Rufo, much later, dedicated to her his *Austriada*.

Don Silves de la Selva (*Amadís*, Book XII): Luis Cristóbal Ponce de León (1518-1573), second Duke of Arcos, patron of the musicians Cristóbal de Morales and Juan Bermudo.
Pedro de Luján, author of *Silves*, later dedicated his translation of *Leandro el Bel*, as he did his *Coloquios matrimoniales*, to Juan Claros de Guzmán (>1518-1556), Count of Niebla, eldest son of Juan Alfonso de Guzmán, Duke of Medina-Sidonia.

Arderique: "Hieronimo de Artes, doncel."

Belianís de Grecia, Parts I and II: Pero Suárez de Figueroa y de Velasco, "dean de Burgos y abad de Hermedes y arcediano de Valpuesta, señor de la villa de Cozcurrita [Zamora]," "suplicando se reciba con aquella voluntad con que todos los antiguos criados de vuestra casa son tratados." He was probably a younger son of the counts of Feria. In *Relaciones de los reinados de Carlos V y Felipe II*, ed. Amalio Huarte, II, Sociedad de Bibliófilos Españoles, 2ª época, Vol. 25 (Madrid, 1950), pp. 183 ff., can be found verses of Bernardino de Avellaneda dedicated to Suárez, "mi señor"; the date is 1546, one year earlier than the first edition of *Belianís*.
"Criado" did not necessarily mean, in this context, *servant*, but could merely mean anyone supported by a noble and who lived with him. Cervantes signs himself *criado* in the dedications to the Conde de Lemos (as does Sancho in his letter to Don Quijote).

Belianís de Grecia, Parts III and IV: "El licenciado Fuenmayor, cavallero de la orden de Santiago, del consejo real y camara de Su Magestad [Felipe II] mi señor." The dedication is by Andrés Fernández, the author's brother, who is the one who tells us how the continuation was written because Carlos V so much liked Parts I and II.

I believe that Fuenmayor, head of the council which granted the book's *licencia*, was Juan Díaz de Fuenmayor, to whom, after the King and the kingdom of Jaén, Argote de Molina dedicated his *Nobleza de Andalucía*.

Cirongilio de Tracia: Diego López Pacheco (1503-1556), second of this name, third Marquis of Villena. He was armed a knight in 1520 (Sandoval, *Carlos V*, BAE, 80, 208), and he was "al lado de Carlos V" in Italy (Fernández de Bethencourt, *Historia genealógica y heráldica de la monarquía española*, II [Madrid, 1900], 226), as was the Count of Astorga (v. *Florambel, infra*; Sandoval, BAE, 81, 366-67, also Pedro Mexía, *Historia de Carlos V*, ed. J. de Mata Carriazo [Madrid: Espasa-Calpe, 1945], p. 550, etc.).

Clarián de Landanís, Part I, Book I: Charles de Lannoy (1482-1527), *caballerizo mayor* of Carlos V and from 1522 viceroy of Naples. (On the honorary office of *caballerizo* see the description in the *Diccionario de Autoridades*.) An extremely important person, with whom the king jousted (Mexía, *Historia de Carlos V*, p. 86, on his later importance see p. 307 and *passim*; also see the *Historia del capitán Hernando Dávalos* of Pedro Vallés [Amberes, 1558], and Léon-E. Halkin and George Dansaert, *Charles de Lannoy, viceroy de Naples* [Brussels, 1934]. The book was allegedly "sacada de lenguaje aleman en italiano por Faderico [sic] de Maguncia obispo de Lanchano, por mandado del serenissimo rey Fernando de Napoles, primero deste nombre."

—————, Part I, Book II (1535 edition): Álvar Pérez de Guzmán, Count of Orgaz, by "maestre Alvaro, fisico suyo."

In the preface, the author says that "vuestra señoria... me mandó que una obra que ovo venido a sus manos, que fue principiada por otro, y es la segunda parte del muy famoso cavallero don Clarian de Landanís, de la qual no estavan aun escriptas treinta hojas, que la acabasse yo, porque fue informado vuestra señoría que la avía llevado a Sevilla e a Valladolid e a Toledo e a otras muchas partes para que la concluyessen."

Considering the lengths to which authors of romances of chivalry went to disguise their part in their works (see my article "The Pseudo-Historicity... " *infra*), this statement, that he is concluding the work of another, could be untrue, and an imitation of the letter of "el autor a un su amigo" of the recent *Celestina*. However, I believe it is true, because there exist, in point of fact, two different continuations of Part I of *Clarián*, the one presently under discussion, and the one treated of immediately following; they are not continuations of each other. I have not been able to examine thoroughly the present book, usually called Part I, Book 2 (however, it and the following "true" Part II begin with the same sentence); probably a proper study would clear up this problem, though the longevity of the controversy over the *Celestina* does not permit excessive optimism.

Floramante de Colonia (*Clarián de Landanís*, Part II, 1550 edition): John III of
Portugal (1502-1577), "por saber de cierto que a semejantes cosas sois
tan inclinado." One of the surviving manuscripts of the Portuguese
Libro de Josep Abaramatia is dedicated to him (Mário Martins, *O Livro de
José de Arimateia da Torre do Tombo* [Lisbon, 1952], pág. 13, *apud* María
Rosa Lida de Malkiel, "Arthurian Literature in Spain and Portugal," in
Arthurian Literature in the Middle Ages, ed. Roger Sherman Loomis [Ox-
ford: Clarendon Press, 1959], pág. 408; in Spanish translation in her
Estudios de literatura española y comparada, 2nd ed. [Buenos Aires: Eudeba,
1969], págs. 134-48).

Despite the fact that in the colophon the author of this part is
stated to be Jerónimo López, "escudero fidalgo de la casa del rey
d'Portugal," who we know wrote the following two parts, it has been
noted by Gayangos, who had a good eye for such things (in Gallardo,
Ensayo, I, No. 540), that in the verses at the end of the book, ostensibly
written by "el trasladador" and directed to John III, there is an acrostic,
formed by the first letter of each stanza, which spells Pedro Cabreor.
Gayangos asks if Cabreor was a misprint for Cabrero, but it is not, and
would be a most unusual Hispanic name. (It should be noted that in
several places López refers to himself as the "trasladador," or translator; *trasladar* meant both to copy and to translate, as *traducir* was a
much newer term and not as widely used.)

In any event, that Jerónimo López is not a pseudonym is firmly
established by the fact that he edited (not wrote, as Gayangos, citing
Cardoso, says in *BAE* 40, p. lxxvª, Fray Álvares' *Cronica do ... Iffante dom
Fernando*, describing himself in the colophon of the first (1527) edition,
which has since disappeared, with exactly the same words: "corregida e
emendada por Ieronimo Lopez escudeiro fidalgo da Caza delRey Nosso
Senhor" (*apud* João Álvares, *Obras*, ed. Adelino de Almeida Calado
[Coimbra: Acta Universitatis Conimbrigensis, 1960], I, xx). In this case,
the only way López could fail to be the true author would be if
someone else published a three-volume work, spread out over several
years, under his name; this is unlikely in the extreme.

The identity and role of Cabreor await further investigation. I think
that we must, however, reject Gayangos' hypothetical edition of this,
the "true" Part II, in 1528 or earlier. Instead, the Toledo printer
Villaquirán, who brought out the complete set (apparently he stopped
printing from 1524 to 1530, which explains why Gaspar de Ávila, who
had underwritten the printing of Part I, published Part IV; F. J. Norton,
Printing in Spain 1501-20 [Cambridge: Cambridge University Press,
1966], p. 54), mistook the work of "maestre Álvaro" as the true Part II
and used it to make up his set, not noticing that Part III was not a
continuation of his Part II.

Clarián de Landanís, Part III: John III of Portugal, "por un fidalgo de sua casa
e criado a las migallas de sua mesa que ha por nombre Geronimo
Lopez."

Lidamán de Ganayl (*Clarián de Landanís*, Part IV): Not stated, but clearly from the same author to John III: "O rey magno y bienaventurado, ¿por que assi vuestra alteza se olvida de un menor siervo e criado suyo, no queriendo recebir ni acebtar mi trabajo y desseo por servicio?"

Claribalte: Fernando de Aragón (1488?-1550?), Duke of Calabria. The circumstances of this dedication are discussed in detail by Antonello Gerbi, in "El *Claribalte* de Oviedo," *Fénix*, 6 (1949), 385-90.

It was mentioned above (n. 9) that the Duke of Calabria had at his death many romances of chivalry in his library, including one (*Leonís de Grecia*) which would otherwise be unknown to us. In 1526, he married Germaine of Foix, who was the widow of Fernando el Católico and of the Elector of Brandenburg, and older than he; they held in Valencia a literary court, described in *El cortesano* of Luis Milán, who later had as patron John III of Portugal. When she died in 1537, he married Mencía de Mendoza (see *infra*, s.v. *Valerián*).

On Germaine de Foix, see J. García Mercadal, *La segunda mujer del Rey Católico* (Barcelona: Juventud, 1942), and José M. Doussinague, *Fernando el Católico y Germana de Foix: Un matrimonio por razón de estado* (Madrid, 1944). I have not been able to see Luis Querol, *La última reina de Aragon, virreina de Valencia* (Valencia, 1931).

Cristalián de España: Prince Felipe [II].

Espejo de cavallerías, Part I (1533 edition): Martín de Córdoba y Velasco, "señor de las villas de Alcaudete y de Montemayor," "corregidor al presente en la imperial ciudad de Toledo."

———, Part II (1533 edition): Diego López de Ayala, "vicario y canonigo y obrero en la santa iglesia de Toledo." One of the most important figures in the sixteenth-century Spanish church, who already in 1516 was Cisneros' agent in Flanders.

———, Part III: "Al muy magnifico señor don Bernaldino de Ayala."

I am pleased to report that the apparently unique Huth copy of the *princeps* of Part III of the *Espejo de cavallerías* (Toledo: Juan de Ayala, 1547), has been located, miscatalogued ("Roselao de Grecia"), in the Chapin Library at Williams College.

Espejo de príncipes y cavalleros [*El Caballero del Febo*], Part I: Martín Cortés (1532-1589), second Marqués del Valle, son of Hernán Cortés.

———, Part II (1617 edition): No dedication.

———, Part III [and IV]: Lucas Rodríguez, Count of Melgar. This romance has introductory sonnets, which was unusual for a romance of chivalry: besides those of the author, there is one of a certain Núñez de Figueroa, "médico andaluz," to Rodríguez, one of Luis Díaz de Montemayor to the same, and one to the author from Lorenzo de Zamora, who two years later was to dedicate his epic *Historia de Sagunto* to Victoria Colona, the wife of Rodríguez.

————, Parts III and IV (1623 edition): Rodrigo de Sarmiento de Silva (1600-1664), Duke of Híjar and later a personage of considerable importance.

Febo el Troyano: Mencía Fajardo y Zúñiga, Marquise of los Vélez, "suplicando se reciba con aquella voluntad con que todos los criados de su casa son tratados." She was the widow of Luis Fajardo (†1575), second Marquis of los Vélez, son of the first Marquis, to whom *Floriseo* was dedicated. This romance has introductory sonnets of Luis Alariv, Josepho Roger, and Benito Sánchez Galindo, the latter of whom published the same year (1576) his *Christi victoria*.

Felix Magno (1549 edition): Fadrique de Portugal, bishop of Sigüenza and viceroy of Cataluña, who ordered it printed, by his "criado," who notes "aunque el principal officio de vuestra señoría sea la milicia ecclesiástica, en el qual, como aya resplandecido, no ay quien no lo conozca y con grande admiración lo publique, no por esso se han embotado en vuestra señoría los exercicios militares, ansí por la línea y descendencia de sus reales progenitores, como por las virtudes y animosidad de su coraçón."

Felixmarte de Hircania: Juan Vázquez de Molina, secretary of the *consejo de estado* of Felipe II, *trece* of the order of Santiago. He was a nephew of Francisco de los Cobos, secretary of Carlos V: see Hayward Keniston, *Francisco de los Cobos* (University of Pittsburgh Press, 1959), *passim*. In 1523 he was already a "criado" of Cobos (Keniston, p. 71). Cobos, Molina, and the author Ortega were all from Úbeda.

Florambel de Lucea: Pero Álvarez Osorio, fourth Marquis of Astorga, Count of Trastamara. An important figure in Carlos V's court, who was faithful to him during the *comuneros'* revolt, and who was at the head of the army in Italy during the sack of Rome.
  The romance was written by a certain Enciso, his *criado*. See also *infra*, *Platir*.

Florando de Inglaterra: "A los caballeros, dueñas y donzellas de Ulixea" [Lisbon].

Florindo: Juan Fernández de Heredia (†1549), count of Fuentes (whom the author refers to as "mi señor").

Floriseo: Pedro Fajardo y Chacón (1477?-?), first Marquis of los Vélez, *adelantado* of the kingdom of Murcia. See Gregorio Marañón, *Vélez* (*supra*, n. 24), pp. 31-57.

————, Book 3 (*Reymundo de Grecia*): No dedication.

————, Part II (?), *Polismán* (Biblioteca Nacional MS. 7839): Juan Franco Cristóbal de Yxar, Count of Belchite.

Lepolemo (Seville, n. d., edition): Íñigo López de Mendoza (1493-1566), eldest son of Diego Hurtado (v. *supra*, *Amadís de Grecia*), and later fourth Duke of the Infantado. The title "Count of Saldaña," which is all that appears on the book itself, was held by the oldest son of the Duke of the Infantado during the life of his father.

At his marriage in 1514 to Isabel de Aragón, cousin of Fernando el Católico, Fernando and Germaine de Foix were *padrinos*. On Íñigo López de Mendoza, see Francisco Layna Serrano, *Historia de Guadalajara y sus Mendozas en los siglos XV y XVI* (Madrid CSIC, 1942), III, 125-32.

Lidamarte [sic] *de Armenia*: Luis Enríquez de Cabrera, Duke of Medina de Rioseco (?). No one since Clemencín, *Biblioteca de libros de cavallerías*, Publicaciones cervantinas, 3 (Barcelona, 1942), p. 36, has seen the printed edition. Clemencín gives the title as Duke of Medina-Sidonia, which must be erroneous; if this information is correct, the person whose biography is found in *CODOIN*, 97, 131-70 must be a homonym. [I would like to thank Mary Lee Cozad for her kindness in sending me information regarding the dedication of this work, which confirms my suspicion that it was dedicated to the Duque de Medina de Rioseco, and not of Medinasidonia. According to her, there was never a printed edition of this work; what Clemencín had seen was a MS—that of Thomas Phillipps, now at Berkeley and used by Cozad—with a printed and factitious title page.]

Lidamor de Escocia: Fernando Álvarez de Toledo (1508-1582), Duke of Alba.

Olivante de Laura: Felipe II (by the printer, not the author).

Palmerín de Olivia: Luis Fernández de Córdoba (1482-1554), son of Diego Hernández de Córdoba, 7th Alcaide de los Donceles, to whom was dedicated the *Cárcel de Amor*. See Diego de San Pedro, *Obras*, ed. Samuel Gili Gaya, Clásicos Castellanos, 133 (Madrid: Espasa-Calpe, 1967), pp. xxviii-xxix, and Bethencourt, IX (Madrid, 1912), 53-60.

—— (1563 and 1566 editions): From Benito Boyer, who had the 1563 edition printed, to Juan Álamos de Barrientos, "capitán de S. M. y regidor de Medina del Campo."

Primaleón: Luis Fernández de Córdoba.

Platir (a continuation of the preceding): Pero Álvarez Osorio and María Pimentel (see *Florambel de Lucea, supra*; it is likely that *Platir* and *Florambel* were written by the same person, and they were published by the same printer, Nicolás Tierri). I believe that María Pimentel was the daughter of Alonso Pimentel (?-1528?), fifth Count of Benavente, who fought with Osorio in resisting the *comuneros*, and that she was widow of Diego Hurtado de Mendoza, who died in 1531, and mother of Íñigo (v. *supra*). *Florambel*, published in 1532, is dedicated to her husband alone, whereas *Platir*, of 1533, was dedicated to the two, suggesting a recent marriage.

Philesbián de Candaria: No dedication.

Policisne de Boecia: Antonio Álvarez Boorques, member of the order of Santiago, "gentilhombre de la casa real de su magestad [Felipe III], y veinticuatro de la ciudad de Córdoba."

Polindo (independent of *Palmerín* and *Primaleón*): No dedication.

Rosián de Castilla: Cristóbal de Guardiola, son of Juan de Guardiola, of the "consejo supremo de su magestad."

Valerián de Hungría: Mencía de Mendoza (1508-1554), second Marquise of Zenete, second wife of the Duke of Calabria (v. *supra*, *Claribalte*). She herself was the widow of Henry, Count of Nassau, another friend of Carlos V. "¿Qué princesa cultivó con más fruto la literatura griega y latina? ¿En quién despertaron más fervor los estudios?" asks García Matamoros, *Pro adserenda hispanorum eruditione*, ed. and trans. by José López de Toro, Anejo 28 of the *RFE* (Madrid, 1942), p. 227. There is an extensive note on her in Marcel Bataillon, *Erasmo y España*, trans. Antonio Alatorre, 2nd ed. (México: Fondo de Cultura Económica, 1966), p. 487; see also Theodore S. Beardsley, Jr., in *HR*, 41 (1973), 170-214, and Oviedo, *Memorias*, ed. cit., p. 666. A letter from Juan Ginés de Sepúlveda to her was published by Ángel Losada in his editon of Sepúlveda's letters (Madrid: Cultura Hispánica, 1966), pp. 79-80.

It is noteworthy that the book was printed in Valencia, where she lived. Gayangos thought that in it were disguised the deeds of her father, Rodrigo de Vivar y Mendoza; I can neither confirm nor deny his statement at present.

The Pseudo-Historicity of the Romances of Chivalry

FICTION, PARTICULARLY PROSE FICTION, did not have an easy birth.* It represented the Renaissance's most radical departure from classical literary models, and even though it met in many cases with overwhelming approval on the part of the book-buying public, it was rejected by purists and theoreticians until it had been established for generations, if not for centuries. This situation was aggravated by problems of vocabulary, as the complicated history of the words *novela* and *roman* illustrates. In Spain, the term *historia* had to serve a number of purposes in the sixteenth and, to a lesser extent, the seventeenth centuries.[1]

To some authors of prose fiction, the ambiguous status of what they wrote was unimportant, or even a source of amusement, but others, especially the authors of the Spanish romances of chivalry, were conscious of it to a considerable degree. The present article is an attempt to examine how these authors resolved the question of the nature of their works by de-emphasizing their fictional quality, and, briefly, how Cervantes was influenced by them.

The difficulty facing the authors of the romances of chivalry was

---

* Published in *Quaderni Ibero-Americani,* Nos. 45-46 (1974-75), 253-59. Since this article was written, William Nelson has published his intelligent *Fact or Fiction. The Dilemma of the Renaissance Storyteller* (Cambridge: Harvard, 1973).

[1] Bruce Wardropper, "*Don Quixote*: Story or History?," *MP,* 63 (1965), 1.

particularly severe because the romances marked the introduction
of this new type of literature into Castile. Faced with a sudden
demand on the part of a noble class turned sedentary after the
conclusion of the reconquest,[2] printers rapidly brought out editions
of whatever chivalric material they could lay their hands on. This
first stage in the history of the Spanish romances of chivalry ended
with the publication of the *Amadís de Gaula* (before 1508), the *Sergas
de Esplandián* (before 1510), and the *Caballero Cifar* (1512).[3] The publication of these works did not satisfy the demand, however, but
rather increased it, and the supply of pre-existing romances having
run low, the time had come for the production of additional ones.[4]

The authors of the new romances, which were printed in large
numbers during the following generation, had a model set for them
by Montalvo, the person to whom we owe the version of the *Amadís*
which has come down to us. At the beginning of his version,
Montalvo says that the book:

> Fue corregido y emendado por el honrrado y virtuoso
> cauallero Garci-Rodríguez de Montaluo, regidor de la noble
> villa de Medina del Campo, y corregióle de los antiguos origi-
> nales que estauan corruptos y mal compuestos en antiguo
> estilo, por falta de los differentes y malos escriptores. Quitando
> muchas palabras superfluas y poniendo otras de más polido y
> elegante estilo tocantes a la cauallería y actos della.[5]

Montalvo clearly presents himself as an editor, not the author,
though taking liberties with his text which would not be permissible
today. The idea of an earlier source, whose provenance is unclear, is
stressed.[6] Throughout the work, he constantly uses formulas of

---

[2] See "Who Read the Romances of Chivalry?" *supra*.

[3] I mention the *Caballero Cifar* together with the above to emphasize
my belief that its publication was not "a testimony to its enduring
popularity" (Alan Deyermond and Roger Walker, "A Further Vernacular
Source for the *Libro de Buen Amor*," *BHS*, 46 [1969], 194, n. 1), but rather a
reflection of the sudden demand, which led printers to hunt for suitable
works to issue.

[4] See *supra*, p. 37.

[5] Ed. Edwin Place, I, 11, ll. 3-9.

[6] See also the comment on the "malos escritores" quoted below.
Although he has not the slightest idea who wrote the book, he does

historical writers: "dize la historia," "la historia contará adelante," "como la historia os ha contado."[7]

Although sixteenth-century readers might have disagreed, we now know that Montalvo was truthful when speaking about an earlier source for Books I-III of the *Amadís*. When he comes to discussing Book IV, now taken to be his own work, he clearly distinguishes it from what he has done with the preceding books:

> ...corrigiendo estos tres libros de Amadís, que por falta de los malos escriptores, o componedores, muy corruptos y viciosos se leýan, y trasladando enmendando el libro quarto con las *Sergas de Esplandián* su hijo, que hasta aquí no es en memoria de ninguno ser visto, que por gran dicha paresció en vna tumba de piedra, que debaxo de la tierra en vna hermita, cerca de Constantinopla fue hallada, y traydo por un vngaro mercadero a estas partes de España, en letra y pargamino tan antiguo que con mucho trabajo se pudo leer por aquellos que la lengua sabían....[8]

He reemphasizes this in the heading to the *Sergas de Esplandián* proper:

> Aquí comiença el ramo que de los quatro libros de Amadís sale llamado las *Sergas de Esplandián*, que fueron escritas en griego por la mano de aquel gran maestro Helisabad, que muchos de sus grandes fechos vio & oyó, como aquel que por el grande amor que a su padre Amadís tenía, se quiso poner en tan gran cuydado.... Las quales Sergas después a tiempo fueron trasladadas en muchos lenguajes....[9]

---

believe that it was the work of more than one person, an interesting detail.

[7] Frida Weber de Kurlat studies this aspect from a different point of view in "Estructura novelesca del *Amadís de Gaula*," *Revista de Literaturas Modernas*, 5 (1966), 29-54, as did previously Raymond Willis, in *The Phantom Chapters of the* Quixote (New York: Hispanic Institute, 1953).

[8] Ed. cit., p. 9, ll. 85-94.

[9] P. 7 of the edition of Dennis Nazak (*supra*, note 49 to Chapter 2); p. 403 of that of Gayangos (*BAE*, 40). It should be noted that Montalvo felt it necessary to speak of the continuation with a metaphor, no doubt because of the novelty of the concept.

We see the character "Montalvo" thus metamorphosized from editor to translator, inasmuch as the language of his "source" has changed from archaic Spanish to Greek. The change in language is, of course, implied by the shift in locale from western Europe to the eastern Mediterranean.[10] Most striking, however, is that Montalvo had to claim it was written in a foreign language at all.

This device (for that it is) solved several problems for Montalvo. It ostensibly freed him of responsibility for the work, except that of "translating" it correctly, while at the same time invested it with the allure of remote places, similar to the later use of eastern European locale in Golden Age drama. Above all, it allowed the book to be presented as the work of an eyewitness, an official chronicler, similar to a historian such as López de Ayala, who both recorded events and participated in them.[11]

Surely this pretense could not have been convincing more than once or twice. Yet with the notable exception of *Palmerín de Olivia*, every major sixteenth-century romance of chivalry I have been able to examine follows the example set by Montalvo, in that they are either "translations," or, in a few cases, "revisions" of an old Spanish text.[12] A considerable variety of "original languages" is represented: English, German, Latin, Arabic ("Chaldean"), Hungarian, and Phrygian, as well as the frequent Greek.[13] Official historians, similar to Elisabat, wrote some of the romances; we can cite Fristón, familiar

---

[10] The eastern Mediterranean was the usual setting of all the later romances of chivalry, and therefore the term "ciclo greco-asiático," used by Gayangos to categorize some of the romances, is not particularly useful. For Montalvo's precedents, see L. Stegagno Picchio, "Fortuna iberica di un topos letterario: la corte di Costantinopoli dal *Cligès* al *Palmerín de Olivia*," in *Studi sul Palmerín de Olivia. III. Saggi e richerche* (Pisa, 1966), 99-136.

[11] See Chapter 18 of the *Sergas de Esplandián*, where Elisabat's reliability is stressed.

[12] Nevertheless, at the end of the *princeps* of *Primaleón* both it and its predecessor are said to have been translated from Greek (quoted by G. di Stefano in his editon of *Palmerín de Olivia* [Pisa, 1966], p. 783.
Aside from this, the exceptions are minor: *Don Clarisel de las Flores*, *Floriseo*, and *Policisne de Boecia* are the only ones I am aware of.

[13] This pretense has contributed to an enormous bibliographic muddle, from which the romances of chivalry have not yet completely ex-

through the *Quijote*, who recorded the deeds of Belianís de Grecia, and Novarco, chronicler of Cirongilio de Tracia.

Many of the later authors went beyond Montalvo's relatively sophisticated device, however, and added additional details strengthening the presentation of themselves as mere translators. In several books we find two separate prologues, one of the "translator" and one of the "author." Such is the case with *Lepolemo*, a particularly interesting romance in view of its setting (North Africa) and the absence of fantastic elements. The Arab Xarton, who recorded the works of this Christian knight, introduces his work in a prologue full of Arabic formulae, and appropriately humble in tone:

PROLOGO DEL AUTOR MORO
SACADO DEL ARABIGO EN LENGUA CASTELLANA

> Alabado sea Dios, grande por todas las cosas que haze. A ti, el gran Soldan Çulema, el mayor y mejor rey moro de tu tiempo, yo, Xarton, el menor y más obediente de tus vassallos, y mayor en la gana de hazer tu mandamiento, te presento este tratado que me mandaste escrevir....[14]

He concludes pointing out that it is not strictly proper for him to be writing about a Christian, and notes that it was only at the Sultan's request.

A second fictional author writes to the Conde de Saldaña under the heading "Prologo del interprete del presente libro." In it he explains how he came upon the book in "aquella barba la lengua araviga" when he was a captive in Tunis, and translated it there. He points out his concern for what critics may say, but he would not want—a topos of historians—that "quedasen tan notables hechos en olvido, haziendo escudo que si la orden dél no está a placer de todos, echen la culpa al moro que lo ordenó, pues en mi traducir no he salido de su estilo."[15]

---

tricated themselves. Additional confusion has been caused by romances of chivalry in other countries, which, following the Spanish example, said they were translations from other languages, including Spanish. Such is the case with *Florimón*, which Nicolás Antonio assumed existed in Spanish, although this is almost certainly false.

[14] Quoted from the Seville, n.d. editon (Biblioteca Nacional R-23,622).

[15] In a similar vein, the author of *Cirongilio de Tracia* discusses in his

Melchor Ortega, author of *Felixmarte de Hircania*, disguised his work through a series of translations, reminiscent of the medieval translation schools. The work was written, he tells us, by a certain Philosio Atheniense, translated from Greek into Latin by Plutarch [!], then from Latin into Tuscan by Petrarch [!!], from which language Ortega translated it into Castilian.

Returning to Montalvo, he also prefixed his own work with a story, at first glance ridiculously contrived, of how his source manuscript came into his fictional author's possession. In the *Sergas* itself (Chapter 99), the character Montalvo describes how he came to know the conclusion of it, and how his writing is really at the request of Urganda la Desconocida. This story should be understood as adding to the historicity of the work, rather than detracting, as it is not as unbelievable as it looks at first glance. Many literary discoveries have been made under similar extraordinary circumstances. Most recently, we have seen the discovery of the Dead Sea Scrolls, or in the preceding century the discovery in Egypt of the largest known fragment of Menander. In Hispanic studies, we can mention the *aljamiado* manuscripts buried in a box in the province of Zaragoza, the fragmentary manuscripts of *Amadís* and *Roncesvalles*, or the *jarchas* in manuscripts from the Cairo *genizah*. How much more common this type of discovery must have been in the early Renaissance! The rediscovery of Heliodorus,[16] the manuscript of Catullus allegedly found in a Verona wineshop, or the discovery of Plautus early in fifteenth-century Italy[17] are only some of the best-known examples.[18]

---

prologue how he was afraid that "la alta fama de la generosa caballería de otros tiempos se escureciesse," and how he was presenting a more accurate translation than any previously available.

Feliciano de Silva, in his *Amadís de Grecia*, also has separate prologues for the author and translator, as well as a "nota del corrector de la imprenta"—probably inspired in Alonso de Proaza's verses which accompany the *Celestina*. It is quoted above, in note 28 to Chapter VI.

[16] Marcel Bataillon, *Erasmo y España*, pp. 620-21.

[17] Raymond L. Grismer, *The Influence of Plautus in Spain before Lope de Vega* (New York: Hispanic Institute, 1944), p. 59.

[18] Dares and Dictys, or the "verdadero historiador" Turpin, would also have been familiar at the time. Today, of course, we are so blasé that an

Various authors used this device of a fantastic story concerning the precedence of their manuscript. One of the more restrained is found at the beginning of *Florambel de Lucea*, where the author Enciso, *criado* of the Marqués de Astorga and presumably the author of *Platir*, claims the help of an unidentifiable friend:

> Sabra V.S. que al tiempo que la serenisima infanta Doña Catalina, hija de los catolicos reyes Don Fernando y Doña Isabel (de gloriosa memoria), que agora es reina de Inglaterra, passó a se casar e intitular por reina y señora de aquella rica isla, se halló a la sazon en su servicio en la ciudad de Londres un notable varon español, cuyo nombre no he podido saber.... Pues como este era inclinado a ver cosas nuevas, y muy dado a saber las antiguas antigüedades, procuró de aver en su poder las historias de los reyes de Inglaterra pasados, y entre las muchas que rebolvio halló esta de aquel invencible y esforçado cavallero Florambel de Lucea. Y pareciole tan bien, y tomó tanta aficion con ella, que se determinó de traduzirla de la lengua inglessa en que estava en la nuestra castellana, y traerla a España...[19]

The role of Enciso was merely that of correcting the translation.[20]

---

author must go to ridiculous extremes if he seriously wishes to deceive readers; no one pays the slightest attention if John Updike puts as preface to *Bech: A Book* a letter from the author whose life is presented, or concludes with a phony bibliography including even a plot outline of one of Bech's supposed works. To fool people nowadays one must do as George Fraser, taking a person from *Tom Brown's Schooldays*, and involving him in a real event (the first Afghan war). Alternatively, one can steal the plot from a Victorian novel (*The Prisoner of Zenda*), then claim the novel was based on the person's life whose memoirs are being edited, taking care to present grounds for "some reappraisal" of Otto von Bismarck, and speaking—most important from our point of view—of a manuscript discovery, with some portions remaining to be found (*Royal Flash* [New York, 1970], p. vii).

[19] Taken from the 1532 edition, Biblioteca Nacional R-4355. English, in contrast with earlier centuries (see the openings of *Tristán de Leonís* and *Oliveros de Castilla*) is not a common source language; the only other work I have found it in is *Florando de Inglaterra*.

[20] Another typical example is found in the preface to *Don Silves de la Selva*; more accessible is the prologue to *Cristalián de España* of Beatriz Bernal, quoted by M. Serrano y Sanz in *Apuntes para una biblioteca de escritoras españolas*, I (Madrid, 1903), 157. It is not, however, a parody, as he calls it.

In two works, *Olivante de Laura* and Marcos Martínez's *Tercera parte del Espejo de príncipes y caballeros*, we find a long prologue, in which the "author" undergoes an adventure reminiscent of that of Montalvo (*Sergas de Esplandián*, 99), which culminates in the receipt of the manuscript which he is charged with translating. In that of Martínez, who was more successful in his romance of chivalry than was Antonio de Torquemada, author of *Olivante de Laura*, the fictional author explains in the prologue the extraordinary series of events which happened to him on Midsummer's Day. Having gone out from Alcalá de Henares to relax in the countryside, through a quarrel of love-struck shepherds he learns of the existence of the cave of Sifronio de Anglante. At first setting off to see it, when he decides to turn back because it is too far a wind picks him up and deposits him at the door, where the evil Selagio threatens to kill him, but is instead killed by Artemidoro and Lirgandeo (on whom see below). These give the bewildered Martínez a sword,[21] telling him he must kill with it "los nueve de la fama," beginning with King Arthur, who guard the cave. Having done this (for the sword was enchanted; presumably the guards were apparitions), he enters the cave, which has now turned into a palace, and is given a tour of all its murals of famous knights,[22] culminating in his receipt of the book, written in Greek and Latin, in parallel columns.

Artemidoro and Lirgandeo are the two "authors" of the *Espejo de príncipes y cavalleros*, characters created by Diego Ortúñez de Calaho-

---

[21] "Juzga, sabio lector," he says, "cual estaria mi atribulada vida, viendo por tantas partes ser acosada con la horrible muerte." The sense of surprise and of events out of control is emphasized.

[22] The use of heroic figures as a subject for murals is an echo of a classic practice found in several places in the romances of chivalry; see, for example, Chapter 3 of *Cristalián de España*. It is particularly interesting in this case because the heroes of earlier romances of chivalry are included (since they were as "historical" as Felipe II or Dom Sebastião, who are also there), providing us with some idea of what romances Martínez knew. We find Amadís de Gaula, with his relatives, and Primaleón, "cercado de sus parientes, que por prolijidad no los cuento," Cristalián de España, Olivante de Laura, Belianís de Grecia, and Felixmarte de Hircania. In a similar display in the prologue to *Olivante de Laura*, we see mentioned, besides the Amadís and Palmerín families, only Clarián de Landanís and his son Floramante.

rra, author of Part I. By adding a second "author" Ortúñez imposed upon himself another requirement of the historian, that of evaluating and combining two different sources. The two occasionally disagree among themselves, as real historians might (one thinks of Alfonso el Sabio's compilers struggling to reconcile Lucas Tudense and Rodrigo Toledano):

> Este valentísimo y bienaventurado príncipe, dize el sabio Artemidoro que nasció luego que el emperador con toda su compañía vino del reino de Lidia, porque quando el fuerte pagano Rodarán pasó en Grecia, ya la emperatriz Briana estava gran preñada. Parece que discordia en esto el sabio Lirgandeo, porque no cuenta cosa del infante hasta que las grandes batallas del emperador Alicandro de Tartaria y el emperador Trebacio de Grecia fueron acabadas, de donde comiença a contar cosas suyas muy maravillosas. Yo creo que la causa desto deve ser que como el sabio Lirgandeo no lo vio hasta que vino en Grecia, que dexó de contar dél hasta que todas las batallas fueron acabadas.... Y ansí, hasta aquel tiempo no se cuenta dél más de en este capítulo, porque después comiençan los dos sabios a escrevir cosas muy grandes y maravillosas dél, y se conforman en todo lo que escriven.[23]

In other romances of chivalry, we see other "histories" mentioned, as in the following quotation from Feliciano de Silva's *Florisel de Niquea*: "Y el principe Anaxartes [quedó] con su esposa, con tanto descanso cuanto con pena lo habia deseado, que fue tanta por ambas partes cuanto su gran historia hace entera relacion, porque como la reina Zirfea aqui de tantos hace relacion, no pudo particularizar las cosas de cada uno, como en sus historias particulares se cuenta...."[24]

Closely related to their pseudo-historicity is a second characteristic of all the Spanish romances of chivalry, their deliberate inconclusiveness. The modern novel is normally expected to arrive at a logical conclusion, and then stop, and although we make allowances

---

[23] Book II, Chapter 52, quoted from Vol. IV of my edition, Clásicos Castellanos, 196 (Madrid: Espasa-Calpe, 1975), 163. For another example, see III, 175.

[24] 1566 edition (Hispanic Society of America copy), fol. ccxi recto.

for certain multi-volume works, no story is permitted to go on indefinitely; a conclusion must be reached sometime.

History, however, is not subject to the same restrictions, and in tacit recognition of the resistance of events to be broken down into logical segments, a certain amount of arbitrariness is accepted in the conclusion of a historical work. The authors of the romances of chivalry recognized this, and further simulated historical writers by deliberately accentuating the artificiality of the endings of their works. Although the physical book had to come to an end, the story does not, just as real events would not. Precisely when a happy resolution seems at hand, something occurs to prevent the "story" from ending. Characteristically, a new element, problem, or character is introduced, creating not only the possibility but the necessity of a sequel to the romance. For example, near the end of Part II of *Belianís de Grecia*,[25] the conclusion of the work seems appropriate, as the various nations (Greeks, Trojans, Babylonians) taking part in the work are at peace, after a series of hostilities. Yet the seed of a new conflict is there, in a marriage designed to cement the peace; two knights desire the lady in question, and open warfare is about to break out again. To prevent this, Fristón, the magician-author of the work, whisks all the ladies of the court away and places them in an enchanted castle. The tranquility in Babylonia ends as the knights start off to seek them out; at this point the book ends.

This inconclusiveness—sometimes only the birth of a son of whom great things are prophesied—might have served at times as a device to permit the author to continue writing, but it was felt as a requirement of the genre quite apart from the author's intentions. Thus, Jerónimo López, author of *Lidamán de Ganail*, Part IV of *Clarián de Landanís*, states that a continuation exists, but "quien saberlo quisiere junte la mano con el papel, y tome alguna parte del gran trabajo que yo he tenido en sacar esta cronica del lenguaje aleman en el vulgar castellano."[26] A similar statement is found at the end of the second *Lisuarte de Grecia*, Book VIII of the *Amadís* family.[27]

---

[25] Parts I and II were written and published together and form a single unit.

[26] Biblioteca Nacional, R-5247.

[27] Quoted by Henry Thomas, *Spanish and Portuguese Romances of Chivalry*, p. 71. The same sentiments are expressed by Jerónimo Fernández at the

Cervantes, of course, was aware of all of this in writing *Don Quijote*. If the authors of romances of chivalry found their manuscripts in remote places and incredible circumstances, his persona will find his being sold as waste paper in Toledo. (What were found under such "honorific" circumstances were the ridiculous verses which conclude Part I.) He speaks, at the end of Part I, of a continuation which could not be obtained, as did Avellaneda at the end of his continuation; perhaps Cervantes would have similarly concluded Part II, if his anger at Avellaneda had not led him to break an unwritten rule of the romances of chivalry and cause his protagonist to die. Cide Hamete has been, if grudgingly, recognized as inspired in the "chroniclers" of the romances of chivalry. In fact, particularly in view of his exaggerated concern for accuracy, he is a parody of them. The whole presentation of the *Quijote* as a history, rather than fiction, is based on this pretense of the romances of chivalry.

---

end of the Cuarta Parte (i.e., Libro) of his *Belianís de Grecia* (fol. 280ᵛ of the ed. of Burgos, 1579): "Lo que en esta estraña aventura subcedio con las espantosas guerras de los nubianos principes... y otras grandes hazañas quisiera contar, porque la aventura deste torneo cada uno cumplio su promesa sin desonor de sus compañeros. Mas el sabio Friston, passando de Grecia en Nubia, juró avia perdido la historia, y assi la tornó a buscar. Yo le he esperado y no viene, y suplire [sic] yo con fingimientos a historia tan estimada sería agravio, y assi lo dexaré en esta parte, dando licencia a qualquiera a cuyo poder viniere la otra parte la ponga junto con esta, porque yo quedo con harta pena y desseo de verla. Y vuestra alteza [Carlos V] me dé licencia, si no basta la que mi enfermedad se tenia, y me mande cosas de otra profision, pues para escrevir amores no me da licencia la edad, y para las armas se me a resfriado la sangre."

⁊⁊ Libro quarto del noble y

esforçado cauallero don Cirongilio que
trata de como fue conocido por rey
de Macedonia y Tracia: y
del casamiéto suyo conla
infanta Regia su
señora.⁖.

Don Quijote y los
libros de caballerías:
necesidad de un reexamen

ON QUIJOTE ERA, sobre todas las cosas, un
hombre que había leído mucho, y es poco pro-
bable que se pueda llegar a una comprensión
satisfactoria de su personalidad sin volver a
leer algunos de sus libros predilectos.* Más
aun, ninguna parodia puede ser adecuada-
mente apreciada si no se estudia sistemática-
mente el objeto que ridiculiza. Sin embargo, en
los últimos años los estudiosos han descuidado el estudio del *Quijote*
a la luz de los libros de caballerías que inspiraron a Cervantes y a su
héroe. Los especialistas en estos libros, como Pascual de Gayangos o
Sir Henry Thomas, no se han condiderado lo suficientemente peri-
tos en la obra de Cervantes como para intentarlo. Los cervantistas,
de otra parte, no han tenido por lo general acceso a los textos de los
libros de caballerías.[1]

---

    * Published in *HR*, 41 (1973), 511-23; revised and reprinted, as transla-
ted by Arcadio Díaz Quiñones, in *Sin Nombre*, 6, No. 2 (October-December,
1975), 54-65.

    [1] Los libros que han sido reimpresos en este siglo han sido objeto de
algún estudio; *El* Amadís *y el* Quijote es el título de una monografía, aunque diste mucho de ser definitiva, del P. Félix Olmedo (Madrid: Nacional,
1947). Sobre las *Sergas* tenemos el trabajo de María Rosa Lida citado más
adelante (n. 24), y *"Las Sergas de Esplandián* como crítica de la caballería bre-

Para el conocieminto de la materia tenemos que volver al único estudio que pretendió ser comprensivo, el de Diego Clemencín. Clemencín, quien es todavía la persona más familiarizada con los libros de caballerías desde el siglo diecisiete, comenzó en 1833 la publicación de su monumental edición del *Quijote*, proyecto concluido póstumamente por sus amigos. Las notas que acompañan su texto son una mina de informaciones sobre los libros de caballerías. Como creía que una de las funciones principales de la crítica literaria era el estudio de las fuentes de la obra, intentó leer el mayor número posible de los libros que Cervantes conocía, incluyendo cuantos libros de caballerías que pudo encontrar. Su proyecto se hizo posible porque tuvo acceso a varias bibliotecas privadas.[2]

---

tona" de Samuel Gili Gaya, *BBMP*, 23 (1947), 103-11. La reproducción en facsímil del *Claribalte* (Madrid: Real Academia Española, 1956) hizo posible los estudios de Guido Mancini, "Sul *Don Claribalte* di Fernández de Oviedo," *Annali dell'Università di Padova: Facoltà di Lingue in Verona*, Serie ii, 1 (1966), 3-21, y de Daymond Turner, "Oviedo's *Claribalte*: The First American Novel," *RN*, 6 (1964), 65-68, aunque ninguno de éstos conocía el estudio de Antonello Gerbi, "El *Claribalte* de Oviedo," *Fénix*, 6 (1949), 378-90, quien trabajó con una fotocopia de otra fotocopia del original. Acompañan la edición de *Palmerín de Olivia* de Giuseppe di Stefano (Pisa: Istituto di Letteratura Spagnola e Ispano-americana dell'Università di Pisa, 1966), dos importantes volúmenes de estudios: *Introduzione al* Palmerín de Olivia de Guido Mancini (ahora traducida al español, en el tomo *Dos estudios de literatura española* [Barcelona: Planeta, 1970]), y *Saggi e richerche*, una colección de articulos sobre varios aspectos de la obra, aunque en ninguno de los dos se examina directamente el problema de la influencia de la obra de Cervantes. El trabajo de Edwin Place, "Cervantes and the *Amadís*," en *Hispanic Studies in Honor of Nicholson B. Adams*, University of North Carolina Studies in Romance Languages and Literatures, 59 (Chapel Hill: University of North Carolina Press, 1966), pp. 131-40, es de poca substancia, y a pesar de las contrarias indicaciones de Ruth El Saffar, *Distance and Control* in Don Quixote: *A Study in Narrative Technique*, North Carolina Studies in Romance Languages and Literatures 147 (Chapel Hill, North Carolina, 1975), p. 16, n. 1, el estudio de José F. Montesinos, "Cervantes, antinovelista," *NRFH*, 7 (1954), 499-514, apenas trata del *Quijote* como parodia de los libros de caballerías. Por otra parte, merece citarse el libro de Hans-Jörg Neuschäfer, *Der Sinn der Parodie im* Don Quijote, Studia Romanica, 5 (Heidelberg: Winter, 1963), pues intenta definir la actitud de Cervantes hacia el *Amadís*, *Palmerín de Inglaterra*, y *Tirante el Blanco*, aunque creemos que sobrevaloriza a éste y exagera la importancia del tema amoroso en los libros de caballerías en general.

   2 Martín de Riquer se aprovecha de muchas de las notas de Clemencín

Francisco Rodríguez Marín hizo mucho por negarle a Clemencín el puesto que merece en la crítica cervantina y caballeresca. En su edición del *Quijote*, el más importante de este siglo, critica en forma detallada, y a veces con gusto evidente, las faltas y defectos de Clemencín, a menudo los del terreno lingüístico.[3] Ello no es una falla grave; después de todo, parte esencial de toda crítica es anotar los errores de los predecesores. Más inquietante, sin embargo, es que Rodríguez Marín no sólo no añade nada importante a nuestro conocimiento de los libros de caballerías (lo cual hubiera sido fácil para él, ya que era Director de la Biblioteca Nacional), sino que da un paso atrás al no incluir en sus notas muchos de los valiosísimos comentarios de Clemencín. Por ejemplo, cuando Don Quijote, al ponerse el nombre caballeresco de *Caballero de la Triste Figura*, explica que lo hace para ser como los caballeros de antaño, que tenían nombres similares, "cuál se llamaba *el de la Ardiente Espada*, cuál, *el del Unicornio*, aquél, *el de las Doncellas*, aqueste, *el del Ave Fénix*, el otro, *el Caballero del Grifo*, estotro, *el de la Muerte*" (I, 19), Clemencín identifica los caballeros a quienes se refiere.[4] Este tipo de ayuda no se encuentra, sin embargo, en las notas de Rodríguez Marín, donde sólo hay un comentario sobre un cambio que introdujo en el texto. Dos veces en *Don Quijote* se menciona a Lirgandeo: en I, 43, donde Don Quijote lo invoca,

---

en su examen de las fuentes del *Quijote* en *Aproximación al* Quijote, 3ª ed. (Barcelona: Teide, 1970). Menos conocida que la edición del *Quijote* de Clemencín (reimpresa, con numerosas erratas, por Ediciones Castilla, 2ª ed., 1966), pero no menos valiosa, es su monografía *Biblioteca de libros de caballerías*. Consiste de notas bibliográficas sobre los libros de caballerías, destinadas a ser la base de un volumen suplementario a su edición del *Quijote*. Hecha a principios del siglo diecinueve, permaneció en forma manuscrita hasta que fue publicada por el cervantista y bibliófilo D. Juan Sedó (*Biblioteca de libros de caballerias. Año 1805*. Publicaciones cervantinas, 3 [Barcelona, 1942]).

[3] Véase la reseña que hizo Américo Castro de la edición de Rodríguez Marín, en *RFE*, 4 (1917), 393-401.

[4] Amadís de Grecia, Belianís de Grecia, un caballero en el *Caballero de la Cruz* y Florarlán de Tracia eran, respectivamente, los primeros cuatro. El Caballero de la Muerte también era Amadís de Grecia. Su identificación del Caballero del Grifo, tomada de Bowle, es insatisfactoria; después ha quedado establecido que se refiere a un caballero de *Philesbián de Candaria* (véase "Búsqueda y hallazgo de *Philesbián de Candaria*," *Miscellanea Barcinonensia*, 11 [1972], 147-57).

junto a Alquife, y en II, 34, donde es una de las figuras que desfilan en el palacio ducal. Clemencín, pero no así Rodríguez Marín, le identifica como un "sabio" que aparece en el *Espejo de príncipes y cavalleros.* No son ejemplos aislados, más bien reflejan la tendencia de Rodríguez Marín de tratar sólo lo mínimo inevitable en sus notas al material caballeresco.[5]

Para poder evaluar el tratamiento de Clemencín a los libros de caballerías desde un punto de vista cuantitativo es preciso determinar cuántos libros conocía Cervantes. Al mismo tiempo podemos estudiar el alcance del conocimiento que éste tenía, si nos detenemos a considerar primero cuántos libros de caballerías había, cuestión que no puede decidirse con certeza. La lista cronológica de Thomas al comienzo del Capítulo V de su *Spanish and Portuguese Romances of Chivalry* incluye 39, excluyendo las obras portuguesas y continuaciones sin nuevo título. A este número hay que añadir dos obras que Cervantes pensó que eran castellanas, aunque se sabe que no lo son, *Palmerín de Inglaterra* y *Tirante el Blanco,*[6] y dos obras que Thomas desconocía, *Lidamarte de Armenia*, de Damasio de Frías (1590),[7] y *Rosián de Castilla*, de Joaquín Romero de Cepeda (Lisboa: Marcos Borges, 1586).[8]

---

[5] La diferencia de enfoque entre Clemencín y Rodríguez Marín es más profunda que el intento del último por engrandecerse a costa del primero (aunque eso fue un factor también); más bien refleja la dictomía que existe en los estudios literarios entre quienes creen que el examen de las fuentes es una forma legítima de crítica, y quienes no lo creen así. Rodríguez Marín trató de encontrar fuentes para las obras literarias de Cervantes en la historia contemporánea; sus descubrimientos, como los de Luis Astrana, todavía son controvertibles.

[6] Para Cervantes, naturalmente, la obra de Martorell era castellana; la traducción de 1511 no indica en ninguna parte cuál era la lengua del original, ni siquiera que era una traducción. Asimismo no se mencionan los autores de la obra; en los comentarios sobre el *Tirant* en *Don Quijote*, I, 6, sólo se puede referir al autor como "el que le compuso." Clemencín sólo conocía el *Tirant* en su traducción italiana.

[7] Esta obra la cita Clemencín (véase n. 2). Sobre el autor, véase Narciso Alonso Cortés, *Miscelánea vallisoletana*, 2ª ed. (Valladolid: Miñon, 1955), I, 225-30, y la edición de Mary Lee Cozad (*supra*, nota 29 al Capítulo II).

[8] Véase Antonio Rodríguez-Moñino, *Curiosidades bibliográficas* (Madrid: Langa y Compañía, 1946), pp. 7-16. En prensa el presente libro, ha salido

De éstos, muchas se mencionan por su título en el *Quijote*. Un buen número se comentan en el "escrutinio de la librería": el fundador del género en España, el *Amadís de Gaula*, así como su progenie, las *Sergas de Esplandián* y *Amadís de Grecia; Olivante de Laura, Lepolemo (El Caballero de la Cruz), Florismarte* (por *Felixmarte) de Hircania*, el *Espejo de caballerías*, mitad italiano, mitad español,[9] *Palmerín de Olivia* y sus descendientes *Platir* y *Palmerín de Inglaterra*, y *Belianís de Grecia*. En otro lugar del *Quijote* se hace referencia al *Espejo de príncipes y cavalleros (El Caballero del Febo* [I, 1]), *Cirongilio de Tracia* (I, 32), *Lisuarte de Grecia* (II, 1), y las obras de Feliciano de Silva (I, 1), por las que hemos de entender los populares "dezeno" y "onzeno del Amadís," *Florisel de Niquea* y *Rogel de Grecia*,[10] y no las otras obras, menos populares y más antiguas, que hoy se aceptan como suyas.[11]

Desde luego, no se sigue necesariamente que el libro haya sido leído porque se cite su título o un personaje. En muchos casos, sin embargo, junto a los títulos de los libros de caballerías hay información adicional que demuestra que Cervantes tenía un conocimiento por lo menos superficial, y en algunos casos profundo, del libro. Por ejemplo, es seguro que Cervantes sabía más del *Espejo de príncipes y cavalleros* que el nombre del protagonista, porque en el soneto preliminar del Caballero del Febo se refiere a varios episodios del libro. El ventero cuenta en el Capítulo I, 32 algunos pormenores de sus libros; Cervantes conocía lo suficiente de *Belianís de Grecia* como para saber cuán belicoso era su protagonista y cuántas curas maravillosas había recibido. El conocimiento que Cervantes tenía de *Tirante el*

---

la edición de Ricardo Arias de *Rosián* (Madrid: CSIC, 1979), reseñada por Cozad en *JHP*, 4 (1980), 266-70.

[9] Esta obra la estudia por primera vez Maxime Chevalier, en *L'Arioste en Espagne* (Bordeaux: Institut d'Études Ibéro-américaines de l'Université de Bordeaux, 1966), pp. 172-75.

[10] Este libro se menciona también en I, 24.

[11] Henry Thomas ha señalado que el nombre de Silva figura en ediciones tardías del Libro IX de la serie de los Amadises, y ofrece evidencia que demuestra que el autor del Libro IX lo fue también del Libro VII. Pero aunque Cervantes lo supiera, las "intricadas razones," rasgo que Don Quijote tanto admiraba, aparecen más en los Libros X y XI. Sobre las obras caballerescas de Silva puede verse ahora el libro de Sydney Cravens, *Feliciano de Silva y los antecedentes de la novela pastoril en sus libros de caballerías* (Chapel Hill: Estudios de Hispanófila, 1976).

Blanco era tan completo que se acordó del insignificante caballero Fonseca.[12]

La otra posibilidad—si uno supone que el conocimiento que Cervantes tenía de los libros de caballerías era muy limitado—es creer que escogió como sujeto de su obra satírica un tipo de literatura de la cual sabía poco o nada, y que para encontrar los motivos para su burla preguntaba a sus amigos sobre lo que les parecía ridículo en los libros de caballerías. Los humoristas no trabajan así, por lo menos no los grandes; y, además, hacia finales del siglo dieciséis si uno quería saber algo de los libros de caballerías, tenía que leerlos por cuenta propia. En los círculos literarios poca gente en España les prestaba la menor atención.

Está claro también, aun de los títulos explícamente mencionados en el *Quijote*, que el interés de Cervantes por estos libros le llevó a investigarlos en serio, y que no quedó satisfecho con hojear los que se conseguían fácilmente. Vemos que estaba familiarizado con los libros más recientes, como *Olivante de Laura*, de 1564, y con los clásicos del género. Sorprende, sin embargo, que conociera *Tirante el Blanco*, pues la obra no tuvo ninguna popularidad en Castilla, nunca se imprimió después de su única edición (1511) y pronto fue olvidada.[13] *Platir*—un "antiguo libro", como anotó el cura—dormía el mismo sueño del olvido.

---

[12] No fue, como sugirió Riquer en la introducción a su edición catalana del *Tirant* (véase W. T. McCready, "Cervantes and the Caballero Fonseca," *MLN*, 73 [1958], 33-35), porque abriera al azar el libro, sino que tenía la intención de ilustrar su opinión del libro. Véase *infra*, p. 157-58.

[13] Aunque, como dice Riquer, "A Itàlia el *Tirant lo Blanc* fruí de certa acceptació" (*Tirant lo Blanch*, ed. Riquer [Barcelona: Selecta, 1949], I, *180), se niega a llegar a la conclusión implícita en su afirmación, es decir, que en Castilla no disfrutó de aceptación alguna. De hecho, Cervantes aparte, sólo mencionan la obra algunos moralistas que la conocían poco o nada: Vives, y algunos que le copiaron, y Jerónimo de San Pedro, quien hace un retruécano con el título en la introducción a su *Caballería celestial*. Es cierto que muchos libros de caballerías nunca se mencionaban—había poca ocasión para ello—pero si el *Tirant* hubiese sido obra bien conocida habría sido comentada por Juan de Valdés en su *Diálogo de la lengua*, escrito poco después, mencionado por Román Ramírez (véase *supra*, p. 105, n. 34), o habría sido citada en la lista de Lope en *Las fortunas de Diana* (véase Rodríguez Marín, *Don Quijote*, nueva edición crítica, I [Madrid: Atlas, 1947], 192, nota), o habríamos encontrado al protagonista en las presentaciones de los

Debemos detenernos un momento y preguntarnos cómo y dónde leía Cervantes esos libros, puesto que era hombre de pocos medios y los libros no eran baratos; Don Quijote tuvo que vender "muchas hanegas de tierra de sembradura" para poder mantener su vicio. Y del mismo modo que Don Quijote debe haber pasado trabajo en obtener esos libros en La Mancha, ni entonces ni ahora un centro cultural, así a Cervantes, aun cuando tuviera el dinero, le hubiera sido difícil comprar esos libros raros de hace varias generaciones. Todo ello lleva a pensar que quizás Cervantes no compró los libros, sino que los leía en alguna colección formada cuando los libros de caballerías estaban en su apogeo. Esto sería aun más probable si fuera cierto que Cervantes "descubrió" los libros de caballerías no en su juventud, para despreciarlos después—el caso de tantos—sino cuando ya era un hombre maduro, y más alejado de la cumbre de popularidad del género.

De los libros de caballerías cuyos títulos están citados en el *Quijote* y que por tanto deben ser los primeros a examinarse como posibles fuentes cervantinas, hay por lo menos cuatro que Clemencín no pudo estudiar. Uno de ellos, *Platir*, es muy raro. Los otros tres también son raros, pero no más que los otros libros de caballerías; son *Felixmarte de Hircania, Cirongilio de Tracia* y *Florisel de Niquea* de Feliciano de Silva, Libro X de la serie de los Amadises. Clemencín no oculta el hecho de que no pudo encontrar ejemplares de dichas obras.[14] Trató de compensar esa situación leyendo muchas obras cuyos títulos no se mencionan. Encontró seña que muestra que Cervantes conocía por lo menos una novela no mencionada en su obra, y Rodríguez Marín encontró indicio parecido respecto a otra. En el debate que el canónigo de Toledo sostiene con Don Quijote sobre los libros de caballerías, afirma: "¿Qué ingenio, si no es del todo bárbaro e inculto, podrá contentarse leyendo que una gran torre llena de caba-

---

caballeros famosos que aparecen en libros posteriores, como las introducciones a *Olivante de Laura* y a la Tercera Parte del *Espejo de príncipes y caballeros* (véase también Irving Leonard, *Books of the Brave* [Cambridge, Massachusetts: Harvard, 1949], pp. 15, 106, y 107, y *supra*, pp. 5 y 6).

[14] Véase notas 15 y 25 a I, 32. Particularmente útil para fijar el alcance de su conocimiento de los libros de caballerías son sus notas más extensas, en las que da ejemplos de algún fenómeno tomados de todos los libros que había leído (nota 14 a I, 49; nota 32 a I, 19; nota 27 a II, 17).

lleros va por la mar adelante, como nave con próspero viento, y hoy anochece en Lombardía, y mañana amanezca en tierras del Preste Juan de las Indias, o en otras que ni las describió Tolomeo ni las vio Marco Polo?" (I, 47). Ésta es, como correctamente anotó Clemencín, una referencia explícita a *Florambel de Lucea*, publicado en 1532 y reimpreso en 1548.

El descubrimiento de Rodríguez Marín es particularmente sorprendente porque ocurrió por casualidad. Mientras ordenaba libros para una exposición cervantina, abrió *al azar* un ejemplar del Libro IV de *Clarián de Landanís*, otra obra que Cervantes nunca mencionó, y encontró allí nada menos que un *Caballero de la Triste Figura*, así como un *Caballero de los Espejos* (uno de los nombres que usa Sansón Carrasco). ¡Quién sabe lo que hubiera encontrado de haber leído el libro completo! Pero se contentó con hojear "una buena parte."[15]

Aunque otros libros de caballerías no mencionados en el *Quijote* no ofrezcan tantas sorpresas, sin duda ha llegado la hora de llenar las lagunas de la obra de Clemencín, y de hacer un estudio lo más a fondo posible del corpus completo de los libros de caballerías, como se conoce hoy en día.[16] Es, sin embargo, igualmente importante dar-

---

[15] "El Caballero de la Triste Figura y el de los Espejos: dos notas para el *Quijote*," *BRAE*, 2 (1915), 129-36, reimpreso en sus *Estudios cervantinos* (Madrid: Atlas, 1947), pp. 373-79. *Philesbián de Candaria* es otro ejemplo de un libro que Cervantes conocía, no mencionado en el *Quijote* (véase mi artículo citado en la n. 4).

[16] En vez de especificar todos los libros de caballerías que Cervantes había leído, es más seguro proceder en dirección contraria y eliminar aquellos que no conocía, reservándose el juicio sobre los otros. Provisionalmente podemos concluir que no estaba familiarizado con *Florisando*, Libro VI de la serie de los Amadises, no sólo porque era una obra temprana, sino porque es tan distinta de enfoque y contenido que habría sido mencionada en uno de los debates sobre los libros de caballerías en el *Quijote* (véase Maxime Chevalier, "Le Roman de chevalerie morigéné. Le *Florisando*," *BHi*, 60 [1958], 441-49. Menéndez Pelayo, quien vio una fuente para el personaje de Sancho Panza en el *Caballero Cifar* (*Orígenes de la novela*, segunda "edición nacional" [Madrid: CSIC, 1962], I, 311-13), estimaba que era "imposible que Cervantes no conociera [el *Cifar*]" ("Cultura literaria de Miguel de Cervantes y elaboración del *Quijote*," en *San Isidoro, Cervantes y otros estudios*, Colección Austral, 2ª ed. [Buenos Aires: Espasa-Calpe, 1944], p. 116), pero ello no es razón para suponer que sí lo conocía (como queda confirmado por Schevill y Bonilla, en su edición del *Quijote*, I [Madrid,

nos cuenta que la mayor parte del trabajo que llevó a cabo Clemencín no puede considerarse aceptable a la luz de criterios y normas
modernos; poca de la crítica literaria de comienzos del siglo pasado lo
es. En muchos casos trabajó con una desventaja, en la medida que
tenía que referirse a libros que había leído y anotado hacía muchos
años que no podía fácilmente consultar de nuevo. Por consiguiente,
encontramos notas como la siguiente: "De la amistad de Alquife con
Urganda, con quien vino a casar en segundas nupcias, se habla larga-
mente, no me acuerdo bien si en la historia de Esplandián o en la de
Amadís de Grecia."[17] Clemencín carecía además de instrumentos críticos que hoy damos por sentado. No tenía conciencia de problemas
de estilo, oral y escrito, de modo que sólo por intuición se conoce
todavía el alcance del lenguaje caballeresco de Cervantes y de Don
Quijote.[18] Tenía conciencia de la trama sólo en el sentido amplio de
los episodios que Don Quijote emprendía o padecía; a menudo no

---

1928], 416, y por Roger Walker, "Did Cervantes Know the *Cavallero Zifar?*"
BHS, 49 [1972], 120-27); pudo haber sido mencionado también, ya que era
un libro antiguo, y por consiguiente de interés para Cervantes. (El *Cifar*
como origen de Sancho ha sido rechazado también por W. S. Hendrix,
"Sancho Panza and the Comic Types of the Sixteenth Century," *Homenaje
a Menéndez Pidal,* II [Madrid, 1925], 485-94, y por F. Márquez Villanueva,
"Sobre la génesis literaria de Sancho Panza," *ACerv,* 7 [1958], 123-55,
aumentado y puesto al día en su *Fuentes literarias cervantinas* [Madrid: Gredos, 1973], pp. 20-94; también véase Erich Köhler, "Ritterliche Welt und
villano. Bemerkungen zum *Cuento del enperador Carlos Maynes e de la enperatris
Seuilla,*" *RJ,* 12 (1961), 229-41. No encuentro en el reciente artículo de
Roger Walker, ya citado, ninguna prueba sólida de su tesis, que Cervantes
conocía la obra, sólo posibilidades y paralelos no concluyentes.) Al otro
extremo, es cierto, como apuntó Rodríguez Marín, que Cervantes estaba
en Valladolid en 1602, cuando se publicó en esa ciudad *Policisne de Boecia,*
pero eso no prueba que lo conociera antes de escribir la Primera Parte de
Don Quijote; tenía pocos amigos y menos dinero, y probablemente no
estaba con ánimo para leer esa obra mediocre. En todo caso no hay nada
en la Primera Parte que refleje dicha obra; el descubrimiento que hace
Rodríguez Marín en ella de la fuente de la historia de Micomicona sólo
revela su ignorancia de los libros caballerescos. Afirmar que fue *Policisne de
Boecia* la causa de que Cervantes, espantado ante tal obra, ampliara su
"novela ejemplar" e hiciera de ella una obra extensa es especulación irres-
ponsable (*Don Quijote,* ed. cit. en la nota 13, IX, 53-56.

[17] I, 43, nota 30. (La obra a que se refiere es ésta.)

[18] Por desgracia la tesis de Howard Mancing, "Chivalric Language and
Style in *Don Quijote*" (Diss. University of Florida, 1970; véase *DAI,* 31

comenta episodios y encuentros menores ni sus fuentes literarias.

Debemos señalar que a Clemencín no le gustaban los libros de caballerías, y los leía sólo por su dedicación al texto cervantino. Creía que Cervantes había escrito el *Quijote* para acabar con ellos, y comenta extensamente la aparente justificación que tuvo para así obrar en el prólogo a su comentario. No deja de ser significativo que una de las notas más largas de Clemencín sea el comentario sobre los "desaforados disparates" que, según el canónigo de Toledo, llenaban las páginas de los libros de caballerías. Comienza así: "¿De qué género los quiere el lector? ¿históricos, geográficos, cronológicos? ¿Ponderaciones monstruosas, relaciones absurdas, desatinos contrarios a la razón, y al sentido común? De todo hay con abundancia en los libros caballerescos..." (nota 34 a I, 47). Este punto de vista le llevó a hacer unos comentarios desfavorables y muy repetidos sobre los libros de caballerías, como su sucinta condena del *Espejo de príncipes y cavalleros*, libro "pesado" y "fastidioso" (nota 16 al I, 1), o su nota sobre las muchas heridas que sufrió Belianís de Grecia: "Sólo en los dos primeros libros de los cuatro de que consta, se cuentan ciento y una heridas graves, y probablemente son más las de los dos libros que siguen; pero no me ha alcanzado la paciencia para contarlas, y no ha sido menester poca para hacerlo en los dos primeros" (nota 11 a I, 1). Es probable que sus comentarios hayan sido afectados por ello de manera aun más profunda.

Unos descubrimientos sobre el *Quijote*, hechos en el curso de un examen preliminar de los libros de caballerías, muestran también la necesidad de un estudio metódico. Una de las aventuras más cómicas del libro, aquella en que Maritornes deja a Don Quijote colgando del brazo en la venta, puede haber sido inspirada por un episodio similar en *Cirongilio de Tracia*.[19] Este libro (como se dijo arriba, uno de los que Clemencín no pudo obtener) sólo es mencionado por Gayangos[20] y

---

[1971], 3556A), es de valor limitado porque el autor dio por sentado que el *Amadís* era lingüísticamente representativo de los libros de caballerías españoles, lo cual no es de ningún modo el caso.

[19] Rodríguez Marín, al comentar este pasaje, sólo pudo señalar una práctica legal. —Ahora James Ray Green ha preparado una edición de *Cirongilio de Tracia* como su tesis doctoral de la Johns Hopkins University, 1974 (*supra*, nota 63 al Capítulo II).

[20] En el "Discurso preliminar" a su *Libros de caballerías*, I (*BAE*, 40), p. lvi.

Menéndez Pelayo;[21] Thomas habla del libro sólo para ridiculizarlo, como hacía tantas veces.[22] Aunque no es necesario estar de acuerdo con el autor del colofón del libro, quien asegura que el lenguaje de la **obra supera al latín ciceroniano**, el libro no carece de mérito, y a ratos se puede notar el marcado esfuerzo del autor para alcanzar un estilo refinado.

Se trata del episodio siguiente: en el *Cirongilio* hay un caballero que se divierte burlándose de los demás. A éste se le llama el Caballero Metabólico, nos dice el autor (confundiendo la palabra con "metamórfico") por los disfraces que usa al llevar a cabo sus trucos (III, 12). Vestido de doncella, logra robarles los caballos a dos caballeros, mediante una serie de engaños (III, 13). No les queda más remedio que comprarle a él sus propios caballos, y le hacen la oferta en las afueras de su castillo. El Caballero Metabólico se niega a abrirles las puertas de su castillo, pero desde una torre les baja una canasta en una soga para subir a un escudero junto con el dinero. Una vez que el escudero ha subido hasta la mitad, amarra firmemente la soga, se va y le deja (III, 14). El escudero se las arregla para escaparse, usando el dinero para sobornar a uno de los criados del castillo que le baje. El mismo criado permite que los caballeros entren al castillo, y ellos con mucho gusto se vengan del Caballero Metabólico, suspendiéndole con sogas por las muñecas.[23]

Otro hallazgo tiene que ver con la Cueva de Montesinos, episodio central de la Segunda Parte del *Quijote*. Pone de nuevo en duda el crédito que merece Clemencín, ya que su fuente se encuentra en una obra que se supone él había estudiado. Entre otros ejemplos de

---

[21] *Orígenes*, I, p. 437.

[22] *Romances*, pp. 140-42.

[23] Paralelo a este truco del *Cirongilio* es el hecho a Virgilio; véase Castillejo, *Obras,* I, Clásicos Castellanos, 72 (Madrid: Espasa-Calpe, 1960), 56. María Rosa Lida, en *Arthurian Literature in the Middle Ages*, ed. Roger Sherman Loomis (Oxford: Clarendon Press, 1959), p. 415, sugiere una fuente para la burla de Maritornes en el *Lancelot*; también véase John J. O'Connor, *Amadis de Gaule and its Influence on Elizabethan Literature* (New Brunswick: Rutgers University Press, 1970), pag. 102. [Sin embargo, me es forzoso confesar que Marie Cort Daniels ha encontrado, en una burla de Fraudador de los Ardides, personaje de Feliciano de Silva, fuente más probable. Véase pág. 228 de su tesis (citado *supra*, p. 26, n. 63)].

cuevas, Clemencín cita uno del *Espejo de príncipes y cavalleros* (última nota a *Don Quijote*, II, 22), pero como ilustración más importante de esta aventura cita un episodio de las *Sergas de Esplandián* (nota 41 a *Don Quijote*, II, 23). María Rosa Lida desarrolló ese paralelo.[24] Pero las semejanzas entre la aventura de la Cueva de Montesinos en el *Quijote* y la Cueva de Artidón en el *Espejo de príncipes* son tan numerosas que sugieren que el *Espejo de príncipes* fue, si no la única, por lo menos la fuente principal de esta importante aventura.[25]

Mientras que en las *Sergas de Esplandián*, 99, es el autor Montalvo quien, por accidente, cae en un pozo innominado, tanto en *Don Quijote* II, 22 como en el *Espejo de príncipes*, II, 4 y 5 es un protagonista quien entra a una famosa cueva en busca de aventuras. Tanto Rosicler, quien lleva a cabo la aventura en el *Espejo de príncipes*, como Don Quijote se preocupan por sus respectivas damas, a diferencia de lo que ocurre con Montalvo. Don Quijote llega a "ver" a su dama, hecho de gran importancia para él; Rosicler se entera de la suya. En ambas cuevas, la de Artidón y la de Montesinos, nos topamos con un amante muerto, en un caso con el corazón al descubierto, en el otro extirpado; ambos hablan cuando es necesario, pero parcamente. En ambos casos la dama deseada se encuentra allí también.

Clemencín tampoco se dio cuenta en su lectura del *Espejo de príncipes y cavalleros* que Lirgandeo, uno de los dos "autores" de la obra, comenta la historia de una manera sorprendentemente similar a la de Cide Hamete en sus "notas marginales." Cuando el autor, Diego Ortúñez de Calahorra, aparece como narrador, su tono es similar al de Cervantes cuando le oímos hablar.[26]

Hay, además, episodios en *Don Quijote* que se destacan por estar claramente inspirados en los libros de caballerías, aunque no sea por ninguno en particular. Por ejemplo, la descripción en I, 9 de la batalla de Don Quijote con el vizcaíno es una deliciosa parodia de los clichés que se usaban en las descripciones de duelos en los libros de

---

[24] "Dos huellas de *Esplandián* en el *Quijote* y el el *Persiles*," *RPh*, 9 (1955), 156-62.

[25] Parece que Clemencín saltó esta parte del *Espejo de príncipes y cavalleros*. Es la misma cueva a la que se refiere en la nota mencionada arriba, pero más adelante en el libro, cuando un personaje secundario lo visita.

[29] **Véase especialmente el comienzo del Capítulo III, 38 en mi edición,** Clásicos Castellanos, 198 (Madrid: Espasa-Calpe, 1975), 88-92.

caballerías: la apariencia feroz, el golpe detenido por la fortuna, el golpe que arranca parte de la armadura. Por otra parte, el hecho de que Don Quijote huya de su casa para iniciar sus aventuras no tiene significado psicológico profundo, como creía Madariaga.[27] Era, de hecho, costumbre de los caballeros andantes iniciar secretamente sus aventuras. Generalmente, sus familiares y amigos estaban interesados en retenerles en casa, puesto que creían por una u otra razón—muchas veces su juventud—que no estaban preparados para la exigente profesión de la caballería andante. Por ello, tenían forzosamente que comenzar en secreto sus aventuras.

En el campo del estilo, Hatzfeld ha visto en el uso que Cervantes hace de las oraciones condicionales irreales "la gran idea de la condicionalidad del ideal."[28] Sin embargo, esa estructura oracional es un rasgo común de los libros de caballerías y otras narraciones caballerescas, que Cervantes imita, con o sin saberlo. Unos ejemplos, fácilmente encontrados, servirán de muestra:

> Don Belianis hiziera lo mesmo [caería del caballo], si no se tuviera con esforçado animo con el braço derecho al cuello del cavallo. (*Belianís de Grecia*, edición de 1587, fol. 40^v)

> El gigante, aunque fue desatinado del golpe, como lo vio tan cerca tirole a la cabeça, y el Donzel del Aventura no tuvo tiempo de apartarse, y alço el escudo, sobre el qual dio el gigante tal golpe que se lo corto hasta que el espada llego al yelmo, y fue tan cargado que le hizo poner la una rodilla en tierra, y a no estar el gigante desatinado del gran golpe que recibio en la cabeça, sin duda con este solo diera fin a su batalla. (*Felixmarte de Hircania*, fols. 72^v-73^r)

> Dio de través por medio de la cintura al Cavallero de Cupido un tan furioso golpe que en dos partes le partiera, si no fueran las armas templadas por el gran saber de Artemidoro. (*Espejo de príncipes y cavalleros*, III, 248).

---

[27] *Guía del lector del* Quijote, 6ª ed. (Buenos Aires: Sudamericana, 1967), p. 101.

[28] Helmut Hatzfeld, *El* Quijote *como obra de arte del lenguage*, trad. [M. Cardona], 2ª ed. (Madrid: *Revista de Filología Española* [Anejo 83], 1966), p. 41. También trata de estas frases Henry Mendeloff, "A Linguistic Inventory of the Conditional Sentence Contrary to Fact in the *Quijote*," *Estudios*

Muchas veces lo que no se descubre en una investigación es tan iluminador como lo descubierto en ella; ejemplo es el papel de la magia en los libros de caballerías. Aunque casi siempre está presente, es generalmente más benigna que mala. Casi todo caballero tenía un "sabio," entre cuyas habilidades se encontraba el poder mágico, para protegerle; es raro que encontremos encantadores malignos, y ciertamente no se transformaban en feas las mujeres hermosas. Y así la paranoia de Don Quijote se destaca aún más: el manchego no explica el mundo en términos de los libros de caballerías, sino en términos de sus propias necesidades psicológicas.

Por último, resulta claro, si ya no lo fuera, que el libro predilecto de Don Quijote era con mucho el *Amadís de Gaula*. Esta obra que, independientemente de la lengua en que fuera escrita originalmente, es poco española en cuanto a su contenido espiritual o amoroso, es mucho más sentimental que ningún otro libro de caballerías español, en los que la acción, más que el amor, es el interés central. La devoción de Don Quijote por Dulcinea, que es una fuerza constante a través de todo el libro, sólo pudo tener como modelo la de Amadís por Oriana.

En conclusión, es imperativo que se estudie a fondo las fuentes caballerescas del *Quijote*, previo al estudio del humor cervantino.[29] Las obras están accesibles a todos, gracias a las colecciones privadas de libros de caballerías que han pasado ya a las bibliotecas públicas; en microfilme se puede reunir todas las obras que es de suponer formaban la biblioteca de Don Quijote, hasta ahora un sueño común pero irrealizable de los bibliófilos cervantinos. La bibliografía española ha progresado hasta el punto de que ahora sabemos donde se encuentra por lo menos un ejemplar de casi todos los libros de caballerías.[30] Basado en una interpretación moderna de todos los aspec-

---

literarios de hispanistas norteamericanos dedicados a Helmut Hatzfeld con motivo de su 80º aniversario (Barcelona: Hispam, 1974), pp. 133-55.

[29] La necesidad de tal estudio puede verse en el estimulante artículo de P. E. Russell, *"Don Quixote* as a Funny Book," *MLR*, 64 (1969), 312-26. —Un paso en el camino es la reciente tesis de Thomas Fonte, "The Evolution of Humor in *Don Quijote*," Diss. Wisconsin 1975; véase *DAI*, 36 (1975), 1555A.

[30] Véase mi bibliografía (London: Grant and Cutler, 1979). De los libros de caballerías españoles conocidos (y probablemente hay algunos

tos del *Quijote*, y sin el prejuicio decimonónico contra los libros de caballerías, tal estudio sería en extremo provechoso, tanto para la comprensión del *Quijote* como para la de los libros que lo dieron origen. Sólo nos falta comenzar.

que no conocemos, como hay varias obras, conocidas sólo por sus títulos, que no sabemos si son caballerescas o no), sabemos donde se encuentra alguna versión de cada uno de los textos, menos *Leoneo de Hungría* y *Lucidante de Tracia*, conocidos sólo por el catálogo de Fernando Colón, y *Leonís de Grecia*, conocido por otro inventario del siglo dieciséis, perdidos quizás en su totalidad.

Don Cirongilio.

Pero Pérez the Priest
and His Comment on
Tirant lo Blanch

HE STATEMENT CONCERNING *Tirant lo Blanch* found in Chapter 6 of the *Quijote* should, by any reasonable standard, by now be a dead issue.* Since Diego Clemencín first labeled this single paragraph as "el pasaje más oscuro del *Quijote*," almost a century and a half have gone by, and fourteen articles, excluding this one, have been devoted specifically to it,[1] as well as a multitude

---

* Published in *MLN*, 88 (1973), 321-30.

[1] Bernardo Sanvisenti, "Il passo più oscuro del *Chisciotte*," RFE, 9 (1922), 58-62; Octavio Díaz-Valenzuela, "Sobre el pasaje más oscuro del *Quijote*," *Hispania*, 16 (1933), 149-53; H. H. Arnold, "The Most Difficult Passage of *Don Quijote*," MLN, 50 (1935), 182-85; Augusto Centeno, "Sobre el pasaje del *Quijote* referente a *Tirant lo Blanch*," MLN, 50 (1935), 375-78; Heikki Impiwaara, "'La portentosa memoria de Cervantes,'" *Neuphilologische Mitteilungen*, 37 (1936), 42-45; Martín de Riquer, "'Echar a galeras' y el pasaje más oscuro del *Quijote*," RFE, 27 (1943), 82-86, later amplified in the introduction to his edition of *Tirant* (Barcelona: Selecta, 1947), pp. *186-*194; Manuel de Montolíu, "El juicio de Cervantes sobre el *Tirant lo Blanch*," BRAE, 29 (1949), 263-77; Francisco Maldonado de Guevara, "El dolo como potencia estética," CHa, No. 7 (1949), 27-55, also in *ACerv*, 1 (1951), 133-57 and in his *Lo fictivo y lo antifictivo en el pensamiento de S. Ignacio de Loyola y otros ensayos* (Granada, 1954), pp. 61-108; less rigorously still in "Martorell y Cervantes," *ACerv*, 4 (1954), 322-26; Margaret Bates, "Cervantes' Criticism of *Tirant lo Blanch*," HR, 21 (1953), 142-44; W. T. McCready, "Cervantes and the Caballero Fonseca," MLN, 73 (1958), 33-35; Giuseppe Sansone, "Ancora del giudizio di Cervantes sul *Tirant*

of treatments of it within larger studies.[2] Yet, astonishing as it may

---

lo Blanch," Studi Mediolatini e Volgari, 8 (1960), 235-53, reprinted with minor changes in his Saggi iberici (Bari: Adriatica, 1974), pp. 168-91; G. B. Palacín Iglesias, "El pasaje más oscuro del Quijote," Duquesne Hispanic Review, 3 (1964), 1-18; later, briefly, in his En torno al Quijote, 2nd edition (Madrid: Leira, 1965), p. 159, n. 1—a book I have read with the greatest of pleasure; the answer of Margaret Bates to Palacín, "Cervantes and Martorell," HR, 35 (1967), 365-66.

[2] The following have come to my attention: the note of Clemencín; Juan Calderón, Cervantes vindicado... (Madrid, 1854), pp. 19-27 (rejected with sarcasm by Menéndez Pelayo); Pascual de Gayangos, "Discurso preliminar" in BAE, 40 (Madrid, 1857 and reprints), pp. xlvi-xlvii; Juan Eugenio Hartzenbusch, Las 1633 notas... a la primera edición de El ingenioso hidalgo (Barcelona, 1874), which I have known only through Menéndez Pelayo; Amenodoro Urdaneta, Cervantes y la crítica (Caracas, 1878), p. 526; Menéndez Pelayo, Orígenes de la novela, second "edición nacional" (Madrid: CSIC, 1962), I, 391-94, and III, 119; Joseph A. Veath, Tirant lo Blanch. A Study of its Authorship, Principal Sources and Historical Setting (New York: Columbia, 1918), p. 2, n. 1; Sir Henry Thomas, Spanish and Portuguese Romances of Chivalry (Cambridge: Cambridge University Press, 1920), p. 39; Homero Serís, "La reaparición del Tirant lo Blanch de 1497," in Homenaje a Menéndez Pidal (Madrid, 1925), III, 57; Rufo Mendizábal, "Más notas para el Quijote," RFE, 12 (1925), 180; F. Rodríguez Marín, "El pasaje más oscuro del Quijote," Appendix XI to his "nueva edición crítica" of the Quijote (Madrid: Atlas, 1949), 179-87 (he transcribes there his earlier note in the "Clásicos Castellanos" edition); Rudolf Schevill and Adolfo Bonilla, eds., Don Quijote, I (Madrid: 1928), 454-55; Luis Astrana Marín, in his "estudio crítico" for the "Cuarto Centenario" edition of the Quijote, published in 1947, 2nd edition (Madrid: Castilla, 1966), pp. lxxxii-lxxxiv; Miguel Herrero Garcia, "Dos apostillas a Cervantes," RABM, 4ª Época, 56 (1950), 141-42, Arturo Marasso, Cervantes. La invención del Quijote (Buenos Aires: Hachette, 1954), pp. 212-14; E. F. Rubens, Sobre el Capítulo VI de la Primera Parte del Quijote, Cuadernos del Sur (Bahía Blanca: Universidad Nacional del Sur, Instituto de Humanidades, n. d. [1959]), pp. 35-37, n. 13, Marcel Bataillon, in Annuaire du Collège de France, 54ème année (1954), 318-20; Frank Pierce, "The Role of Sex in the Tirant lo Blanc," Estudis Romànics, 10 (1962), 292; Hans-Jörg Neuschäfer, Der Sinn der Parodie im Don Quijote, Studia Romanica, 5 (Heidelberg: Winter, 1963), pp. 23-25; Martha M. Alfonso, "Influencia de la literatura catalana en Don Quijote de la Mancha," Estudios Lulianos, 10 (1966), 111; E. C. Riley, Teoría de la novela en Cervantes, trans. Carlos Sahagún (Madrid: Taurus, 1966), pp. 48-52 and 145; Sylvia Roubaud, "Chevalier contre chien: L'Étrange Duel du Tirant lo Blanc," Mélanges de la Casa de Velázquez, 6 (1970), 131; Cesáreo Bandera, "Cervantes frente a Don Quijote: Violenta simetría entre la realidad y la ficción," MLN, 89 (1974), 159-72, now reprinted in his Mimesis conflictiva (Ficción literaria y violencia en Cervantes y Calderón) (Madrid: Gredos, 1975), pp. 39-56; Ciriaco Morón-Arroyo, Nuevas meditaciones del Quijote (Madrid: Gredos, 1976), pp. 196-97, n. 4.

seem, there has been virtually no agreement on the questions raised about the passage: whether it was intended as praise or censure of the *Tirant*, the motives for such praise or censure, whether the words mean what they seem to mean,[3] and whether the text may be trusted.[4] Without being able to evaluate individually each of the interpretations proposed, this paper attempts to present additional evidence leading to an interpretation which is in harmony with the text as it stands, and with the normal meaning of the words and expressions in the passage.

I would like to pause briefly to read the paragraph to you. After deciding to dispose of the remaining romances of chivalry without further examination, "por tomar muchos juntos," one fell on the floor, and it turned out to be *Tirante el Blanco*. The passage continues as follows:

—¡Válame Dios!—dijo el Cura, dando una gran voz—. ¡Que aquí esté *Tirante el Blanco*! Dádmele acá, compadre; que hago cuenta que he hallado en él un tesoro de contento y una mina de pasatiempos. Aquí está don Quirieleisón de Montalbán, valeroso caballero, y su hermano Tomás de Montalbán, y el caballero Fonseca, con la batalla que el valiente de Tirante hizo con el alano, y las agudezas de la doncella Placerdemivida, con los amores y embustes de la viuda Reposada, y la señora Emperatriz, enamorada de Hipólito su escudero. Dígoos verdad, señor compadre, que, por su estilo, es éste el mejor libro del mundo: aquí comen los caballeros, y duermen, y mueren en sus camas, y hacen testamento antes de su muerte, con estas ["otras," in Cuesta's second and many later editions] cosas de que todos los demás

---

[3] Juan Calderón, Riquer, Sansone, and Morón Arroyo, in particular, have attempted to explain the passage through what can only be called distortion of the meaning of the words in it; Riquer has been refuted by Montolíu and Sansone, but he has twice said that despite criticism he still holds the same opinion (in his edition of the *Quijote* of Avellaneda [Madrid: Espasa-Calpe, 1972], III, 13, l. 8, n. and in his "Cervantes y la caballeresca" chapter in the *Suma cervantina* volume [London: Tamesis, 1973], p. 278, n. 6).

[4] Various nineteenth-century editors and critics, among them Menéndez Pelayo, sought to give the sentence coherence removing the negation; Arnold proposed making the central statement a question, a suggestion that was refuted by Centeno. More recently, Sansone has also attempted to reinterpret the passage by changing the punctuation.

libros deste género carecen. Con todo esto, os digo que merecía el
que le compuso,[5] pues no hizo tantas necedades de industria, que
le echaran a galeras por todos los días de su vida. Llevadle a casa y
leedle, y veréis que es verdad cuanto dél os he dicho.

The problem which has received so much comment is the apparent
inconsistency between the priest's enthusiasm for the book, and the
condemnation of the author to the galleys.

I think that this passage can be understood properly only by
examining the personality of the character whose words we hear:
Pero Pérez, the priest who carries out the "escrutinio"—or rather,
destruction—of Don Quijote's library, following the suggestion of
the housekeeper that the books be burned. Pérez is one of the most
significant among the minor characters of Part I of the *Quijote*. He is
usually mentioned in the same breath as his friend and companion
the barber, but the priest is by far the more important of the two,
and, especially at the beginning, dominates his companion in a
manner not unlike that in which Don Quijote dominates Sancho. It is
the priest, for example, who initiates the expedition to return Don
Quijote to his village, and it is he who discusses literature with the
canon from Toledo. It is not until the conclusion of Part I that the
barber initiates a conversation or expresses an independent point of
view.[6]

The priest is a particularly intriguing figure since, although there
is a great deal to laugh at in Part I, usually accepted as the more
humorous of the two parts, the priest is one of the few characters

---

[5] Many editions, including those of Rodríguez Marín, here read "el que lo
compuso," but the correction is unnecessary, since the pronoun *le* was used
for all masculine direct objects by Castilian and northern writers (Hayward
Keniston, *The Syntax of Castilian Prose* [Chicago: University of Chicago Press,
1937], 7.132). Cervantes also uses "le" as the masculine direct object pronoun
in the comment on Lofrasso's book, quoted below, I, 40 ("abriole" [el papel]),
and II, 4 ("no sé yo quién recibe gusto de no tenerle").

[6] I would not wish to take the Don Quijote-Sancho priest-barber parallel
too far; but certainly the barber becomes more like the priest as Part I
progresses, although the corresponding change in the priest does not occur.
They have both read romances of chivalry, as we can tell from Chapter I, 1,
but the priest is much more familiar with them, as well as better educated in
general. As Don Quijote is a knight, and single, so the priest also practices a
demanding profession with a high social standing, and is celibate.

who are funny by intent, rather than involuntarily.[7] He is, from the very beginning, presented as a humorous character, since he was a graduate of the University of Sigüenza. Clemencín, in a note which Rodríguez Marín did not see fit to reproduce, pointed out that because of its intellectual level, even to name this university was humorous; Cervantes drives the humor home by slyly observing that the priest was an "hombre docto." It is, in fact, the priest who, in view of his knowledge of romances of chivalry, suggests the extremely comical, although logical, disguise as a damsel in distress by which to trick Don Quijote into returning to his village, and the priest encourages his chivalric talk, "gustando de oírle decir tan grandes disparates" (II, 1). It is the priest who baits Don Quijote by mentioning the *galeotes* who had been freed, rumor had it, by "algún hombre sin alma y sin conciencia" (I, 29). It is the priest who would have Sancho worry about his master becoming an *arzobizpo andante*; it is the barber who allays his fears (I, 26).

This, then, is the person who takes it upon hemself to examine the contents of Don Quijote's library, and who delivers in the process of the examination a series of most remarkable literary judgments, though perhaps not so remarkable as the fact that they have been repeatedly taken as completely serious.[8] There are 27 titles commented on specifically, out of the more than 300 books which Don Quijote had in his library (I, 24); three others are also mentioned which were not found in it. The priest, who insists on at least reading the titles of the books before burning them, selects 16, or more than

---

[7] We can also mention the people Don Quijote meets on his *primera salida*, and, of course, the *galeotes*, "gente que recibe gusto de hacer y decir bellaquerías."

[8] By Riquer and Montolíu, for example; also William E. Purser, Palmerin of England. *Some Remarks on this Romance and on the Controversy concerning its Authorship* (Dublin, 1904), p. 204: "No one will deny that he [the priest] is merely the channel through which Cervantes expresses his own views"; Stephen Gilman, "Los inquisidores literarios de Cervantes," *Actas del Tercer Congreso Internacional de Hispanistas* (Mexico: El Colegio de México, 1970), p. 6: "los juicios que expresan [the priest and the barber] son los de Cervantes." In this paper, without wishing to accept some of his more general remarks, much less his affirmation that Cervantes wrote the *Quijote* to criticize the drama of the time, Gilman has made a real contribution by calling attention to the religious imagery in the examination and condemnation, which explains the personification of various of the books.

half, as worthy of salvation (of which more later); if Don Quijote's shouts had not interrupted the process, very little would have been burned.

In only a few cases does the priest give any meaningful justification for his decision to destroy a book, and even then we can see his sense of humor at work. He says of *Felixmarte de Hircania* that its style is hard and dry, which is meaningful enough, yet quite irrelevant to the book's content, moral or otherwise, and to its potential for contributing to Don Quijote's madness. On the other hand, *Olivante de Laura* is condemned because of its content, yet it is not clear how the priest would have a romance of chivalry be other than *mentiroso*, or fictional; in any event, the book may be *disparatado*, but why does he call it *arrogante*? His criticism of Feliciano de Silva's works is understandable,[9] but he illustrates his disapproval with a most unusual image; he would, to be able to destroy these books, burn his father as well, *if his father were a knight-errant*.

With the remaining books condemned to the flames, except for three pastoral novels and the chivalric romance *Platir*, which are condemned without explanation, he abandons subtlety and makes a humorous remark, in two cases a pun: such as, that the novel of Gil Polo should be preserved as if it were of Apollo.

Of the books which are saved, many receive their reprieve only with a condition attached. The *Diana* of Montemayor must undergo major surgery; the *Tesoro de varias poesías* requires some excisions. Perhaps we are to understand that pages must be ripped out, but I fail to see how *Belianís de Grecia* could conceivably cure itself, no matter how long a time is allowed. Similarly, humor can be the only reason for ordering all the books about "estas cosas de Francia" to be placed in a dry well, as if they contained something poisonous that could not be allowed indoors (as *Belianís* can, if no one reads it), nor left on the ground, for fear an animal might eat it.

There is little consistency to be found in the priest's comments, but we can deduce, parenthetically, the following with regard to his literary tastes: first, he has a sense of the history of literature, and

---

9 Sydney Cravens has suggested that the priest's otherwise inexplicable censure of Queen Pintiquinestra was because of her name ("Feliciano de Silva and his Romances of Chivalry in *Don Quijote*," *Inti*, No. 7 [Spring, 1978], 28-34, at p. 32).

will condemn the *Amadís* for giving the romances of chivalry birth, while pardoning the *Diana* of Montemayor in part because it started the pastoral novel in Spain. Secondly, the priest likes to see good language. He censures the language of Feliciano de Silva and that of *Felixmarte de Hircania*, as well as the translations of Ariosto; on the other hand, he commends the language of *Palmerín de Inglaterra*. Finally, the priest is not much intereted in lyric poetry. Not only do Darinel's eclogues displease him, but López Maldonado's could also be a bit shorter; the *Diana* of Montemayor must have its major verse removed, and the *Tesoro de varias poesías* is too long, as well as in need of some purification. Even the verses of Cervantes himself do not satisfy him.[10]

Besides *Tirant lo Blanch*, there are two other books about which the priest is particularly enthusiastic. His comments on one of them, *Palmerín de Inglaterra*, have been discussed in an excellent book-length study, that of William E. Purser (Dublin, 1904), and we need not speak of them here; however, his comments on the second, Antonio de Lofrasso's *Los diez libros de Fortuna de amor*, are very much to the point. If one would still believe that the priest's ambiguous judgments are to be taken as those of Cervantes—that we are to take him seriously when he calls Turpin a true historian and Ariosto a Christian poet—his comments on Lofrasso prove decisively that the books the priest is enthusiastic about would not necessarily receive Cervantes' praise.

I would like to read his comment on Lofrasso:

> —Por las órdenes que recibí—dijo el Cura—que desde que Apolo fue Apolo, y las musas musas, y los poetas poetas, tan gracioso ni tan disparatado libro como ése no se ha compuesto, y que, por su camino, es el mejor y el más único de cuantos deste género han salido a la luz del mundo; y el que no le ha leído puede hacer cuenta que no ha leído jamás cosa de gusto. Dádmele acá, compadre; que precio más haberle hallado que si me dieran una sotana de raja de Florencia.

We know what Cervantes' true opinion of Lofrasso was, since in the *Viaje del Parnaso*, the bitterest of satire is applied to him: it is

---

[10] "Mas versado en desdichas que en versos" can be taken as a comment on Cervantes' poetry, as well as on his life.

proposed that he, as the most expendable on the literary boat, be thrown to the waves, to enable the boat to pass between Scylla and Caribdis. It should be no surprise, then, that the priest is enthusiastic about Lofrasso's book not because it is well written, but because it is funny and ridiculous, or, in his words, *gracioso* and *disparatado*. This is the sense[11] in which it is "el más único de cuantos deste género han salido a la luz del mundo." It is because it is such a bad pastoral novel that the humor-loving priest is going to take it home with him, in order to laugh at it.[12]

And so we finally arrive at the work which is the focus of our discussion, *Tirant lo Blanch*, a book which certainly would be no better known than the other romances of chivalry were it not for the passage we are examining. I would like to pause before discussing the priest's statement to mention briefly the most common interpretation of Cervantes' attitude toward the *Tirant*, that of Menéndez Pelayo. Menéndez Pelayo's position, briefly paraphrased, is that Cervantes realized that the realistic nature of the *Tirant* was a valuable contribution, but that he felt obliged to censure the book because of its obscenities and licentious scenes. Realism no longer

---

[11] *Por su camino* supports the interpretation that *por su estilo* in the comment on the *Tirant* means "in its own way," and has nothing to do with Martorell's use of language.

[12] Palacín, Rodríguez Marín, and Montolíu all mention Lofrasso, although they do not all draw this conclusion from the passage. That the novel of Lofrasso was in fact a very inferior work is confirmed by Juan Bautista Avalle-Arce, *La novela pastoril española*, 2nd edition. (Madrid: Istmo, 1974, pp. 176-83, who says (pp. 177-78) "resulta increíble que estas opiniones de Cervantes se puedan entender en sentido favorable.... La crítica ha actuado con rara unanimidad y ha condenado nuevamente a Lofrasso al equivalente literario del infierno dantesco. ¡Bien hecho!" [I am surprised to see that Edward Aylward believes that "gracioso" and "disparatado" are favorable terms ("gracioso," to him, means "tener gracia"), and that Cervantes is praising Lofrasso in the *Viaje del Parnaso*, when Mercury makes him *cómitre* of the boat so he can whip the other poets with his verses; Mercury calls him "pobretón" and "ignorante," and the narrator calls him "marchito y laso." Mercury wants to save him from the waves because of the *quantity* of the verse which he wrote, fearing worse seas if he is thrown overboard. It is most significant that Lofrasso does not appear among the poets praised in Chapter II of the *Viaje*. (Edward Aylward, "The Influence of *Tirant lo Blanch* on the *Quijote*," Dissertation, Princeton, 1974; abstract in *DAI*, 35 [1974], 1085A.)]

inspires the reverence in the literary world that it did in the preceding century, and I think that modern Cervantine criticism would resist the picture of a Cervantes enamored of realism in its varied forms and opposed to the usual literary modes of his time, which were not realistic in the sense which that word normally has today. Without being able to enter here into an indeed complicated and controversial area, I would merely remind you that while Cervantes wrote *La Gitanilla*, he also wrote *El amante liberal*; that while he wrote *Rinconete y Cortadillo*, he also wrote *Las dos doncellas*; that he considered his *Persiles*— scarcely a "realistic" work—superior to his *Quijote*, and that at the end of his life he was working on Part II of the *Galatea*, and the *Semanas del jardin*, which from its title alone must have resembled the idealized world of Boccaccio or of *Los cigarrales de Toledo*.

With regard to the second part of Cervantes' alleged attitude, that he was censuring the *Tirant* for its immorality, there is a great deal that could be said. First of all, the *Tirant* is not a particularly dirty book,[13] and its "obscenities" are confined to a small section; it seems to me absurd to call it, in the words of Francisco Maldonado, "una apoteosis del erotismo,"[14] or to say, as Rodríguez Marín does, that "*La lozana andaluza*, con ser lo que sabemos, no le echa el pie delante más que en una escena."[15] Secondly, Cervantes is being quite inconsistent in singling out the *Tirant*, as various other romances also have licentious elements, which he never mentions.[16] But most important, I think that in the *Quijote* alone there are too many explicit or implied sexual references for us to accept its author as a Victorian prude, and I mean more than the scabrous episodes associated with the *aventura*

---

[13] I hope that Frank Pierce would agree with this statement, for although, in his article cited in n. 2, he says that the sexual element in the *Tirant* is "pervasive," he admits that it is restricted to the parts dealing with the court of Constantinople. He is more concerned with the type of presentation—natural and accepting—rather than the quantity of sexual scenes.

It should be noted that the emphasis on the sexuality of the *Tirant* began in an attempt to find an explanation for the *necedades* the priest finds in it, other than the one given below.

[14] "Martorell," p. 322.

[15] *Don Quijote*, ed. cit., IX, 186.

[16] This is particularly true in the case of Feliciano de Silva's works. [See Chapter VI, *supra*.]

de los batanes (I, 20) and Don Quijote's imprisonment in the cage (I, 48), or the delightful semantic discussion of the term "hideputa" (II, 13). Don Quijote himself calls the office of *alcahuete* a necessary and important one, and Otis Green feels he speaks for Cervantes.[17] There are, in Part I, several women whose virtue is open to question (as is Aldonza Lorenzo's; see I, 25) or nonexistent (Maritornes, la Tolosa). Sexual lust is what moves the muleteer to seek Maritornes, bringing on the hilarious scene in the inn; in the equine world, it brings on the adventure with the *yangüeses*, contributes to Maritornes' trick on Don Quijote, is a concern of the Caballero del Verde Gabán (II, 16), and is the source of the conflict of two of the justice-seekers who appear before Sancho (II, 45). There are explicit, yet casual references to homosexuality in the Historia del Cautivo[18] and in the tale of Ana Félix, Ricote's daughter (II, 63). And beyond this, there are other references of such questionable taste that I hesitate to mention them in public.[19]

---

[17] "Don Quijote and the *Alcahuete*," in *Estudios dedicados a James Homer Herriott* (Madison: University of Wisconsin Press, 1966), pp. 109-16, reprinted in *The Literary Mind of Medieval and Renaissance Spain* (Lexington: University Press of Kentucky, 1970), pp. 193-200.

[18] III, 188, ll. 2-3 of Rodríguez Marín's editon, cited above: "le quiso tanto, que fue uno de los más regalados garzones suyos." *Garzón* in an Arabic context meant "un sodomita mantenido por un señor árabe" (Haedo, cited by Corominas).

[19] Sancho's etymology of Ptolomeo (II, 29), a scatological reference in Teresa Panza's letter to her husband (II, 52), an allusion to menstruation (II, 23) and no doubt others I have missed.

I said "in the *Quijote* alone," because I am sure that a systematic survey of the Cervantine corpus would turn up many more sexual allusions. There is a constant sexual undertone to *El celoso extremeño* (and *El viejo celoso*), there are references to syphilis in *El casamiento engañoso*, and various types of sexual allusions in *El coloquio de los perros*. (My thanks to Ruth El Saffar for a stimulating discussion of this topic.)

In his introduction to *Tirante el Blanco*, I (Barcelona: Asociación de Bibliófilos de Barcelona, 1947), li-liii, and almost verbatim in his *Aproximación al* Quijote, pp. 68-69, Riquer maintains that Cervantes criticized the romances of chivalry as a genre as "incitadores de la sensualidad." He cites three passages in support of this allegation, two of which are spoken by the canon from Toledo, whose identification with Cervantes is in any event not to be taken for granted (see Alban Forcione, *Cervantes, Aristotle, and the*

Having said all this, we can return to the priest's statement. The key, to my mind, to understanding this passage is that the priest says the *Tirant* is full of *necedades*, idiocies, and by saying "tantas necedades" he makes it clear that he is referring to the details he has just given. In a chivalric context, the book is ridiculous. We see a knight fight with a dog, and an empress in love with a squire; there is also the merry widow, a figure completely alien to the chivalric world, in the person of Reposada, whose sexual desires lead to her suicide. Knights die of old age—a dishonorable death[20]—taking the precaution of making a will before. Finally, even the names knights have are ridiculous: Kirieleisón de Montalbán, which Cervantes must have understood as a ludicrous attempt to create a Greek-sounding name (like "Polifebo"), such as many other knghts in the Spanish romances had, and whose association with the famous Montalbán family was doubly funny, and the knight Fonseca, an insignificant character who

---

Persiles [Princeton, 1970]). The first of the quotations ("¿Qué haremos de la facilidad con que una reina o emperatriz heredera se conduce en los brazos de un amante y no conocido caballero?") was cited by the canon as an example of lack of verisimilitude, not of licentiousness; in the second, the canon compares them to the Milesian fables, then goes on to explain that he means by this that they lack a moral lesson, which is the point made by Cervantes' obvious source, López Pinciano (*Philosophía antigua poética*, II, 12), as well as the earlier Pérez de Moya (cited by Blecua, "Libros de caballerías" [*supra*, note 31 to Chapter IV], pp. 152-53)—not that they are obscene, as Riquer tries to show from other texts. The final quotation Riquer uses to prove his point is spoken by the Caballero del Verde Gabán, who says that knights-errant were "en daño de las buenas costumbres," an extremely vague comment that by no means need refer to sensuality.

Although not mentioned in this context by Riquer, others have seen Cervantes as criticizing the *Celestina* for its licentious elements, in the comment of Donoso, "libro en mi opinión divino/ si encubriera más lo humano" (D. W. McPheeters, "Cervantes' Verses on *La Celestina*," *Romance Notes*, 4 [1963], 136-38; Pierre Ullman, "The Burlesque Poems which Frame the *Quijote*," *ACerv*, 9 [1961-62, publ. 1965], 220-23). I would venture the opinion that to see these lines as referring to sex reflects our modern prejudices, and that by "lo humano" Cervantes meant the whole spectrum of human passions presented in Rojas' work.

It is noteworthy that Cervantes never criticized Avellaneda for his greater crudity in these matters.

[20] At Don Quijote's death, the *escribano* said that "nunca había leído en ningún libro de caballerías que algún caballero andante hubiese muerto en su lecho tan sosegadamente y tan cristiano como don Quijote."

could only have caught Cervantes' eye because of his name. Because of its very familiarity, we find nothing noteworthy in the name Fonseca, but it is an unwritten rule of the Spanish romances of chivalry that the characters in them never have Hispanic names, so much so that it would seem a hilarious blooper for one to appear, above all, as a Greek.[21]

In short, the book is "un tesoro de contento y una mina de pasatiempos" because of details like these which the priest found in it. If it had been Martorell's purpose to write a humorous or farcical book—that is, if he had in fact written these idiocies "de industria"— he would not deserve any punishment. It is because he attempted to write a serious romance of chivalry, and failed so badly, that he should be sent to the galleys.

Of course, this is only the opinion of a country priest of a mediocre education, and is not to be taken literally, or perhaps even figuratively, as expressing Cervantes' true opinion; no doubt Cervantes would not have really sent Martorell to the galleys, any more than he would have really placed the books dealing with the *matière de France* in a dry well. What should be clear is that there is in this passage no praise of *Tirant lo Blanch*, on the part of Cervantes,[22] or of anyone else.

---

[21] This does not mean that Fonseca is the most unusual name in the *Tirant*, nor that there were not chivalric figures, such as Bernardo del Carpio, who had Spanish names. But within the context of the sixteenth-century Castilian romance of chivalry (and Cervantes had no way of knowing that the *Tirant* was not such a work), the appearance of any Spanish element is striking. Following the lead of the *Amadís*, the books had neither a Spanish setting nor Spanish characters, and though occasionally a Spanish knight might turn up at a tournament, he would have a fantastic name, undistinguishable from those of the other knights. This is the case even in those books whose titles would lead one to believe otherwise: *Cristalián de España, Rosián de Castilla, Florando de Castilla.*

[22] The other, briefer allusions to the *Tirant* in *Don Quijote* are no more indicative of a favorable attitude on the part of Cervantes. Aside from the list in Don Quijote's speech at the beginning of I, 20, the description in I, 13, "el nunca como se debe alabado Tirante el Blanco," is ambiguous, and the adjectives *acomodado* and *manual* used to describe him in II, 1 are frankly insulting, despite Riquer's attempt in a note to his edition of the *Quijote*, 6th ed. (Barcelona: Juventud, 1969), II, 548, to explain them away. *Acomodado*, in the *Diccionario de Autoridades*, is "el que es muy amigo del descanso, regalo y conveniencias"; *manual*, citing this very passage as its example, is "el hombre que tiene el genio dócil, y es muy fácil en hacer quanto le mandan."

Two Little-Known Discussions of the Romances of Chivalry

I. Juan Arce de Otálora's *Coloquios de Palatino y Pinciano*

The following is a previously unpublished comment on the romances of chivalry, taken from Juan Arce Otálora's *Coloquios de Palatino y Pinciano*, an Erasmian dialogue dated by Norine Patricia O'Connor, who has studied and partly translated the work as her dissertation (University of Texas, 1952), as "no earlier than 1550 or later than 1555" (p. 10). The work is conserved in British Library MS. Eger 578, of which a microfilm copy is in the Library of Congress. The following is the untitled Estancia Octava of the Jornada Sexta of the work.

> PINCIANO No negaré yo lo que aveis dicho en este articulo;
> que por expiriencia sé algo de lo mucho que se
> gana y recrea el animo con un rato de buena lec-
> tion. Y entiendo que no ay exercicio tan noble ni
> provechoso, ni amigo tan leal y sabroso, ni arte-
> sano de tan buena conversacion y tan sin pesadum-
> bre como los buenos libros. Pues como dizen, *Jussi*
> *tacent jussique loquntur.* Mas en essos tambien, como
> en los demas, me paresce nos hazen ventaja los
> que no estudian para ser letrados, pues pueden
> emplear toda la vida en leer excelentes libros, y tie-
> nen más tiempo y aparejo para ello que nosotros.
>
> PALATINO En la corte, mal peccado no se dan a essos libros,
> sino a las fabulas e mentiras de Feliciano e sus con-
> sortes. Que si fuesse en mi mano, los haria quemar

todas, como a libros de mala doctrina, que traen
yesca e fuego para encender malos pensamientos e
abusos [fol. 198] para effectuarlos.

PINCIANO Otros ay mejores, pero tanbien dessos se pueden
sacar buenos exemplos y avisos. Que si no fuesse
assi, no los consintirian imprimir ni bender, ni los
leerian frailes ni personas doctas y religiosas.

PALATINO Si solamente los leyesen essos, no sería tanto el
damno, porque se aprovechan de lo bueno, si lo ay,
y no les damna lo malo. Mas un moço, que está en
la primavera de su hedad, y una donzella o monja o
casada o viuda que anda en esta misma renta, no
es posible sino que se les dañen los buenos pensamientos, y se les acaben de corromper los malos,
pues dize S. Pablo *Corrumpunt bonos mores colloquia*
prava. [See 1 Corinthians 15:33.] En estos tiempos
y en estos tales se cumple la otra prophecia, que
dize *Erit tempus cum sanam doctrinam non substinebunt e*
ad fabulas autem convertentur [see 2 Timothy 4:3-4],
pues aviendo tantos buenos libros en el mundo, de
doctrina y erudiction, se dan a las mentiras de
Amadis e Primaleon y sus descendientes, que aina
haran creer que es verdadera su historia. Y rezare-
mos una Ave Maria e un Pater Noster por su alma,
como dezia una señora que presumia de devota,
que todos los dias rezava por el anima de Amadis e
Oriana.

PINCIANO Piadosa señora era essa. No he visto yo ninguna
tan devota de los finados. No es possible sino que
los aya sacado de purgatorio. No os maravilleis.
Que yo conozco un mi amigo que es ya letrado y
honrrado que tuvo mucho tiempo creido que ubo
Amadis y que passó todo lo que dél se quenta, y
entre labradores y officiales se tiene por cosa averi-
guada. A no se aver dilatado tanto, su linaje alla
passaria la primera jornada genealogia, porque pa-
ramentira, fue bien compuesta y más honesta que
otras. Yo he oido de un predicador señalado, que
no se desdegnaba tenerle entre sus libros, y averle
leido tres o quatro vezes. Y conosco uno de mi tierra que tenia sacado dél un cartapacio de buenas
razones.

PALATINO Demasiada curiosidad me parescia essa de ambos. Tantas y tan [fol. 198ᵛ] dulzes y notables pudieran hallar en otros libros. Igual fuera sacarlos de los libros de Salamon y S. Agustin y Sanct Gregorio. De un echacuerbo he oido dezir que alegava en el pulpito a don Tristan de Leonis y del Lanzarote del Lago y a otros tales.

PINCIANO No se pueden condenar de todo puncto essos livros, que a rrato dan recreacion y estorvan otros peores exercicios, y por esto se han de permitir. Que por ventura algunos que gastan el tiempo en ellos si no lo hiziessen jugarian o hurtarian. Y deste fin, por huir de un mal grande permite la republica otro menor. En Sevilla dizen que ay officiales que las fiestas a las tardes llevan un libro dessos a las gradas y le leen y muchos moços y officiales y trabajadores que avian de jugar o reñir o estar en la taberna se van alli a oir. E si fuesse menester pagarian a maravedi porque los dixassen. S. Pablo dize *quaecumque scripta sunt ad nostram doctrinam scripta sunt* [Romans 15:4].

PALATINO Por algunos respectos particulares podra ser que sean licitos essos livros, pero absolutamente yo los tengo por perniciosos y por tiempo mal gastado el que se gasta en leerlos, de que Dios pedira quenta al que los hizo y al que los lee, por que ellos son concebidos en ociossidad, y no pueden dexar de dar mal fructo. Si los lacedemonios, con ser gentiles, mandaron echar de sus andades los [?] los libros del poeta Archilocho, solamente por tenerlos por algo desonestos y lascivos, y no quisieron que sus hijos gustassen de tan dulze beneno, aunque perdiessen de conocer tan eloquente poeta, y por la misma causa desterró Platon de su republica los poetas, y por mucha honrra dize que vaya con los demas el divino Homero, coronado de rosas y muy ungido con fiestas de danças y regocijos, muy más justa la ay para que entre christianos se destierren todos estos malos y occiosos libros, que tanto pueden dañar las buenas inclinaciones. Yo, a lo menos, [fol. 199] razon tengo de estar mal con ellos, porque un señor escolar me pidio una parte de Bartholo para oir al doctor Peralta, y fuesse a su tierra, y dexómela empeñada en cinco reales de alquileres de libros de Amadises y Esplandians.

PINCIANO Agora no me maravillo que esteis mal con ellos, pues sin leerlos, os han echo daño. No me podeis negar sino que como es plazer ver una imagen o una obra de pinzel de un maestro singular, aunque sea fingida e imaginada, solamente por la policia y arte que tiene y por la imitacion de lo real y propio, assi se recrea el entendimiento en ver una imaginacion e mentira bien compuesta y de subtil imvencion y artificio, y si aquella pintura se alaba y aprueva por solo el contentamiento de los ojos, ¿por que se reprobrará lo que da contentamiento al entendimiento, que es principal sentido?

PALATINO Porque la imagen da contentamiento a los ojos, sin perjuizio de la vista ni de la virtud. Mas los libros tales, aunque le den, es con tan damno y estrago del entendimiento y de la voluntad. Y porque si de solo mirar la imagen de Jupiter, sturpador y deshonesto, sé como vio a mal deseo el otro mancebo-...tiano, quanto más se deve de conmover con leer la misma deshonestidad, especialmente qu'es el mayor peligro de los que menos saven y entienden, como son los moços y donzellas, que tienen los animos tiernos e inocentes, y se ceban más dellos. Pero mayor culpa merezen los que aventuran menor damno, como son estudiantes y otras personas que más saben porque podrian hallar el mesmo gusto y passatiempo que hallan en aquellas mentirosas y falsas historias en otras verdaderas, y verian otros más notables echos y más dulzes y avisados dichos y mejores exemplos. Porque si en ellos por dicha se halla algo bueno, está tan enbuelto en aquella vanidad que es dificultoso aprovecharse de lo bueno sin participar de lo malo, y llevar el cebo sin quedar en el anzuelo. Yo tengo por cierto que aunque Celestina es buen libro y de [fol. 199ʳ] grandes avisos y sentencias, ha estragado tanto a los lectores como aprovechado, y mucho más sus subcesoras, la Feliciana y Muñona, y las demas, porque no sé si son tan agudas y graciosas, y sé que son más deshonestas.

PINCIANO   Por fuerza avia de ser assi, porque la primera es
           más vieja, y por esto avia de ser más sabia y no tan
           deshonesta. Estotras son agora moças, y no sabran
           tanto ni ternan tanta authoridad hasta que lleguen
           a la edad de la primera. Una cosa quiero que me
           digais: ¿que diferencia ay entre essos libros de
           romançe que tanto condenais a los libros de latin y
           poesia que se leen en las escuelas publicamente
           para enseñar a los que aprenden, como son Ovidio,
           Virgilio, Horatio, Persio, Marcial y Juvenal, y otros
           tales, pues algunos son más deshonestos y no tan
           dulzes? Y vemos que estos no tan solamente son
           admitidos, pero las leen publicamente en las scue-
           las y estudios, y nos enseñan por ellos en la niñez.

PALATINO   La differencia y mejoria que ay es que no son tan
           faciles de entender, ni se comunica tanto su daño,
           por estar en latin, y que estan más llenos de avisos
           y doctrina, y que oyendolos y entiendolos, se
           aprende philosophia moral, y el mismo latin que
           con su capa y velo cubre lo deshonesto dellos, aun-
           que tambien los confessaré que muchos dessos se
           podrian desterrar por ruines con ...ones, especial
           los poetas fabulistas, pues los destierra S. Agustin
           de su Ciudad de Dios, y Platon no las admitia en su
           Republica, ni Ciceron en la romana, porque demas
           de sus fabulas y mentiras, han sido maliciosos y
           perjudiciales. Socrates dezia que quien quisiesse
           guardar su fama, que se guardasse de poetas, por-
           que no perdonavan a nadie con sus mentiras,
           minos con ser justissimo. Por aver movido guerra
           a los athenienses, le persiguieron los poetas grie-
           gos hasta ponerle en el infierno. A Penelope, con
           ser castissima, infamó Licofroon. A Dido infamó
           Vergilio y Anacreonte y otros muchos, y poor esto
           vino a tanto su desverguença y atrebimiento que
           en Roma les dieron censores. Y fue tan aborrescida
           la poesia que dizen Gelio y Platon que el [fol. 200]
           que se dava a ella era infame, y le tenian por roba-
           dor publico. Y assi Marco Caton mató a Quinto
           Fulvio, porque yendo por proconsul a Etolia, llevó
           consigo al poeta Eguio [?]. Y no solamente los
           romanos no dieron entrada a los poetas, pero aun
           los griegos de Athenas desterraron a Homero, que

era principe dellos, y le condenaron en cinquenta
drachmas, y escarneçieron a ...tes como hombre
pobre de juizio. S. Agustin llama a la poesia vino
que enbriaga y Ovidio como ladron de casa, dize:

> Eloquar invictus teneros ne tange doctas
> Enervant animos etc.
>   [*Remedia Amores*, 753, 757].

S. Iheronimo dize que su lection es manjar del diablo y arte de mentir. Y assi les hizo unos versos
campano [a proper name?] que dizen:

> Vinunt carmine ansam poetae
> Si nugas adimas fame peribunt
> His mendacia sunt opes et aurum
> Fingunt quaeque volunt putant palmam
> Mentiri

PINCIANO   Alguna razon tiene; que a esto algunas vezes yo no
puedo en fin sus fabulas y mentiras aquellos partos
de Venus, la pelea de las titanes, la criança de Jupiter, los engaños de Rea, la prision de Saturno, la
revelion de los gigantes, el .... de Prometheo, el
Labirintho de Dedalo, los trabajos de Hercules, la
muerte de Pitho, las asechanças de Erao, el dibujo
de Enchalion, los celos de Juno, el robo de Elena, el
rapto de Proserpina, la batalla del Sol y de Nep-
tuno, la locura de Lidamante, los ojos de Argos, los
cabellos de Medea, la muerte de Agamenon, la ven-
ganza de Clytemnestra, la peregrinacion de Uixes,
la pena de Tantalo, el vellocino dorado, la ascen-
dencia de Bacho y de Semeles [?], los amores de
Eneas, el juizio de Paris, los equinas... de Edipo,
las transformaciones de Castor y Polus, de Daph-
ne,de Europa, de Phedra, de Ariadne, de Pasiphe,
de Dedalo, de Icaro, de Glauco, de Atalante, de
Piramo y Tisbe, y aquellos centauros y satiros y
silenos y otras mill mentiras que cansan. De las
quales, algunas son tan resabidas por el vulgo que
las tienen por verdades, y aun algunos humanistas
hazen tanto caudal dellas y se fatigan tanto en
explicallas como los sanctos theologos en explicar
las visiones y prophecias de [fol. 200ᵛ] Daniel o del
Apocalypsi. Pero dexemoslos en buen hora; no

echemos la culpa en los poetas ni a sus libros; que todos tienen buen fin y buenas cosas, sino que nuestra flaqueza y malicia se aprovecha mal dellas, y no sabemos moralizar sus fabulas y fictiones como lo han sido Horatio y Plutarcho en sus Epistolas, que de los dichos y exemplos de Homero sacaron excelentes moralidades y avisos. No es razon que desterremos a essos buenos hombres, Virgilios y Ovidios, Horatios y Terentios, pues aprendimos por ellos. Tantos años los ha sufrido el mundo sin murmuracion, y por ser gentiles tienen menos culpa. Para ser un hombre perfecto y universal no tengo yo por inconveniente que aya leido y oido todos essos libros; que por más apocrifas y mentirosos que sean, siempre tienen algo de provecho, y son dulzes de oir. Que como dize Plinio el moço, no ay libro tan malo que no tenga algo bueno. Y si con lo bueno el dulze, llegan al puncto que dize Horatio:

Omne tulit punctum, qui miscuit utile dulce.
[*Ars Poet.*, 343]

Ellos son propios para pasar tiempo y para hazer compania a un enfermo y para cosas semejantes.

PALATINO Si no oviese en romance otros verdaderos tan dulzes y sabrosos, disculpa avria. Mas teniendo como tenemos las choronicas de nuestra España, y las romanas y latinas, y griegas traducidas, y la historia eclesiastica, que andan en romance, que es cosa digna de ser sabida de todo christiano, y arto sabrosa, gran culpa es dexar la sombra y mentira por la verdad, y andar a buscar mentiras estrañas, dexando las verdades y historias propias, las quales somos obligados a saber, como curiosos y celosos de nuestra patria, y despues dellas las romanas, por ser patria comun de todos. De mí os digo que si fuesse casado, no consintiria en mi casa estos libros prophanos, Amadises, ni Felicianos, ni Celestinas, sino un Flos Sanctorum o un Cartuxano y otros deste xaez, donde se leen y oyen exemplos de Christo Nuestro Señor, y de sus sanctos.

Two other references found in the *Coloquios* to the romances of chivalry are the following quotations: "Muchos desos deven ser de mi tierra, que son hombres de bien y muestran todos sus bienes.... Ellos siempre son buenos christianos, y traen essos sanctos, y la reina Isea, y Lançarote de Lago, y Amadis y Oriana, y Paris y Elena, y el endriago, y otras mill historias campestres. No sé como no gustariades desto; que yo mucho olgaria, y más de conocer las naciones y condiciones de tantos e informarme de sus tierras y sinales, que valdría tanto como una leccion de cosmographia de Ptolomeo o Pomponio Mella" (Jornada XIII, Estancia 3; fol. 451 of O'Connor, 446 of the MS). "No las metamos en platicas que les den atrevimiento para perder la verguença, ni las hagamos terceras ni mensajeras, Que quien a su hermana pone en tal officio, licencia le da para que se pague en la misma moneda. PALATINO Esso va muy en seso. Parece ausiliaria de Amadis y reprehension de lo que yo he dicho vos me lo rogastes, y mandastes passe con las otras" (Jornada X, Estancia 9; fol. 368 of O'Connor, 380 of the MS).

II. Some Comments of Pedro Mantuano

The following comments, written in the 1610's, are found in a manuscript in which Pedro Mantuano, author of the *Advertencias a la* Historia de España *de Juan de Mariana*, answers criticisms made of his work by an unknown correspondant. Found in Academia de la Historia MS. Salazar Est. 7, Gr. 2, no. 60, fols. 108-17, this extract was published by Georges Cirot, *Mariana historien* (Bordeaux, 1904), pp. 192-93. I would like to thank Alan Soons for calling it to my attention.

Mantuano had offered a series of arguments explaining why La Cava and Bernardo del Carpio had never existed. When the unknown reader of his work protested this, and said that they should remain as examples to the readers, Mantuano first makes a series of points about the terrible example these two would offer, and then suggests that the romances of chivalry would be better reading, if examples to improve readers are what is wanted:

Y si semejantes vanidades an de mouer los animos de los españoles a seguirlos como quiere esta persona. Lean de aqui adelante al cauallero de febo, amadis, don Belianis el cauallero de la ardiente espada, el de la cruz de Trapissonda, D. Policisne de Boecia, Cirobante [?] de Dinamarca, Traquitantos [?] del Ponto, el Constantinopolitano rei de los Godos, D. floriponesio de Vngria [?; these three interrogations by Cirot], al gran almirante de la Valaquia, Don Rolando y si mas modernas haçañas quissieren ai esta D. Quixote que en la Mancha passa tantas auenturas por defender la lei de cauallero como Achiles y Diomedes se [?] Troia y los demas, que las ociosidades de los Griegos an inuentado.

Index

Characters of romances of chivalry are indexed under the work in which they are found.

Publishers/Printers of romances of chivalry are not indexed separately, but are found in the combined entry "publishers/printers."